T0319529

# *Japan's Protoindustrial Elite*

Harvard East Asian Monographs, 179

# Japan's Protoindustrial Elite

## THE ECONOMIC FOUNDATIONS
## OF THE GŌNŌ

Edward E. Pratt

Published by the Harvard University Asia Center
and distributed by Harvard University Press,
Cambridge (Massachusetts) and London

Printed in the United States of America

The Harvard University Asia Center publishes a monograph series and, in coordination with the Fairbank Center for East Asian Research, the Korea Institute, the Reischauer Institute of Japanese Studies, and other faculties and institutes, administers research projects designed to further scholarly understanding of China, Japan, Vietnam, Korea, and other Asian countries. The Center also sponsors projects addressing multidisciplinary and regional issues in Asia.

Library of Congress Cataloging-in-Publication Data

Pratt, Edward E.
    Japan's protoindustrial elite : The economic foundations of the *gōnō* / Edward E. Pratt.
        p.   cm. — (Harvard East Asian monographs : 179)
    Includes bibliographical references and index.
    ISBN 0-674-47290-X (alk. paper)
        1. Elite (Social sciences)—Japan—History—19th century.
2. Rural industries—Japan—History—19th century—Case studies.
3. Japan—Social conditions—1864–.   4. Landowners—Japan—
History—19th century.   4. Merchants—Japan—History—19th
century.   I. Title.   II. Series.
HN730.Z9 E447     1999
305.5'.2'095209034—dc21                                          98-40615
                                                                      CIP
                                                                      r98

Index by the author

♾ Printed on acid-free paper

Last figure below indicates year of this printing
08   07   06   05   04   03   02   01   00   99

*To My Father, Earl Edward Pratt*

*And in Memory of My Mother, Mary Christina Ellis Pratt*

# Acknowledgments

A number of people provided invaluable assistance during the preparation of this manuscript. My greatest debt is to Gary D. Allinson of the University of Virginia, who oversaw the project first in its dissertation stage and later in various stages of revision. His advice and encouragement every step of the way proved indispensable in its completion. A thank-you hardly does justice to the guidance and many kindnesses he has extended to me over the years.

In Japan, I had the great fortune of being affiliated with Hitotsubashi University, which provided not only a community of scholars active in my field but a congenial atmosphere in which to conduct my research. Nakamura Masanori facilitated my research there and assisted in a number of other ways. Sasaki Junnosuke offered counsel and criticisms on countless occasions. I have fond memories of the research trips I made with him and other members of his seminar. Although our research concerns may differ, his influence on my thinking concerning the *gōnō* has been enormous. Sugano Noriko, Mori Yasuhiko, Iwata Kōtarō, and Hayashi Reiko provided tremendous assistance in reading and interpreting Tokugawa-period documents.

I would also like to thank Ann Jannetta for her perceptive comments on my dissertation. Alice Davenport, Carol Sheriff, and Cindy Hahamovitch read and commented on later drafts. Their suggestions for improvement came at a critical stage in the writing process.

Finally, I am grateful for financial assistance from several institutions. A Fulbright grant awarded by the Japan–United States Educational Commission facilitated my initial dissertation research in Japan. The Reischauer Institute for Japanese Studies at Harvard University provided a fellowship to begin the process of turning the dissertation into a book. Summer grants from the University of Wisconsin-Milwaukee and the College of William and Mary allowed me to continue the process of revision by providing funds to purchase materials and visit libraries in the United States.

E.E.P.

# Contents

# Maps and Tables

# A Note on Japanese
# Names and Dates

All Japanese names follow the Japanese convention, with the family name preceding the given name. *Gōnō* often adopted the merchant house practice of using hereditary given names upon assumption of the family headship; for example, Nakano Kyūjirō VI was the sixth-generation head of the Nakano household. It was not always possible, however, to determine the generational sequence, especially before the mid-Tokugawa. In the case of the Fukami (Chapter 4) and Ōhashi families (Chapter 5), I adopted a makeshift designation among known heads (e.g., Sahei I, Gizaemon II) to avoid confusion. Ishikawa family heads, examined in Chapter 6, used the hereditary name Yahachirō, but I employed their names before assumption of the headship (Kamesaburō, Wakichi, etc.).

Before 1873 Japanese used the lunar calendar and era names to designate the year. Tenpō 13, for example, refers to 1842 in the Gregorian calendar. In the text, I have adopted the format month/date/year, with the lunar month and date followed by the Gregorian year.

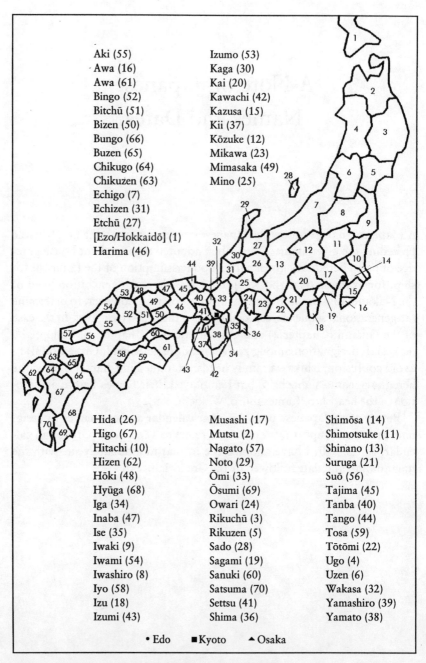

Aki (55)
Awa (16)
Awa (61)
Bingo (52)
Bitchū (51)
Bizen (50)
Bungo (66)
Buzen (65)
Chikugo (64)
Chikuzen (63)
Echigo (7)
Echizen (31)
Etchū (27)
[Ezo/Hokkaidō] (1)
Harima (46)

Izumo (53)
Kaga (30)
Kai (20)
Kawachi (42)
Kazusa (15)
Kii (37)
Kōzuke (12)
Mikawa (23)
Mimasaka (49)
Mino (25)

Hida (26)
Higo (67)
Hitachi (10)
Hizen (62)
Hōki (48)
Hyūga (68)
Iga (34)
Inaba (47)
Ise (35)
Iwaki (9)
Iwami (54)
Iwashiro (8)
Iyo (58)
Izu (18)
Izumi (43)

Musashi (17)
Mutsu (2)
Nagato (57)
Noto (29)
Ōmi (33)
Ōsumi (69)
Owari (24)
Rikuchū (3)
Rikuzen (5)
Sado (28)
Sagami (19)
Sanuki (60)
Satsuma (70)
Settsu (41)
Shima (36)

Shimōsa (14)
Shimotsuke (11)
Shinano (13)
Suruga (21)
Suō (56)
Tajima (45)
Tanba (40)
Tango (44)
Tosa (59)
Tōtōmi (22)
Ugo (4)
Uzen (6)
Wakasa (32)
Yamashiro (39)
Yamato (38)

• Edo   ■ Kyoto   ▲ Osaka

Map 1. Provinces of Japan in the Tokugawa Period

Aichi (19)        Kumamoto (42)     Tochigi (10)
Akita (4)         Kyoto (29)        Tokushima (37)
Aomori (2)        Mie (25)          Tokyo (13)
Chiba (12)        Miyagi (5)        Tottori (31)
Ehime (39)        Miyazaki (43)     Toyama (21)
Fukui (23)        Nagano (17)       Wakayama (27)
Fukuoka (40)      Nagasaki (46)     Yamagata (6)
Fukushima (7)     Nara (26)         Yamaguchi (35)
Gifu (20)         Niigata (8)       Yamanashi (16)
Gunma (11)        Ōita (41)
Hiroshima (33)    Okayama (32)
Hokkaidō (1)      Osaka (28)
Hyōgo (30)        Saga (45)
Ibaraki (9)       Saitama (14)
Ishikawa (22)     Shiga (24)
Iwate (3)         Shimane (34)
Kagawa (36)       Shizuoka (18)
Kagoshima (44)
Kanagawa (15)
Kōchi (38)

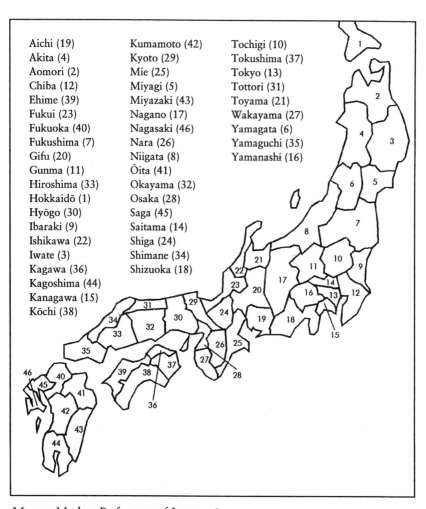

Map 2. Modern Prefectures of Japan, 1890

*Japan's Protoindustrial Elite*

# Introduction

> My mother's family, the Kondō, served as hereditary headman until the
> establishment of the village head (*kochō*) system after the Meiji Restora-
> tion, and they were a big landlord in the region. According to my mother,
> until the early Meiji you could walk in any direction one-half *ri* [about
> 1.22 miles] from the main house without setting foot on someone else's
> land. Most of the land was tenanted out, but they also cultivated a large
> portion themselves, and they had many horse drivers (*umakata*), a farm
> foreman (*kuwagashira*), and male and female farm hands. . . . Their
> house was also large. I have a faint memory of it as a child. There were
> any number of buildings, including the large main house, storehouses,
> and sheds. The garden was beautiful, and the house was enclosed by a
> moat, called a *kamaebori*, almost like that of a castle. . . . As a family of
> great means, it also ran a pawnshop. For generations it was known as
> Shichirōemon. That was the name of the shop, but villagers added
> "*sama*" to the name.
>
> Hashimoto Denzaemon, *Nōgyō keizai no omoide*

FARMERS IN THE late Tokugawa and Meiji periods would have
found much familiar in Hashimoto Denzaemon's description. Serving
as village officials, owning extensive lands and large residences, hiring
outside labor to tend to their fields and help in the family business, running a pawn business—powerful households like the Kondō could be
found in most regions of Japan, though few had the same magnitude of
landholdings. Such families also engaged in extensive interregional commerce or in manufacture. Perhaps in the late Tokugawa they wore samurai garb on important occasions and used their surnames in communications. They were also probably on close terms with their political overlords, be they domain or bakufu officials or civil servants of the new Meiji
state after 1868.

Contemporary commentators frequently remarked on the appearance
of families of substantial means in the countryside. The famed nativist
scholar Motoori Norinaga noted in a 1786 treatise that some peasants

(*hyakushō*) were acquiring wealth through commerce, moneylending, and the practice of superior farming techniques. Many such people, he stated, were no different from merchants in the cities and towns. Writing in the early nineteenth century, Takemoto Kunryū, himself from this stratum of farmers, stated that a small number had enriched themselves not through agriculture but by running sake and oil-pressing establishments, engaging in commerce, and operating pawn shops. For both writers, the rise of such families was a cause for concern, not celebration. The gulf between rich and poor in the countryside had widened to an unacceptable degree, and most farmers were mired in deep poverty.[1]

These families of means were the *gōnō*, the rural elites of late Tokugawa and Meiji society. Literally, *gōnō* means wealthy farmers (sometimes translated as "wealthy peasants" or "rural entrepreneurs"), but farming was only one of several pursuits. In addition to cultivating their own lands, they often served as merchants in interregional commerce, as the owners of small-scale manufacturing operations, such as sake brewing, as moneylenders, as landlords, and as village officials. The term itself is largely a contrivance of Japanese historians. Although it appears to have been first used in the Meiji period to describe people of wealth in the countryside, it was not used by Japanese historians to refer to a particular socioeconomic class until the postwar period.

Most of what we know about the *gōnō* in English stems from the works of Thomas C. Smith, the first to bring them to the attention of Western readers. In his classic 1959 work, *The Agrarian Origins of Modern Japan*, Smith described the *gōnō* as those who acquired wealth in the latter half of the Tokugawa from the land or from activities outside agriculture, or both.[2] Many engaged in extensive moneylending, commerce, and industry, often all at the same time. By the end of the period, he noted, they were clearly a class distinct from the mass of peasant cultivators. Smith's primary concern, however, was the totality of agrarian change in Tokugawa Japan and how the transformation of the countryside laid the basis for the economic changes that transpired after the Meiji Restoration of 1868, rather than to record the history of a particular socioeconomic class.

Smith's most important contribution to the study of Tokugawa rural society, subsequently reinforced by the studies of E. S. Crawcour, William B. Hauser, Susan B. Hanley, and Kozo Yamamura, was the assertion that it was not a time of stagnation and decay, as had been depicted in much of the early literature.[3] Indeed, there was considerable economic growth, and this growth, he postulated, was spearheaded by entrepreneurial elites in the countryside. In a 1960 article, Smith provided quantitative support for his contention. In examining the career activities of landlords' sons, he found that they occupied key positions in business, politics, and intellectual and artistic endeavors, far more, in fact, than their percentage of the general population would warrant. He attributed this to their possession of particular values and qualities that were conducive to economic growth.[4]

There is little doubt that the gōnō played prominent roles in the transition to capitalist society. Examples of their contributions are numerous. Shibusawa Eiichi (1840–1931) graces every Japanese history text as the consummate promoter of modern industry in the Meiji period. After working for several years in the bureaucracy, Shibusawa quit his post to help in and encourage the creation of modern enterprises. In 1872 he established Japan's first modern bank, Daiichi Ginkō, and in later years he assisted in founding what were to become some of the country's leading companies, including Ōji Paper Company and Osaka Cotton Spinning Company. During his lifetime he began or was involved with over 500 firms.[5]

Shibusawa is the best known of the Meiji-era entrepreneurs with rural origins, but there are many others. Itō Denshichi became active in the spinning industry. His family had brewed sake in the late Tokugawa, but Denshichi soon became all-consumed in a quest to introduce modern industry. To learn more about the cotton-spinning industry, he went to work for Sakai Spinning in 1877, and within a few years he had established his own company. Despite successive years of difficulties, Denshichi's firm became one of the country's leading mills by the end of the century.[6] Wakao Ippei, who started as a petty merchant in the 1840's, became active in the raw silk trade after the opening of the ports in 1859, and in the 1870's he began investing in banking, railroads, and various industries. At the time of his death in 1913, he had become one of the wealthiest men in Japan.[7] Such figures have become the grist of legend.

Annual personal income data corroborate the gōnō's importance in the Meiji economy. Of the twenty-six people with annual incomes over 70,000 yen in 1898, twelve were members of the peerage, former daimyo in particular. At least half of the remainder hailed from the countryside.[8] Of 664 people included in a 1912 publication listing the country's highest taxpayers, over 52 percent lived in villages.[9] Because of the amalgamation of villages into towns and the exodus of some rural elites to urban areas, the number of those with rural roots was undoubtedly much higher.

Beginning in the 1980's, historians of early modern and modern Japan added to our understanding of the gōnō and rural society in general by

moving the discussion away from "origins," instead examining Tokugawa and Meiji society and economy on their own terms. Several works on
peasant revolts, in particular, introduced the critical dimension of contention and conflict. With the increasing commercialization of the economy
from the mid-Tokugawa, a widening disparity in fortunes appeared between the mass of the farming class, many of whom lived at the subsistence level, and a few wealthy farmers, the gōnō, who had accumulated
substantial assets. Conflict in late Tokugawa Japan often took the form of
collective action by the former against the latter, leading to "house smash-
ings" (uchikowashi) and demands for the return of pawned items and reductions in interest rates.[10]

Through her studies of "house styles" and farm women, Anne Walthall
provided additional insight into the privileged position of the gōnō in rural society. Wealthy farm households composed diaries and family histories, in which they recorded for family members and later generations the
"household history, its culture, and occupation" in an attempt to impose
certain values and standards of behavior. Walthall showed how such
"house styles" had clear ideological functions, intended to distinguish
"rural entrepreneurs" from other peasants. These families also lavished
far more resources on their daughters than others in the farming class:
they provided them with several years of education, and they sent them to
work in high-ranking samurai and daimyo households, where they could
learn the proper "feminine deportment."[11] The resulting picture from
these studies is of a rural populace with a growing consciousness of social
and economic class and of a society beset by inequality.

Historians have long recognized the critical role of the gōnō in Japan's
modern economic transformation, both as dynamic elements of change in
the late Tokugawa and as the sources of entrepreneurship and capital accumulation in the Meiji. Scholarship on this pivotal class, however, has
been largely impressionistic and episodic, with only a few notable exceptions. Thomas Smith's works, in particular, which continue to dominate
our understanding of this class, have left the lingering image of the gōnō as
unmitigated success stories, blazing the path toward industrial society. In
reality, Japan's protoindustrial economy was far more volatile, indeed far
more dynamic, than portrayed in most studies to date. Very few rural
elites, including the Kondō family described in the epigraph, survived the
extremely competitive and unstable climate of the protoindustrial era. A
combination of factors—government policy, crop failures, competition,
market fluctuations, and household dynamics—hurtled many rural elite
families into decline, and there was rarely a shortage of newcomers to take

their place. The search for origins has always been alluring, whether it be in the seeds of England's Industrial Revolution or American industrial decline, but it is time to return the *gōnō* to the context of their times.

The compartmentalization of the historical profession has also led to a dearth of studies examining the *gōnō* across the Tokugawa/Meiji divide. There have in fact been no substantive attempts in English to analyze this class over the long term.[12] Particularly glaring is the paucity of studies relating to their continuing role in the traditional sector of the economy in the Meiji period. We have valuable studies by Ann Waswo and Richard J. Smethurst of the *gōnō* as landlords in the late Meiji and the reasons for their eventual abandonment of direct cultivation of their lands.[13] We also have a number of vignettes of Meiji-era *gōnō* entrepreneurs who actively promoted modern industry. The preoccupation with modern, transplanted, industries and the origins of Japan's industrial might, however, has been at the expense of the traditional, indigenous, sector. As Nakamura Takafusa has shown, traditional industry was a most vibrant sector of the Meiji economy. Even in 1892, the total value of cottage industry production was around twenty times greater than factory production, and it was only at the close of the Meiji era in 1912 that their positions reversed.[14]

Even historians in Japan, who have produced prodigious scholarship on the *gōnō*, have traditionally confined their attention to one period or the other, and there has been scant commonality in their primary concerns, or problematic.[15] A central concern of many Tokugawa historians has been to interpret the events leading to the Meiji Restoration of 1868, and they have debated whether Japan had an indigenous bourgeoisie comparable to that found in Western Europe on the eve of its Industrial Revolution.[16] Meiji historians, on the other hand, have focused on the landlord system, especially the rise of "parasitical landlordlism," which developed from the mid- to late Meiji, and by implication the decidedly unprogressive nature of prewar rural society.[17]

This book examines the evolution of the *gōnō* from their emergence in the mid-eighteenth century until the early twentieth, when many abandoned agriculture for other pursuits. I also analyze how *gōnō* shaped—and were shaped by—economic and political forces, both in the locales where they were prominent and in the country as a whole. My focus is on *gōnō* in industries critical to the economy at the time, especially tea, sake, and textiles and their raw and intermediate materials.

In terms of Japan's trajectory of economic development, the *gōnō* can best be viewed as a transitional class, historically situated between a society in which the bulk of the population engaged in limited market-related activities and one that was moving steadily toward industrial modes of production. In that sense, the gōnō were the products of Japan's protoindustrial era. Although there is far from a consensus as to what the term protoindustrialization entails, I adopt the broad definition offered by Sheilagh Ogilvie and Markus Cerman in a recent comparative study of Europe: " 'Proto-industrialization' is the name given to the expansion of domestic industries producing goods for non-local markets. . . . Often, although not always, such industries arose in the countryside where they were practised alongside agriculture; usually, they expanded without adopting advanced technology or centralizing factories."[18]

In many ways, the protoindustrialization rubric is tailor-made to characterize the Japanese economy and the activities of rural elites between the mid-eighteenth and early twentieth centuries. The economy and the nature of regional production changed in significant ways. Rural elites experimented with new seeds and cultivation methods. They also introduced to their communities advanced technologies, such as looms for weaving high-quality silks, and techniques, such as those used to produce superior teas and sake, all of which resulted in a spectacular growth of domestic industries. Japanese farmers, of course, had been involved in market-related activities well before the mid-eighteenth century, because political authorities—the bakufu and domains alike—demanded that a significant portion of their taxes be paid in specie. The commercialization of the economy after the mid-Tokugawa, however, was of a far different order of magnitude. Large numbers of farmers around the country began to engage in new forms of market-related activity—and not simply to obtain specie for taxes. Rural elites shipped many of their products to distant markets, especially to the country's three largest cities, Edo (renamed Tokyo in 1868), Kyoto, and Osaka. As the protoindustrial economy developed, farmers became not only major producers of goods but consumers, leading to growing levels of inter- and intrarural commerce.

The two decades bracketing the year 1900 witnessed a paradigmatic shift in the nature of the Japanese economy, and the protoindustrial era gradually came to a close. The establishment of government experiment stations, bureaucratically controlled agricultural societies, and research institutes made redundant many of the rural elites' traditional roles. The advent of modern industry, too, displaced those who had been active in interregional trade in the past. Many gōnō abandoned direct cultivation, instead emphasizing landlord operations or investments in modern banks and industry.

In a very real sense, historians of protoindustrial Japan owe their greatest intellectual debt to Thomas Smith. Although he never employed the term protoindustrialization in his writings, his descriptions of the processes at work anticipated many of the arguments later made by historians of early modern Europe. In his study of by-employments in one overwhelmingly agricultural county in Chōshū domain, Smith found that over half of the residents' income derived from nonagricultural sources, salt and cotton cloth production, in particular. Area merchants shipped large quantities of goods to outside markets, and they also imported fuel and foodstuffs not supplied locally.[19] Smith later described this process as rural-centered premodern growth. Unlike the European pattern, where urban areas witnessed population growth before the advent of industrialization, Japan's urban centers declined or stagnated, while rural areas dominated key sectors of the economy.[20]

More recently, David Howell and Kären Wigen explored the protoindustrialization process in rich and suggestive ways by focusing on particular regions. In his study of the Hokkaidō fishing and fertilizer industries, Howell found vibrant protoindustrial production for distant markets, dominated by powerful merchants with close ties to domain officialdom. Policies of the new Meiji government after 1868 advantaged capitalist entrepreneurs, eventually generating a system of capitalist production and the commodification of labor.[21] Wigen depicts a thriving protoindustrial entrepôt in the Shimoina valley, where farmers engaged in numerous by-employments, including transport, papermaking, textile weaving, and lacquerware production. With the opening of the ports in 1859, sericulture and silk reeling at first coexisted with and later replaced these once vital forms of side employment, while at the same time creating a number of spin-off industries.[22]

The concept of protoindustrialization, like any concept purporting to explain the totality of socioeconomic change, must be employed advisedly. In particular, the teleological assumptions on which the term protoindustrialization was initially predicated must be revised. If we understand protoindustrialization to signify a particular confluence of factors at work in the economy—the growth of rural industry, the expansion of production for the market, and interregional trade—then the term is indeed useful for our understanding of the transition to industrial society. It does not follow, however, that a protoindustrial regime must necessarily lead to an industrial one, particularly when viewed at the regional level. The transition was far more complex, as Wigen has shown in her study of Shimoina. Some regions steeped in a protoindustrial economy made the transition to industrial modes of production, but many did not. As we shall see in Chapter 3, many rural elites did not survive the wrenching transformation. This finding also comes out in my case studies of the northern Kantō bleached cotton region (Chapter 4) and the Sashima tea production region (Chapter 6). Both had been fairly vibrant protoindustrial centers but by the early twentieth century had largely deindustrialized, with commercial agricultural dominating the economy.

The term also fails to take into account production in urban centers, as several historians of European protoindustry have recently argued.[23] Thomas Smith was correct in arguing that rural areas were responsible for much of the growth in the late Tokugawa economy, but Japan's cities and towns were by no means moribund. City merchants exercised controls, especially financial, over much of the initial protoindustrial activity in rural areas. Even in the Meiji era, the ultimate desire of many rural merchants was to establish ties with wholesalers in the major cities, where there was vast, concentrated demand.

An examination of any class requires a look not just at individual actors but at the structure in which they act. As Anthony Giddens and others have argued, society cannot be viewed simply as a composite of unfettered individuals. Individuals act within a particular structure or milieu that both constrains and enables their actions. Structure constrains individuals to act within their society's given norms, beliefs, practices, institutions, and economic systems. At the same time, it enables them to pursue individual choices and actions within the structural constraints, but these choices and actions often have the effect, intended or otherwise, of altering the structure itself. Structure, in other words, is both the medium and the outcome of individual practices.[24]

To examine the *gōnō* as both actors and as individuals acted upon, this study takes a twofold approach. Part I, "The Political Economy of Japanese Protoindustrialization," looks at the broader milieu in which the *gōnō* operated, while Part II, "Case Studies," analyzes the activities of particular families, as well as conditions at the local level. The merit of this approach is that it highlights the fact that villages and their rural elites were not isolated entities divorced from processes at work in the political economy as a whole. The latter assumption is implicit in the works of Thomas Smith, who creates the image of *gōnō* acting of their own volition, free from outside encumbrances or pressures.[25]

Within the context of this study, structure includes several elements. The policies of political authorities had an immediate bearing on rural elites' activities. As I demonstrate in Chapter 1, beset by burgeoning deficits, domains increasingly turned to rural elites for loans and contributions. By the end of the Tokugawa, their demands became so burdensome that many *gōnō* were forced into bankruptcy or into reducing the scale of their economic activities. My case study of the Ōhashi family in Chapter 5 demonstrates how seriously rural elites viewed such demands and just how disastrous they could be. Similarly, demands on sake brewers, both before and after 1868, oftentimes propelled rural elites' businesses onto the precipice of ruin. Ishikawa Wakichi and his successors (Chapter 6) survived the tumultuous first decades of the Meiji, but few others did.

The protoindustrial economy itself infused a tremendous element of instability into the *gōnō*'s economic endeavors. As seen in Chapter 2, the transformation of regional production generated intense interregional competition for market share. There were clear winners and losers in this competition, but even the winners had no guarantee of continued success. The dynamic nature of the economy required rural elites to continually adjust and respond. My case studies suggest how tenuous the positions of the rural elites could be.

*Gōnō* were also subject to the demands of distant markets, both domestic and international. In the initial stage of protoindustrialization, many rural elites were subordinate to the dictates of city merchant houses. Wholesalers provided them money in advance for purchases, and they prohibited them from selling to outsiders. They sometimes forced rural elites to lower their costs and appointed new merchants as purchasing agents to foster competition and lower prices. The opening of the ports in 1859 decimated Japan's silk-weaving industry for a time, and merchants active in the silk cloth trade suffered correspondingly. This was an important contributing factor to Nakano Kyūjirō's bankruptcy (Chapter 5). Even merchants handling raw silk, which became the country's leading export item, found it difficult to shift the locus of their trade to export markets. This was certainly the case with Ōhashi Gizaemon (Chapter 5).

At the same time, the *gōnō* were not simply victims of dark forces beyond their control. They consciously tried to shape their environment to advantageous ends. They experimented with new crops and techniques, went on inspection trips to regions producing superior products, and purchased superior seeds and seedlings from advanced regions. They organized agricultural discussion societies, trade and industry associations, and producers' cooperatives, in an attempt to improve the quality of local products (Chapter 2). They actively established ties with distant markets, whether in the major cities or in Yokohama, the major site for foreign trade. Nakayama Motonari, for example, was among the first to sell

Japanese tea to Western merchant houses (Chapter 6). The *gōnō* aggressively launched into rural commerce and manufacture, as was the case with Ishikawa Wakichi (Chapter 6). They also petitioned political authorities for the enactment of policies beneficial to their industries and worked to ameliorate political authorities' excessive exactions. In the Meiji many rural elites strongly opposed government policies, especially those detrimental to the traditional sector of the economy.

The search for the prototypical rural elite, as with any socioeconomic class, is a most elusive undertaking, and the choice of subjects for this study proved a most formidable task. A defining characteristic of the *gōnō* is their participation in diverse economic activities—as farmers cultivating their own lands, landlords, moneylenders, merchants, and manufacturers—but the particular mixture and weight of these activities changed over time. Chapter 2 presents examples of improving farmers and diffusionist elites, those striving to increase the productivity of their crops or those introducing superior cultivation techniques and manufacturing technologies to their communities. With the exception of the Nakayama family (Chapter 6), however, those *gōnō* examined in my case studies concentrated on commerce, moneylending, and landlord operations. They were in many ways quite unlike improving farmers and diffusionist elites, because they took advantage of technological advancements already introduced. Both types of *gōnō* existed, and most probably were a composite of the two forms. To be successful, though, rural elites could not rely solely on profits from agriculture; agriculture was simply too volatile, and land productivity was relatively low in the regions analyzed. Interregional commerce and moneylending, in particular, were critical in their rise to positions of economic prominence.

Moreover, the vastness of the body of materials available made it necessary for me to confine my attention primarily to the main island of Honshū. The material presented in Chapter 3 focuses largely on rural elites and markets in central and eastern Japan, so as to avoid duplicating findings presented in earlier works, especially William Hauser's study of the Kinai cotton trade.[26] My case studies, too, focus on these regions. In part this focus was dictated by the greater abundance of materials for in-depth studies of particular families, but the regions were also the home of *gōnō* actively engaged in extensive interregional trade, both for distant and, after 1859, for international markets. Many *gōnō* in regions not a part of this study, especially where agricultural productivity was very high, such as the Kinai and western Honshū along the Seto Inland Sea, engaged far less in interregional commerce, and landlord operations and moneylending assumed far greater importance in their economic endeavors. In the Meiji period, especially, protoindustrial elites were far more numerous in eastern Japan than in the west, because this was the primary locus of export-oriented industries.

Readers may be disappointed that most of my case studies include scant mention of the *gōnō*'s political activities, such as their stance during the disturbances in the closing years of the Tokugawa, their role in the Popular Rights Movement, and their participation in politics after the convening of the new national Diet in 1890. This stems from my choice of subjects, the sources for which did not facilitate such an all-encompassing examination. But it must also be emphasized that, although the *gōnō* were hardly apolitical, not all of them sought political participation. As Chapter 1 demonstrates, they sought policies advantageous to their economic endeavors, not necessarily administrative posts. At any rate, more studies are needed to flesh out the full range of rural elite experience.

# PART I

# The Political Economy of Japanese Protoindustrialization

# 1

# Political Authorities and
# the Rural Elite

A FUNDAMENTAL PREMISE of the Tokugawa order was the division of society into four distinct status groupings: samurai, farmers, artisans, and merchants. During the period of consolidation of the Tokugawa state, the bakufu and daimyo bound farmers to the land and ordered that they engage only in limited forms of commerce and manufacture. Political authorities and ideologues cherished an idealized view of the rural economy, one in which self-sufficient farmers blissfully tilled the soil and paid their taxes to benevolent overlords, with little concern for the workings of the market. But from the mid-Tokugawa, everything began to change. A vibrant commodity economy permeated villages across the country, and increasing numbers of farmers joined the ranks of merchants and produced goods for sale in distant parts of the country.

Political authorities slowly began to reconcile themselves to these changes in rural society. By the mid-eighteenth century they had largely accepted rural commerce and production for the market. Many daimyo, in fact, came to fully embrace the growth of the rural economy. As a result of growing budget deficits, they encouraged greater production for the market and increasingly turned to the rural elite—the gōnō—both as a source of funds and as facilitators of the sale of commodities produced within their territories to central markets. The overthrow of the Tokugawa bakufu in 1868 and the creation of a new centralized regime heralded still greater changes in rural society. After abolishing the last vestiges of controls over rural production and commerce, the Meiji leadership aggressively enacted policies to lay the groundwork for modern growth, both through critical investments in infrastructure and through the introduction of Western industrial technology and agricultural methods. Through its experimental farms, competitive exhibitions, and financial inducements, the government encouraged the rural elites' local development efforts, especially in the export sector.

Rural elites received numerous benefits in recompense for their new role in the political economy. In the Tokugawa many acquired samurai status and other perquisites of social power and prestige. They won tacit approval of their activities outside agriculture, as well as their acquisition of other farmers' lands. A few rural elites even acquired positions in domain administration. By abolishing formal status distinctions, the Meiji government recognized the critical role rural elites were to perform in the creation of a modern industrialized nation state. It increasingly appointed them as key figures in government efforts aimed at modernizing the traditional sector of the economy.

But old notions were slow to die out. Despite their importance in the economy, rural elites learned that political authorities, both in the Tokugawa and in the Meiji, had very limited visions of the role they were to play in society. Although rural elites at times won important concessions from their overlords, the priorities of political authorities always took precedence over the needs of the rural elite. Little changed in the Meiji period. Rural elites were to do the government's bidding in encouraging growth, but without exercising any real power within the political economy.

## Tokugawa Political Authorities and the Rural Economy

Contrary to early historical accounts depicting an intense disdain by samurai officialdom toward the merchant class and the workings of the market, all political authorities—the bakufu and domains alike—shared a profound concern for commerce. Indeed, their very existence depended on the vitality of markets—whether in the castle towns, in rural towns, or in the major cities—and the merchants active in them. With the majority of the country's samurai concentrated in the major cities and castle towns, it was necessary to have merchants and artisans there to cater to their needs. All domains were dependent on outside markets as well, both for the purchase of necessities not produced on their own territories and for the sale of surplus rice, collected from farmers in partial fulfilment of tax obligations, to obtain specie. While dependent on commerce, political authorities devised policies to ensure that merchants and artisans conducted their trades within clearly prescribed limits, especially with an eye toward maintaining status distinctions and an orderly system of commerce. The bakufu, too, periodically issued edicts ordering farmers to dedicate themselves to farming alone and not to engage in commerce.[1]

Many types of territorial entities muddled the Tokugawa economic landscape. Lands directly controlled by the Tokugawa house, amounting to about one-sixth of the productive capacity of the country's fields, could be found in every part of the country, though many were concentrated in the Kantō and Kinai regions. The Tokugawa apportioned another 10 percent of the country's land among its bannermen (*hatamoto*), who controlled lands assessed at under 10,000 *koku*. Bakufu and bannermen lands were scattered and noncontiguous; they rarely constituted discrete territorial entities of more than a handful of villages.

Most of the remaining lands took the form of domains under the control of feudal lords, or daimyo, who numbered around 260 by the eighteenth century. As Harold Bolitho has shown, here too there was a broad range of territorial entities. Some small domains, often with little more than 10,000 *koku*, derived income from only a few dozen villages, while larger domains encompassed areas roughly corresponding to modern prefectures, with several hundred thousand *koku* or more.[2] Some domain territories were fragmented, with lands scattered over different parts of the country. There were also smaller territories—including lands controlled by domains, the bakufu, and bannermen—that were under the custodial jurisdiction (as *azukarichi*) of larger domains, which collected the taxes and otherwise subjected farmers to their rule.

Likewise, the nature of territorial rule varied. Most daimyo with sizable holdings ruled from castle towns, where they forced their samurai to reside. This was often not the case with small domains. Many *fudai* daimyo (personal vassals of the Tokugawa house) with small holdings worked permanently in bakufu administrative posts in Edo, Kyoto, or Osaka and only maintained administrative offices, often known as *jinya*, in a town in their territories. The bakufu, too, ruled not through castle town administrations but through intendants (*daikan*) appointed to oversee its lands. Bannermen lived in the major cities and had their retainers, bakufu intendants, or village officials collect taxes and maintain order.

Because of differences in territorial integrity and the nature of rule, controls over commerce varied. Most daimyo ruling from castle towns accorded merchants there monopolistic rights over commerce, both in handling goods produced on their lands and in transactions with the outside. They did the same with artisans: they designated particular establishments in the castle towns to produce such necessities as sake, soy sauce, and lacquerware or to provide particular services, such as carpentry. They allowed residents of designated rural towns to engage in commerce and manufacture, but they were to supplement activities undertaken in the castle towns, not compete with them. When rural commerce or manufacture appeared to threaten the privileged positions of castle town establishments, officials intervened. The actions of Takashima domain in the Suwa area of southern Shinano were typical. In the first half of the Tokugawa, Takashima officials sought to protect the commercial monopoly of castle town merchants and periodically issued bans on rural industry, including sake brewing and new cloth dyeing establishments.[3]

For small domains, bakufu territories, noncontiguous areas of domains, or areas where others' territory was included within one's boundaries, controls on rural commerce and manufacture were far less effective. If a small domain instituted controls on silk cloth its residents produced, for example, the production or market center would frequently move to a neighboring territory where no such controls existed. Obviously, there were clear limits to the control political authorities in these areas could exercise over rural commerce and manufacture.

Even those areas of highly fragmented rule—with no castle towns and no resident political authorities—were not without some controls over commerce. Such areas had designated markets where merchants conducted business on particular days of the month. Merchants there zealously guarded the special rights they had been accorded in handling local products. If new markets arose, merchants in already-existing markets would appeal promptly to political authorities. In the first half of the Tokugawa, rural commerce was still in an early phase of development, so such conflicts were rare.

POLITICAL AUTHORITIES AND THE MARKET ECONOMY

The growth of the market economy made it increasingly difficult to restrict rural commerce and manufacture. The enforcement powers of political authorities had always been weak. Most domains forced samurai to reside permanently in castle towns, while entrusting the implementation and enforcement of regulations concerning farmers to village officials, all farmers themselves. Although political authorities set rigid guidelines within which farmers were to act, farmers were in most ways quite autonomous, free from outside supervision of their day-to-day activities.

Political authorities were also somewhat ambivalent toward the activities in which farmers engaged. While trying to uphold the monopolistic rights of castle town and rural town residents and clamping down on transgressors, political authorities recognized that all farmers were dependent to some degree on the market economy. Indeed, by compelling farmers to pay a significant portion of their annual tax in cash, they forced farmers to engage in market-related activities. At times, political authorities even enacted policies to encourage farmers to produce more for the market, to ensure that farmers had the means to continue as farmers and thus to pay their annual taxes.

By the mid-eighteenth century, political authorities began to embrace the market economy in far more overt ways. Beset by burgeoning budget deficits, they devised new measures to increase their revenue. Most domains faced financial difficulties from the early years of the Tokugawa. Some were burdened with excessive numbers of samurai who could not be put to productive use in administration. In addition, the system of alternate attendance, which dictated that daimyo live in Edo every other year and that their wives and children reside there permanently, often consumed one-third or more of their annual revenues. Compounding their burdens, the bakufu frequently ordered them to pay large sums for extraordinary expenditures.

In the early years, daimyo, large and small, covered their deficits by turning to Kyoto and Osaka financiers and by increasing taxes on farmers' lands. By the eighteenth century, though, financiers had become very stringent in their loans to domains; too many daimyo had defaulted on their debts, causing the bankruptcy of many a moneylender. Moreover, by the 1720's to 1750's it had become difficult to levy more exactions on the rural populace; major uprisings in the countryside forced the domains to search for other sources of revenue.

From the mid-eighteenth century, many domains launched an unprecedented series of reforms to revitalize their economies. Specific policies differed, but most sought either to reduce expenditures or to find new sources of income. Expenditure reductions often took the form of sumptuary edicts and rarely remained in effect for more than a few years. Daimyo and their retainers were unwilling to accept long-term reductions in their standards of living. Of greater importance in covering deficits were new sources of revenue. Those, too, took multifarious forms, but one of the most common practices was for domains to borrow from their retainers, usually by reducing their stipends. Probably every domain did this at one time or another.[4]

Equally important were policies to encourage commodity production in the countryside. Political authorities recognized clear benefits from such policies. Farmers earned more by selling goods in demand in local and central markets. When farmers earned more, domains profited, because fewer farmers defaulted on their tax payments and abandoned their fields. Also, through the institution of monopolies, domains could collect a portion of the profits from the sale of farmers' goods in central markets.

From the mid-Tokugawa, growing numbers of domains adopted policies to encourage greater rural production. In 1748 Matsue domain in western Japan encouraged the cultivation of wax trees. In 1767 Yonezawa domain in northeastern Japan initiated a project to plant one million trees each for lacquer, silk mulberry, and paper mulberry. It also introduced the technology for weaving crepe. By the 1820's sericulture—the raising of silkworms to produce cocoons and the cultivation of mulberry trees to feed them—had become such an important industry in the domain that nearby Akita domain sought to emulate Yonezawa's policies. It invited Ueki Shirōbei of Yamaguchi village in Yonezawa to teach Akita farmers mulberry cultivation methods.[5]

In the 1780's Aizu domain, also in northeastern Japan, introduced the technology for sericulture and safflower cultivation and instituted stricter quality controls on its lacquer industry. It also began to produce sake by bringing in brewing technology and brewmasters from the Osaka area. The domain's goal was to produce superior sake for sale outside the domain and to improve sake-brewing technology in the domain as a whole.[6]

Some domains encouraged the diffusion of the weaving technology of Kyoto's Nishijin district, which was the country's preeminent production center for high-quality silks. In 1711 Sendai domain invited textile workers from Nishijin to produce various silks, which the daimyo presented as gifts. In the 1830's Kaga domain employed Nishijin textile workers in a domain factory to produce high-quality brocades. Other domains introduced tea cultivation and tea-processing technology. Around the 1830's the daimyo of Mito invited in a tea specialist from Uji, an area near Kyoto that produced superior teas. The specialist opened a tea grove in a village near the castle town and traveled to tea cultivation regions in the domain to instruct farmers on Uji production methods.[7]

Bakufu intendants charged with overseeing Tokugawa lands enacted similar measures. In the 1780's Nakai Seidayū, bakufu intendant for lands in Kai province, encouraged the cultivation of potatoes from Kyūshū, which he distributed to farmers for experimental cultivation. Yamaguchi Takakazu, an intendant in the northern Kantō in the 1790's, ordered farmers to plant lacquer trees around their residences.[8] The bakufu itself, however, rarely enacted sweeping policies for encouraging industry. Its lands were scattered over different parts of the country, making such policies difficult to implement, if not meaningless considering the varied terrains.

From the mid-Tokugawa, political authorities' encouragement-of-industry policies signified an unmistakable shift in official attitudes: instead of seeking to confine and regulate rural commerce and manufacture, political authorities actively fostered it. Indeed, they came to consider greater rural production of tremendous benefit, not just to farmers but to themselves. An examination of domain monopolies makes this point especially clear.

DOMAIN MONOPOLIES

In the mid- to late Tokugawa, growing numbers of domains increased revenue by instituting monopolies on commodities produced within their territories. Although some had existed in the early Tokugawa, they were few in number: only an estimated fifty-four until 1735, as compared with 323 instituted between 1736 and 1871.[9] Whereas samurai officials or their agents in the castle towns operated early monopolies, from the second half of the period domains increasingly incorporated people at all levels of the purchasing hierarchy, in particular the rural merchant class. This, too, represents an important concession on the part of political authorities. Not only were rural commerce and production for the market to be encouraged, but rural elites were to be instrumental agents in the implementation of domain economic policy.

Examples of the rural elites' participation in domain monopolies are numerous. In 1821 Himeji domain attempted to reduce its staggering debt, which had reached 730,000 ryō in 1808, by initiating a monopoly on the cotton cloth produced by its residents. Village merchants were an integral component of the monopoly: rural jobbers bought the cloth from weavers; rural wholesalers purchased the cloth from the jobbers and sold it to castle town wholesalers, who shipped the cloth to Edo. Himeji collected a 1.5 percent tax on cotton cloth sales, bringing in massive profits to the domain and enabling it to pay off its debts within a relatively short time.[10]

Other domains in western Japan instituted monopolies on cotton cloth around the same time. Hiroshima domain maintained few controls over cotton cloth until 1842, when officials ordered all cotton exports to be shipped to a designated Osaka wholesaler. Hiroshima next established three inspection stations where it stamped the cotton cloth and shipped it on to Osaka. At the district level, the domain appointed village officials and other high-status farmers as its agents in ensuring adherence to the official sales network. The process was much the same in Tottori domain, which instituted a monopoly on cotton cloth in 1853. The monopoly office appointed six people, four of them from villages, to collect the cloth at the local level.[11]

Domain monopolies proved profitable to a number of parties. If they were successful, they could be extremely lucrative for domains, as happened with Himeji. Monopolies also sometimes benefited producers. One of the reasons Himeji instituted its monopoly on cotton cloth was to bring greater profits to its weavers. Previously, merchants had sent Himeji's cloth to Osaka wholesalers, who shipped much of the cloth to Edo for sale in consumer markets. By establishing a direct route to the Edo market, the monopoly eliminated the Osaka middlemen, thus generating greater profits for Himeji's producers.[12]

Those monopolies that inspected for quality also furthered the interests of producers. Inspection was especially important from the mid-eighteenth century because of intense interregional competition for market share. With greater production for the market, farmers oftentimes produced goods with little concern for quality, thus damaging their region's reputation in central markets. This was the case with safflower produced in the Mogami region of northeastern Japan. Because of the highly fragmented nature of rule there, there were few controls on commerce and production. Producers sometimes mixed rice flour in their safflower cakes, and merchants cheated on the weights of what they sold. As a result, the region's reputation suffered a serious decline in the Kyoto market, the primary destination of safflower. The safflower produced in other regions, such as Sendai, acquired a better reputation, in part because domain monopolies closely inspected for quality.[13]

Domain monopolies directly benefited merchants as well. Castle town merchants profited because they assumed an indispensable role in their operation. Many castle town merchants had seen their fortunes decline in the past, because rural merchants had usurped much of their business by shipping directly to outside markets. Monopolies also served the interests of those rural merchants responsible for local purchases, because they received commissions on the goods they handled.

The catalyst for monopoly formation, in fact, especially in the closing decades of the Tokugawa, was sometimes the rural merchants themselves, not domain officials. This was the case with the institution in 1859 of Himeji domain's monopoly on *shinomaki*, ginned cotton that was beaten until soft and the fibers straightened and bundled in preparation for spinning into yarn. Rural elites were also instrumental in establishing Hikone domain's monopoly on silk crepe.[14]

## DOMAIN FINANCES AND THE RURAL ELITE

Another manifestation of an unmistakable shift in political authorities' stance toward the market economy was their increasing reliance on wealthier residents for contributions and loans. Many domains had done this well before the mid-Tokugawa, but those providing loans had usually been merchants from the castle towns. Beginning in the mid-eighteenth century, in contrast, growing numbers came from villages. By the end of the Tokugawa, rural elites providing funds often far outnumbered those from towns.

This growing reliance on the financial might of rural elites can be seen in Nagaoka domain in Echigo. Nagaoka suffered from budget deficits from the early Tokugawa.[15] It periodically issued retrenchment edicts, encouraged commodity production, and ordered residents of the domain to provide loans (goyōkin), but a series of natural disasters and extraordinary budgetary outlays from the second half of the eighteenth century forced Nagaoka further into debt. In the nineteenth century it increasingly turned to its residents for funds. In 1831 it imposed 15,000 ryō of loans on the populace at large. In 1843 officials asked residents for another 30,000 ryō, two-thirds to be collected from rural areas and one-third from its three major towns. It also encouraged wealthy residents to contribute funds in exchange for status increases.

In 1849 Nagaoka again ordered residents to provide 80,000 ryō in loans (saikakukin). Perhaps embarrassed by its fiscal ineptitude, the domain promised not to seek any more loans in the future. At the time, the domain debt totaled over 230,000 ryō, about 98,000 ryō of which it owed to Osaka and Edo financiers and 134,000 ryō to residents. Of the 80,000 ryō the domain requested that year, Nagaoka castle town itself was responsible for 17,000. The domain asked three individuals, two of whom were from villages, to pay a total of 5,800 ryō and apportioned the remainder among villages in the domain. Only three years later, the domain again called upon local notables for financial assistance. It requested twenty-one wealthy merchants and farmers in the domain to underwrite loans totaling 40,000 ryō, again to repay outstanding debts.

In 1854 Nagaoka sought another 50,000 ryō in loans and for this purpose summoned its purported wealthiest resident, Imai Magobei of Yoshida village, who was reported to have assets of 200,000 ryō. The domain offered Imai samurai status and a stipend of 100 *koku* but he refused, claiming that he did not have such funds. He also criticized the domain, arguing that such a loan would not fundamentally solve its fiscal crisis. After further negotiations, Imai asked the domain to appoint him to oversee its finances, and the domain consented.

Within a few decades Nagaoka had thus radically altered its means of financing. Although most of its early funding came from outside sources and from extraordinary levies assessed on residents of the domain as a whole, by the end of the Tokugawa it turned increasingly to selected wealthy residents alone. That people like Imai won concessions from the domain testifies to their new role within the political economy.

Other domains pursued similar policies. In western Japan Tatsuno domain's finances worsened in the 1730's. A famine resulted in a decline in tax revenue, and lower rice prices in 1735 decreased its cash income. Conditions had improved by around 1740 after officials enacted a series of retrenchment measures, but a far more serious fiscal crisis ensued in the 1770's. Tatsuno implemented new retrenchment measures and borrowed large sums of money from Osaka merchants, other domains, and wealthy residents. In 1777 alone it borrowed 600 *kan* from wealthy town and village residents, which it promised to repay with 25,000 bags of rice a year for five years. But when the bakufu assigned the daimyo to a new administrative position, requiring 15,000 *ryō* in annual expenses, even such a liberal repayment schedule proved impossible to meet. Tatsuno borrowed 7,500 *ryō* of this from Osaka financiers and 5,500 *ryō* from its own town and village residents. The repayment of the original loan of 600 *kan* had to be considerably delayed.

In the nineteenth century Tatsuno relied all the more on loans from residents, and frequently used them as intermediaries in obtaining loans from other parties. The domain also began to appoint residents, several of them from villages, as its financial purveyors (*goshakuyōsuji goyōkiki*). Those from villages frequently borrowed money from outside the domain, putting their lands up as collateral. In exchange, the domain permitted many of them to wear swords outside the castle town and granted them stipends and samurai status. It did the same for those making outright contributions.[16]

Hiroshima domain enacted such measures from the 1830's, when a series of poor harvests drastically reduced its income from the land. In 1853 its debt rose to over 43,000 *kan*, 48.5 percent of which was owed to residents of the domain, 43.1 percent to Osaka financiers, and the remainder to Edo financiers. It encouraged lenders from towns and villages in the domain to convert their loans into outright contributions in exchange for the granting of surnames, the right to bear a sword, and status increases.[17] In the Ashikaga region, daimyo frequently imposed extraordinary levies and demanded that the annual tax be paid in advance. They, too, turned to the rural elite for loans and contributions. Some bannermen appointed rural elites as their intendants, charging them with the responsibility of keeping order and tax collection.[18]

As with monopolies, rural elites received several benefits from political authorities in return for their loans and contributions. Obviously, the growing dependence on such funds provided a degree of assurance that political authorities would continue to approve tacitly of rural elites' activities. Land accumulation was one such activity in which rural elites were involved. Never formally sanctioned by most political authorities, the buying and selling of land had become quite common in many parts of the country by the mid-eighteenth century.[19]

Similar tolerance can be seen in political authorities' attitudes toward the rural elites' commercial and manufacturing activities. Domain officials increasingly ignored the protestations of castle town merchants and artisans whose monopolies were being usurped by these upstarts in the countryside. Here, too, Takashima domain provides a clear example of this new stance. Faced with unstable finances and unable to confine commerce and industry to the castle town, by the mid-eighteenth century Takashima reversed course. Rather than restricting rural commerce and industry, it began to actively encourage them. In 1824 the domain even offered farmers gifts of mulberry seedlings to encourage the growth of the sericulture industry.[20]

Rural elites also profited from the interest they received on their loans. The Watanabe family of Shimoseki village in Echigo, for example, loaned almost 62,000 *ryō* to Yonezawa domain between 1749 and 1784. The family received numerous honors from Yonezawa in return, including an annual stipend, the use of a surname, and appointments to official positions. The family's financial resources were so important that when domain officials learned that the sixth-generation head Yoshitomi was seriously ill, they sent a doctor to treat him. But to the Watanabe family, who earned over 8,850 *ryō* in interest on the above loans, this was above all a profit-making activity, and the family lent money to other domains in the area, as well as to bakufu officials.[21]

Rural elites also enjoyed short-term loans from political authorities to support their business activities. Maeki Kyūhei of Naka village in Shindatsu received loans from time to time from the domain office in Hobara to facilitate his purchases of raw silk. Shimosato Jirōhachi, a rural brewer on the Chita peninsula, petitioned Owari domain for a loan of 1,300 ryō in 1802 to launch into sake brewing. In 1805 he asked for another 5,000 ryō and in 1807 for a loan of 500 koku of rice.[22] We do not know if the domain granted Shimosato's requests, but they do suggest that such appeals for financial assistance were not at all uncommon.

Rural elites' financial might sometimes provided them important leverage over decisions taken by samurai officials. When Sakata Kichisuke of Kamiyada village in western Mikawa petitioned Nishio domain in 1865 to become a rural agent (kaitsugi) for an Edo cloth wholesalers guild, officials at first rejected his request. Sakata immediately asked them to reconsider, arguing that there was demand in Edo for Nishio cloth and that he would be able to provide around 1,000 ryō to the domain, should the need arise. The domain soon reversed its decision.[23]

There were also important symbolic benefits to this new relationship with political authorities. As Herman Ooms has observed, status distinctions were an integral component of Tokugawa village life, even with the growth of the market economy. What distinguished the rural elite from others in rural society was not only their economic status ("economic capital") but also their accumulation of "symbolic capital."[24] The status increases and gifts granted them by political authorities accorded them prestige, both among their peers and among the rank and file in their communities. They could use their surnames in communications with others. They could wear the swords and the dress restricted to the samurai class. They received preferential seating at village festivals and ceremonies. All were intoxicating symbols of their new position within the Tokugawa order.

But the gōnō were quite unlike those French entrepreneurs who, in the words of historian Claude Maruié, committed "treason of the bourgeoisie," using their profits at every turn to gain seigneurial privileges and eventual ennoblement.[25] Japan's rural elites obviously considered samurai status important, but there is little evidence that they wanted to become like samurai. They used that status to further their prestige and reputation among fellow rural elites and businessmen in other parts of the country, not necessarily to gain high administrative positions. With few exceptions, the pursuit of profit took precedence over the quest for political power.

By the closing decades of the Tokugawa, the views of political authorities toward rural commerce and production for the market had changed in significant ways. Faced with burgeoning deficits and unable to stem rural commerce and manufacture, domains increasingly encouraged commodity production within their territories. They also turned to the rural elite for funds and to ensure compliance with domain monopolies. In so doing, political authorities began to accept many of the activities in which the rural elite engaged and accorded them legitimacy as important economic actors. Rural elites profited from their new relationship with political authority in a number of ways, notably in the relaxation of restrictions on their activities. As recipients of various status increases, their social positions were elevated within their communities. They also reaped handsome profits from the loans they extended to domains.

## RURAL ELITES AND POLITICAL AUTHORITIES: A MUTUALITY OF INTERESTS?

Fujita Gorō, the first Japanese historian to systematically analyze the *gōnō*, characterized the new relationship between political authorities and rural elites from the mid-Tokugawa as one of "rising and transforming" (*jōshō tenka*). Rural elites, in Fujita's view, increasingly "entered the world" of the daimyo.[26] Daimyo accorded them various special rights, including status increases, positions in domain monopolies, and tacit acceptance of their land accumulation and commercial activities. Indeed, as this chapter has demonstrated, many rural elites had ingratiated themselves into the ranks of political authorities by the closing years of the Tokugawa. That some rural elites were able to marry their daughters into sometimes powerful samurai households testifies, as well, to their new importance in the Tokugawa social order.[27]

It is also true that rural elites in some parts of the country allied with anti-bakufu forces in the closing years of the Tokugawa. Rural elites in Chōshū domain joined lower-ranking samurai and others in militia fighting for the restoration of imperial rule. The same happened on a much larger scale in Mito domain. By the 1830's rural elites had allied with the conservative and reform factions in domain administration. When the bakufu forced the Mito daimyo Nariaki into resignation and domiciliary confinement in 1844, large numbers of rural elites joined reform faction samurai in a petition drive to have him reinstated. In the closing years of the Tokugawa, rural elites aligned with opposing sides in the growing confrontation between reform and conservative factions.[28]

Nonetheless, it would be difficult to conclude that rural elites were in an alliance with political authorities, as some historians in Japan have claimed. Those rural elites who actively participated in the political disturbances before the bakufu's collapse—and my readings of village histories suggest that far more did not take part than did—played at best only a supporting role, and there is little evidence to suggest that even the most reform-minded samurai officials desired to bring them into the political process as full participants.[29]

The exactions of political authorities, in fact, inflicted tremendous hardships on many rural elites. Requests for loans and contributions, in particular, oftentimes proved disastrous. Initially, rural elites saw few problems with such requests. They earned interest on their loans, and the contributions they provided were not especially onerous, especially in the light of the status increases they acquired in return. But in the closing decades of the Tokugawa, such demands came with alarming frequency and, in the case of loans, with little likelihood of repayment. The Nakajima family of Hitachi provided loans to a number of local bannermen and daimyo. In the 1790's three daimyo owed Nakajima almost 11,000 ryō, forcing him to borrow to meet expenses. Nakajima's financial condition became so precarious that the head of the household stated in his will that the family should no longer lend to domains. The Watanabe family of Echigo fell upon trying times in the last two decades of the Tokugawa as a result of onerous demands, both from area domains and bakufu officials, for contributions and loans. It had to put much of its land into pawn and borrow heavily from others.[30]

The bakufu also adopted a number of policies detrimental to the rural elite. In addition to the supervision of lands under its control, the bakufu faced a far greater economic imperative—the political and economic stability of the system as a whole. Bakufu officials were particularly concerned about the prices of goods in the Edo and Osaka markets, and for obvious reasons. The prices the domains and bakufu received for their goods determined the vitality of the Tokugawa system itself. If rice prices fell, so too did money going into bakufu and daimyo coffers, because much of their income derived from the sale of surplus tax rice in the Edo and Osaka markets. If rice prices remained the same while the prices for other goods or services rose, their annual expenditures increased, leading to budget deficits; moreover, samurai, living on fixed stipends, were pushed further into debt.

Bakufu officials attempted to restrain price fluctuations by instituting price controls. Whereas early policies focused on merchants in Osaka and Edo, from the 1790's the bakufu began to increasingly extend its reach down to the local level. In its 1790 price edict, it ordered reductions in the prices producers received for their goods, as well as the prices at which jobbers sold these goods, commensurate with the fall in rice prices. In

1819 it ordered domains to lower the prices of the goods produced within their territories. And during the Tenpō reforms of the 1830's, the bakufu ordered both city merchants and domains to implement price reductions of 20 percent or more on a host of products.[31]

Bakufu officials were particularly concerned with the sake industry, both because rice was its primary ingredient and because vast quantities were consumed. Between 1634 and 1867 the bakufu issued sixty-one edicts ordering reductions in the quantities brewed countrywide, regardless of territorial affiliations; also, in 1657 it instituted a licensing system, which designated the maximum rice usage per brewer. Curtailment edicts frequently called for drastic cutbacks. In 1671, for example, the bakufu ordered production slashed to one-eighth of the amount stipulated on licenses issued in 1666; a 1708 edict cut production to one-fifth the amounts stipulated on 1702 licenses.[32]

Fortunately for brewers, the restrictions rarely remained in place for long. Almost three-fourths of the edicts, in fact, were concentrated in five periods, the years 1666–75, 1699–1708, 1786–94, 1828–42, and 1859–68. In most other years there were no limitations in place, and the bakufu sometimes even encouraged greater production to prop up rice prices in central markets. It was during these periods that Japan's rural sake industry witnessed phenomenal growth. Nadame, a rural coastal area to the west of Osaka, became an important sake production region in the decades before 1786, when few restrictions existed. Between 1803 and 1828, again when there were few restrictions, Nadame and nearby Imazu increased their sake shipments to Edo by over 47 percent.[33]

Despite numerous periods of relative freedom, the periodic reinstitution of controls meant that the brewers suffered violent swings in their fortunes. Between 1786 and 1788, a time of strict controls, total countrywide sake shipments to Edo declined by almost 23 percent. Between 1821 and 1853 sake shipments to Edo from the twelve major production centers in the provinces of Settsu and Izumi, including Nadame, Imazu, Osaka, Itami, and Nishinomiya, dropped by 35 percent.[34] Large Nadame brewers, such as the Kanō family of Mikage village, had accumulated enough capital to remain in business until the bakufu relaxed its restrictions, but smaller brewers in other parts of the country were less fortunate.[35]

Rural elites had a few tools at their disposal to combat the more egregious demands of political authorities. Perhaps their most powerful weapon was evasion or noncompliance, as was evident in the brewing industry. When no curtailment orders were in place, brewers increased production to meet market demand, regardless of stipulations on their licenses concerning rice usage. The licenses for brewers in Imazu village in 1785, for example, stipulated a maximum rice usage of 1,364 *koku,* but the actual amount used was over seventeen times greater, or 23,376 *koku.*[36] But the bakufu did not consider this a serious problem; it only enforced rice-usage stipulations when curtailment orders were in effect.

Rural elites were most successful in evading the purchasing networks of domain monopolies. These monopolies were of benefit to castle town merchants and selected rural merchants, but merchants outside the official network continually sought to bypass them and to sell directly to outside markets. Domains responded by incorporating larger numbers of rural merchants into their monopolies, but it proved impossible to completely remove transgressors. Officials did not have the power, or political will, to patrol coastlines or all roads leading to the outside.

As a result, few monopolies remained in operation for more than a few years. Even Hikone's monopoly on crepe, which was unusual in that it lasted until the Meiji Restoration, was not without its problems. From the late eighteenth century, more and more weavers evaded the domain's monopoly and sold crepe to other areas, such as Osaka, regions neighboring Hikone, and the Kantō.[37] Himeji's cotton cloth monopoly faced similar problems. To tighten its hold over sales, in 1836 the monopoly incorporated more rural merchants into its network and established a supervisory body at the local level. Dissatisfied with the prices they received from the domain, growing numbers of producers soon abandoned weaving altogether; in its place, they began selling the raw and semi-processed materials (raw cotton and *shinomaki*) outside the domain. In Tottori domain it proved impossible to ensure that all cotton cloth went through official channels, and domain edicts aimed at tighter control did little to guarantee compliance. Hiroshima's monopoly, too, increasingly met with opposition from producers, forcing officials to rescind many of their restrictions in the late 1860's.[38]

But there were clear limits to the rural elites' ability to ameliorate political authorities' exactions. This was especially true of requests for loans and contributions. Rural elites sometimes feigned insufficient funds; perhaps, too, they negotiated reductions through face-to-face talks with officials. But rural elites, especially in the final decades of the Tokugawa, had little choice but to acquiesce. Fear of retribution was certainly a compelling reason to do so. When Ishiuraya Mosuke failed to comply with a request from Kaga domain for a mere 4 *ryō,* officials responded with a vengeance. For a period of three years, they prohibited the family from wearing dignified dress (*hakama* and *haori*) and wooden clogs (*geta*), tying their hair with a paper cord (*motoyui*), and using a formal umbrella (*kasa*).[39] If officials wanted to send a message to the family and to others considering similar actions, this was the way to do it. Shaming the family by taking away symbols of its status was a powerful deterrent in the very status-conscious Tokugawa society.

Rural elites no doubt felt tremendous ambivalence toward political authorities in the closing years of the Tokugawa. Their positions had changed dramatically over the last century. They had become important economic actors, and many had ingratiated themselves into the ranks of their social betters, in limited but important ways. That many samurai leaders of the overthrow-the-bakufu movement argued for bringing "men of talent" into administration must also have provided some consolation that their talents would be more fully recognized under a new political order. But there were equally persuasive reasons for concern. Judging from the endless requests for loans and contributions, political authorities viewed the rural elites primarily as a source of funds, not as a wellspring of administrative talent.

Did protoindustry and the activities of the rural elite contribute to the collapse of the Tokugawa feudal order? The answer must be ambiguous. On the one hand, protoindustry provided a means to prolong the traditional order, not undermine it. As we noted earlier, many political authorities came to embrace and even encourage greater market activity. The domain monopoly itself was predicated on robust market activity. In addition, the domains' ability to tap rural elites for loans and contributions undoubtedly contributed to a prolongation of their rule. In that sense, protoindustry itself was not at all antithetical to feudal rule. Similar conditions obtained in many European states, where protoindustry coexisted for long periods of time with a wide variety of political institutions. In eastern Europe, for example, feudal lords often encouraged rural protoindustry, financed trade, and operated manufacturing establishments, with no apparent diminution or corrosion of their power.[40]

On the other hand, many of the *gōnō*'s endeavors subverted fundamental premises of the traditional order. Farmers no longer simply engaged in farming, and a few even amassed considerable fortunes, while many samurai sank deeper and deeper into debt and degradation. The status rural elites gained led to a considerable blurring of the once rigid hierarchy, giving rural elites and samurai alike cause to reflect on the importance of talent, not birth, in the proper functioning of society. Equally important, protoindustrialization complicated political authorities' economic decisions. No longer could they hope to control the economy by simply regulating city merchants' activities or regulating prices. Especially in the last decades of the Tokugawa, political authorities thrashed about in search of policies to bring their budgets under control, but there were no ready solutions in sight. With the overthrow of the Tokugawa house in 1868, most came to realize that radical changes were necessary to correct society's ills.

## The Meiji State and Rural Elites

The arrival of Commodore Matthew Perry's "black ships" in 1853 unleashed a series of events that propelled the power of the Tokugawa bakufu into steep decline. In 1868 a coalition of powerful domains in the southeast ended over two-and-a-half centuries of Tokugawa rule, and within a decade Japan's political landscape had radically changed. The Meiji leaders abolished the domains in 1871 and replaced them with a system of prefectural administration, under the close direction of the leadership and bureaucracy in Tokyo. In 1872 the leadership granted farmers the right to buy and sell land. The government overhauled the land tax system in 1873. In the past each domain had had its own tax rates and particular customs for collecting taxes. Under the new system, farmers were to pay their taxes completely in cash, and there was now a unified tax rate nationwide based on land value.

Official conceptions of social structure changed radically as well. In 1870 the government accorded non-samurai the right to use surnames. The following year it allowed them to intermarry with samurai and nobility and granted them freedom of employment, residence, and travel. With the initiation of a system of national conscription in 1873, the samurai lost their monopoly on the right to bear arms, and farmers and townspeople joined the ranks of the military. In 1876 the Meiji leadership abolished samurai stipends, in effect eradicating them as a class. These were certainly welcome reforms for rural elites, who were now in a position of equality with everyone else in society. Talent, not birth, was to be the primary criterion of advancement.

Other reforms beneficial to the rural elite followed. With the creation of a modern tax system and prefectural administrations, the never-ending rounds of loans and contributions from rural elites came to an end. Expenses for prefectural government were to come from the local tax, not from loans by residents or outside moneylenders.[41] The Meiji government's decision to assume the debts of the former domains in 1873, too, came as welcome news. Those debts incurred before 1843 became null and void; those acquired between 1844 and 1867 were to be paid off without interest over fifty years; and those acquired between 1868 and 1872 were to be returned over twenty-five years at 4 percent interest.[42] These were hardly compassionate repayment terms, especially for those rural elites whose businesses had been ruined as a result of incessant exactions, but at least they could hope for greater stability in their future endeavors.

The abolition of domains ushered in a period of fewer restrictions on rural trade, especially as a result of the eradication of monopolies and the remaining special privileges accorded castle town merchants. Regions and their elites could, and did, continue to compete for market share, but economic advantage was now to stem largely from market forces, with encouragement and modest financial inducements from the state and local governments, not through the clearly visible hand of domain overlords. The focus was on the state, not territorial advantage.

In the economic realm, the new central government and its agents in local administration continued to encourage industry, just as domains had done in the past. Indeed, "enriching the country, strengthening the military" (fukoku kyōhei), became the central focus of government policy throughout the Meiji period. To create a powerful nation-state on a par with the Western powers, the Meiji leaders sought to implant Western models of development, both in industry and in agriculture. In the industrial sphere, the government expanded existing shipyards and armories, built by the Tokugawa bakufu in the final years of its rule, and created new ones. It established several modern factories, including a silk filature at Tomioka, spinning mills in Aichi and Hiroshima, and cement and glass factories, all of which it directly owned and managed. The government also began to build railroads, lay telegraph lines, and establish a system of modern banking.

Even in agriculture, the government worked to introduce Western crops and farming practices. At government experimental farms, specialists bred livestock and tested Western seeds, fruits, and agricultural implements and disseminated the results to prefectures. The government also promoted the amalgamation of fields—to move the country toward a system of large-scale farming, as practiced in the West.

Because of a serious trade imbalance with the Western powers, the government actively encouraged export-oriented industries. Its experimental farms explored new techniques in, for example, sericulture, silk reeling, and tea production. To prevent inferior products from being shipped out of the country, and thus to ensure Japan's reputation in international markets, in 1873 the government initiated a system of inspection stations for raw silk and enacted tough regulations for the manufacture of silk-worm egg cards, or trays of silkworm eggs.[43] The following year it appointed an official to the Home Ministry to encourage the tea industry and to ensure the production of superior teas. In 1879 the government convened a competitive tea exhibition in Yokohama and awarded prizes to those submitting superior products. It held another such exhibition in Kobe in 1883.[44]

Prefectural governments, although given some initial autonomy in devising policies to encourage industry, largely followed the wishes of the central government. They, too, promoted large-scale farming and the introduction of Western agricultural methods and seeds. The Osaka metropolitan government, for example, experimented with raising pigs and the cultivation of Western grains and fruits. Ibaraki prefecture hired a Western instructor in 1875 to develop a pasture and invited students from around the prefecture to learn the techniques of sheep husbandry. The following year it established an experimental farm on which it tested Western crops and farming methods. Similar farms could be found in almost every prefecture.[45]

Prefectural administrations were especially eager to encourage profitable export-oriented industries. Tottori prefecture, which had had a relatively insignificant sericulture industry before the opening of the ports, provided loans of mulberry seedlings to its residents. In 1874 it purchased two million mulberry seedlings from the Ibaraki area, and in later years it purchased more seedlings from other parts of the country. Aichi prefecture did the same in 1874, when it purchased 150,000 mulberry seedlings from a village in Ōmi. Mie prefecture, hoping to encourage silk reeling, dispatched an official in 1874 to Kumagaya prefecture to purchase equipment and to hire an instructor and workers. Okayama prefecture's experimental farm at Tsuyama, established in 1877, hired specialists from Gunma to assist in sericultural training. Fukui prefecture encouraged the weaving of habutae, a soft, lightweight plain-weave silk, by bringing in an expert from Kiryū in 1886 and held training sessions for weavers. This proved most fortuitous, for habutae became an important export item at the end of the century. Gunma prefecture purchased high-quality mulberry seedlings from Fukushima, which officials then distributed to farmers upon request.[46]

The convening of competitive fairs and exhibitions was especially vital to local development efforts. In 1879 Okayama prefecture held an exhibition that displayed 5,294 items and attracted over 150,000 visitors. Mie prefecture held an exhibition in 1878 attended by over 70,000, with 3,214 people submitting more than 10,000 products for display. An exhibition held in Kitamuro district in Mie in 1883 attracted some 14,000 people, and another in Taki district the same year brought in over 5,700.[47]

A few prefectures offered loans to enterprising residents. In 1877 officials in the Shindatsu area agreed to lend 23,000 yen over a period of five years to rural elites to establish a silk-reeling factory. The following year officials provided an additional loan of 1,000 yen to expand the factory to include a silk-weaving division. Ibaraki offered technical guidance and financial assistance to those opening silk filatures. When Sakurai Masatarō launched into machine reeling with other rural elites in 1880 and established the Taiseisha, he received both technical guidance and a loan of 500 yen from the prefecture. Several others received similar forms of assistance.[48]

The Meiji leadership's early policies were most welcome developments for rural elites. At long last, status restrictions and feudal privileges had been swept away, and their talents could now be more fully recognized under the new order. They also felt a strong sense of nationalism. They, too, wanted to propel Japan into the front ranks of the world powers. They thus became enthusiastic participants in the government's modernization efforts. Some served in prefectural administration as encouragement-of-industry officials. Tajima Yahei, one of Gunma's largest egg card producers, served as an official in the central government's egg card inspection system.[49]

Some rural elites experimented with the new crops and agricultural techniques being promoted by the central government. Itohara Gonzō of Shimane prefecture cultivated Western vegetables, including asparagus, eggplant, and sunflower. He established two private experimental farms in his district, where he tested 250 domestic and foreign seeds. Mutō Kōitsu in Gunma opened a large-scale farm, on which he demonstrated the superiority of modern plowing methods. He also planted grapes, launched into wine production, raised goats, and engaged in carp farming—all potent symbols of the government's emphasis on Western-style farming.[50]

Others introduced export-oriented industries, both to revitalize their communities and to reduce their country's trade deficit. Furuhashi Terunori in Mikawa began experimenting with tea cultivation in 1870. In 1874 he requested the prefecture to provide technical support for mulberry cultivation and mulberry seedlings, and he donated money for a sericultural training center. Likewise, Iwamoto Renzō of Tottori prefecture purchased mulberry seedlings from the Tanba area and distributed them to area farmers. In 1878 he hired someone from Nagano to teach silk-reeling methods, and in 1887 he established a sericultural training center, employing someone from Gunma as an instructor.[51]

In 1881 the government adopted a new approach to encourage industry. Faced with an inflationary spiral resulting from the overprinting of paper currency, Finance Minister Matsukata Masayoshi adopted severe retrenchment measures, resulting in drastic cutbacks in government expenditures. At the same time, Matsukata and other government leaders argued that it was not the government's responsibility to get involved in private enterprise; government involvement, Matsukata argued, impeded private initiative. Largely as a result, the government abandoned efforts to manage the economy directly, instead focusing its efforts on indirect means.[52] This was most evident in the industrial sector: the government sold off many of its factories, almost all of which had been operating at a deficit, to private enterprise.

In the agricultural sector, it was clear to government leaders that previous policies too had been dismal failures: despite the examples cited above, few farmers had adopted Western crops and methods, and efforts to promote land amalgamation proved fruitless. To rectify the problem, the government turned its attention to the country's so-called rōnō (literally, "old farmers"), improving farmers who were actively involved in experimentation and encouragement of industry at the local level. The government had made the first tentative moves in this direction in 1878, when it initiated a system of agricultural communications agents. By appointing rural elites to these positions, the government found a means by which its directives and recommendations could be transmitted to the local level and put into practice, while making few substantive changes in its agricultural policies.

To exploit more fully the talents of the rōnō, in 1881 the government established the Agricultural Society of Japan (Dai Nippon Nōkai), which brought under its aegis local agricultural societies already in existence at the local level. The same year, the government sponsored the first National Agricultural Discussion Conference, bringing together rōnō from across the country to exchange information on improved farming methods and crop varieties. As part of this policy to utilize the talents of the country's improving farmers, the government convened numerous competitive fairs and exhibitions. In 1883 it established a system of encouragement-of-industry advisory committees, and in 1885 a system of agricultural circuit agents.[53]

Prefectural administrations were particularly eager to tap the enterprising spirit of improving farmers. Ibaraki prefecture's yearly encouragement-of-industry bulletin frequently cited the activities of *rōnō*, including their participation in agricultural discussion societies and competitive exhibitions. Fukushima prefecture invited experts from other parts of the country to impart their expertise on such things as horse plowing methods.[54]

Despite these efforts, by the 1880's government encouragement-of-industry policies had been thoroughly discredited at the local level, and rural elites around the country voiced opposition to government policies. Even the Agricultural Society of Japan saw its membership and influence plummet. By the late 1880's the government had sold off or shut down many of its experimental farms, agricultural schools, and training centers.[55]

Rural elites had cause to be disenchanted. Despite efforts to encourage traditional industry, the overwhelming thrust of early Meiji policy—as senior officers of the Agricultural Society of Japan made clear in their pronouncements—was still on modern industry and on Western agricultural practices, to the neglect of the traditional sector.[56] In addition, the goal of many government projects was not to better the lot of farmers but to provide employment for samurai. Moreover, the majority of the students at the government agricultural schools were samurai, not farmers, and many of the instructors were British.[57] The same was true even at the prefectural stations. At Okayama prefecture's Tsuyama station, for example, twenty of twenty-five students trained between 1877 and 1880 were samurai.[58]

Another problem concerned financing for industrial promotion programs. In the view of many rural elites, the central government had done little to encourage traditional industry and agriculture. Most funds had gone toward the establishment of government enterprises and to the so-called *seishō*, the large merchant houses and other firms with close ties to the government, such as Mitsui, Mitsubishi, Yasuda, and Furukawa. This was true even after 1881, when the government enacted severe retrenchment measures. While the government virtually terminated financing for traditional industries, it continued to provide benefits to the *seishō*. This was clear from the sale of government enterprises to the *seishō* at well below market rates and on favorable terms.[59] Even during the retrenchment years, the government still granted large subsidies to *seishō* enterprises.

At the prefectural level, despite numerous examples of financial assistance for local projects, the total amounts allocated were inconsequential. The proposed budget submitted to the Ibaraki prefectural assembly in 1879 included 11,400 yen for encouragement of industry, or about 4.5 percent of its total budget. In 1882 Gunma prefecture spent 8,206 yen on encouragement of industry, about 2 percent of all expenditures that year. The greatest expenditures were for police, public works, salaries and official expenses, and jails.[60]

This situation, too, was largely the result of actions taken by the central government. With the initiation of new codes for prefectural administration in 1878, expenses for construction and prisons, as well as for prefectural encouragement-of-industry efforts, had to come out of the local tax, not from the central treasury. As a result, local taxes soared, increasing by 50 percent between 1879 and 1884. This came at a time when prices for agricultural products were declining as a result of Matsukata's deflationary policies; rice prices alone dropped by over 50 percent between 1881 and 1884.[61]

Rural elites also bristled at the fact that they had little real power in either central or prefectural administration. Immediately after the Restoration of 1868, a few domains demonstrated a willingness to bring "men of talent" into the administration by establishing deliberative assemblies composed of both samurai and non-samurai, and some prefectural administrations did much the same upon their establishment in 1871. These assemblies, though, served primarily as conduits through which directives were to be relayed to localities.[62] By the end of the 1870's little had changed. Almost all the high-ranking prefectural officials in Gunma were samurai from other parts of the country. In 1879 it was unusual for commoners to serve even as district heads. They dominated local administration only at the district secretary level and below.[63]

Sake brewers had their own grievances with government policy. In 1871 the Meiji government lifted all restrictions on the numbers of brewers and the amount they brewed. The latter was certainly good news for existing brewers, but they soon faced impositions far more onerous than had existed under the old regime. In an effort to increase revenues to finance modernization projects and a growing military complex, the Meiji government instituted oppressive taxes on the sake industry. Sake's share of government tax revenue increased from a mere 3.7 percent in 1876 to 34.4 percent in 1900, outstripping revenue from the land tax.[64] Until the late Meiji, increasing the land tax had been a political impossibility: there had been a number of rebellions in various areas against the new land tax in the first place, and rural elites voiced strong opposition to any increase. The leadership also believed that a move to more indirect forms of taxation would bring Japan into line with practices in Western countries, where the land tax occupied a relatively insignificant proportion of government income.

As a result, increases in the sake tax came in rapid succession. In 1871 the government imposed a flat fee of ten *ryō* on each new brewer of refined sake, regardless of size, a yearly operating fee of five *ryō*, and a 5 percent tax on sake sales. In 1875 it abolished the fee for new brewers but increased the yearly operating fee from five yen to ten yen and the sales tax from 5 to 10 percent. In 1878 it replaced the sales tax with a tax of one yen per *koku* of sake brewed. Further changes came in 1880: the government abolished the licensing system, but it increased the yearly operating tax to thirty yen; and the per *koku* tax doubled to two yen.[65]

It was no coincidence that many rural elites opposed to the government's economic policies had strong links to the Popular Rights Movement (*jiyū minken undō*), joining the ranks of samurai around the country in calling for the enactment of a Constitution and the institution of an elective national assembly. Brewers were among the first lobbying groups active in the movement. They held a nationwide conference in Osaka and Kyoto in 1882, under the auspices of leaders of the Popular Rights Movement. Representatives from eighteen prefectures and two metropolitan areas drafted a petition calling for a reduction in sake taxes.[66]

Many of the agricultural discussion societies and encouragement-of-industry associations the rural elites formed in the early Meiji became important forums for criticism of government policy. The Kōunsha, formed in 1873 and centered on rural elites in Kumamoto prefecture, worked to introduce cash crops into the area and operated an experimental farm. At the same time, members criticized the government for failing to assist local development efforts. The Aishinsha, established in the Aizu area of Fukushima in 1878 to promote industry, became one of the major groups in the region for Popular Rights activity. The Tokushinsha, established in Yamagata prefecture in 1880, encouraged local industry, while simultaneously part of a movement calling for a nationally elected assembly.[67]

Many of those most outspoken in their attacks on government policy had been enthusiastic supporters of government efforts in the past, often serving in local encouragement-of-industry positions. This should be not at all surprising. Those active in the Popular Rights Movement were ardent nationalists. They differed with the government not over the ultimate aim of policy—propelling Japan into the front ranks of the world powers—but over the best means to achieve it.

Lacking a political voice, rural elites used the only political institution at their disposal to express discontent with government policy—the prefectural assembly. To assuage the demands of rural elites for political representation, the government had initiated a system of prefectural assemblies in 1878. There were substantial income and residence requirements for both candidates and the electorate, so the assemblies were composed entirely of people of wealth, the rural elite in particular. Moreover, the Meiji leadership accorded the assemblies little power. They were to consult on expenditures from the local tax and on the means of tax collection, but assembly proposals needed the governor's approval before taking effect.[68]

Prefectural assemblies in succession voiced opposition to what they saw as the government's misguided policies. Fukuoka prefectural assemblymen recommended the abolition or suspension of many of the offices and institutions championed by the central government, such as encouragement-of-industry officials and agricultural communications agents. Fukushima abolished its system of agricultural schools in 1886 and its agricultural experiment station in 1891. In 1881 the Okayama prefectural assembly decided to terminate funding for its experimental farms. Ibaraki assemblymen voted in 1879 to end funding for experiment stations for sericulture and raw silk, paper manufacture, and black tea.[69]

The Gunma prefectural assembly voted to slash the proposed encouragement-of-industry budget in seven of the twelve years between 1879 and 1890; in only two years did it approve an increase. The most the assembly appropriated was 7,695 yen for 1882, but thereafter it drastically curtailed such expenditures. In 1888 it appropriated only 135 yen. The assembly voted to cut or severely slash all initiatives relating to encouragement of industry, including funds for officials, salaries for managers and cultivators at the prefecture's experimental farm, and funds the prefecture allocated to purchase mulberry seedlings for distribution to residents.[70]

The reasons for these actions varied. For some, the differences were philosophical. Hagiwara Ryōtarō of Gunma prefecture believed that the government should not be involved in fostering and protecting private industry; what was needed among the people of Japan was a strong spirit of independence and self-reliance, not subservience to government dictates. Many in the Fukushima prefectural assembly argued along the same lines. From the 1880's there was much debate about how much of a role the government should have in promoting agriculture. Many asserted that government interference in private industry was no longer necessary, and some even called for the abolition of the Ministry of Agriculture and Commerce.[71]

Especially important in the prefectural assemblies' decisions were the wretched economic conditions of the early 1880's, forcing rural elites to reconsider which areas the government should be involved in. Indeed, the assemblies voted to reduce spending not just for encouragement of industry but in all areas, including funds for police and construction. In 1881, for example, the Shiga prefectural assembly actually voted to abolish funding for prisons and prison construction and repairs.[72] If they wanted to send a message to the law-and-order Meiji leadership, there was no better way.

Mounting protests from rural elites forced government leaders in 1881 to announce the enactment of a constitution, providing for an elected national assembly, by the end of the decade. But few other concessions were forthcoming. This was especially true for brewers. Despite mounting protests, the government imposed even greater exactions on the industry. In 1882, only months after brewers held their conference, the government defiantly doubled the sake tax from two yen per *koku* to four. By 1908 the tax had increased to twenty yen.[73]

Onerous taxes proved disastrous for brewers across the country. Between 1880 and 1908 the number of brewers dropped from 25,480 to 10,804.[74] Most larger establishments, such as those in Nadame, survived, but countless small and medium establishments ceased operations. Conditions for brewers were especially poor in the 1880's, when the government's deflationary policies greatly restricted demand. In Niigata prefecture sake production fell by almost 57 percent between 1882 and 1887. Production recovered slowly thereafter, but even at the end of the Meiji it was 20 percent below that of 1882. In Okayama the number of sake brewers dropped from 891 in 1882 to 459 in 1887, and production declined by over 40 percent. Even brewers on the Chita peninsula, which had become one of the leading sake production regions in the late Tokugawa, saw their businesses collapse as a result of high taxes, the poor economic climate of the early 1880's, and inability to compete with superior brands from Nadame.[75]

By the end of the 1880's government encouragement-of-industry policies aimed at the traditional sector of the economy were in complete disarray. Faced with implacable resistance at the local level to its policies and institutions, the government finally abandoned attempts to introduce large-scale farming and Western cultivation methods. Rather than relaxing its hold, however, it enacted a broad range of measures to provide greater central direction to improvements at the local level, especially in agriculture. By the early twentieth century there was in place across Japan a network of experimental farms and agricultural societies under the supervision of bureaucrats. Also, by enacting laws for trade and industry associations (*dōgyō kumiai*) and producers' cooperatives (*sangyō ku-*

*miai*), the government provided an organizational and regulatory structure through which localities, and their rural elites, could work toward improvements in traditional industry.

Calls for fundamental change in Japan's policies toward agriculture and traditional industry came both from rural elites and from the members of the government itself. As to the former, many rural elites had been active in encouraging local industry and agriculture for decades. Since at least the early 1870's, they had been organizing agricultural discussion societies, seed exchange societies, and forums for encouragement of industry. Even after voting to slash funding for government institutions and policy initiatives in the early to mid-1880's, rural elites continued to establish agricultural discussion societies, though on a completely independent footing, with no ties to the Agricultural Society of Japan.[76]

Until the 1890's, rural elites concerned with local improvements were, at best, loosely organized and lacked a united political voice. The organizing activities of Maeda Masana changed this situation. Maeda, who had been forced from his position in the Ministry of Agriculture and Commerce in 1890 over policy disputes with Matsukata Masayoshi and other officials, had argued that the government should focus its efforts more on fostering and protecting indigenous industry, and less on implanting Western factories on Japanese soil, and that it should avoid over-reliance on the *seishō*. Now in a totally private capacity, in 1892 Maeda launched a movement at the grassroots level. He traveled around the country, arguing the need for improvements in local industry and agriculture, urging elites to devise plans for community revival, and organizing farmers and other producers into local and national associations.[77]

Organizing efforts were especially vital to Maeda's goals. Beginning in 1893 with a national organization for tea producers, by 1895 Maeda had organized twelve producers' associations nationwide, covering almost every area of agriculture and traditional industry, with branch associations across the country. Maeda also assumed the leadership of the National Agricultural Association (Zenkoku Nōjikai) and lobbied the government for the creation of a nationwide system of agricultural societies. Originally part of the Agricultural Society of Japan, under Maeda the National Agricultural Association became an independent organization in 1895 as a result of differences with officers of the parent organization, most of whom were Ministry of Agriculture and Commerce bureaucrats.[78] By 1898 the National Agricultural Association included forty-two prefectural agricultural societies, 500 at the district level, and over 8,000 in towns and villages.[79]

What made Maeda's local-improvement movement a success was the zealous participation of rural elites across the country. Hoshino Chōtarō, active in organizing raw silk cooperatives in Gunma since the 1870's, was particularly involved in Maeda's organizations. Ishikawa Rikinosuke of Akita prefecture traveled around Kyūshū for several months in 1894 explaining the need for agricultural improvements and agricultural societies. When he returned, he began organizing a network of agricultural societies in Akita prefecture.[80]

Ishikawa, Hoshino, and countless other rural elites in Maeda's movement vigorously lobbied government officials and members of the new national Diet for the enactment of measures to facilitate their efforts. Implicit in their demands was the conviction that the government could play a critical, albeit indirect, role in facilitating local improvement efforts. They called for regulations to make membership and dues in agricultural societies compulsory—this was the only way to truly effect improvements—but they wanted the societies themselves to remain independent from government control and to not receive subsidies. They requested the establishment of prefectural agricultural experiment stations, agricultural banks, and inspection systems for raw silk and egg cards. They also sought regulations allowing for sericulture and raw silk producers' cooperatives, so that farmers could engage in collective sales and establish credit associations to facilitate their improvement efforts.[81]

There were also influential voices in the government calling for change. Bureaucrats in the Ministry of Agriculture and Commerce, as well as those with close ties to the ministry, increasingly argued the need for a network of agricultural societies. Inoue Kaoru, a powerful leader in the Meiji government and one of the greatest proponents in the past of Western farming methods, actively promoted the issue as Minister of Agriculture and Commerce in 1889.[82] Around the same time, the Association of Agricultural Sciences (Nōgakukai), composed of graduates of the country's leading agricultural schools, called for a network of agricultural societies and prefectural experiment stations.[83]

Shinagawa Yajirō and Hirata Tōsuke were especially active in sponsoring measures aimed at preserving Japan's small-farming system and promoted a bill for the establishment of rural credit associations. Both were influential members of the government: Shinagawa served in important posts in the Ministry of Finance and Ministry of Agriculture and Commerce before becoming Minister of the Interior from 1891 to 1892; and Hirata served in the Ministry of Finance before joining the House of Peers and Privy Council in 1890. There were countless others in the bureaucracy who believed that the government needed to do more to improve the lot of Japan's small farmers.[84]

As a result of the efforts of Maeda, rural elites in his movement, and influential ministers and bureaucracts, the government implemented a number of important measures aimed at agriculture and traditional industry. In 1893 it (re)established a national agricultural experiment station and several branch stations around the country. It also encouraged prefectures to establish or revive experimental farms, many of which had been abolished in the previous decade. By 1900 a network of agricultural stations spanned the country, enabling the government to effect improvements at the local level.[85] The government enacted regulations for agricultural societies in 1899. There were now to be associations in every prefecture, in every district, and in many towns and villages across the country, all of which were to receive subsidies from the central treasury.[86]

The government also adopted measures aimed at producers in traditional industries. In 1897 it passed a law for trade and industry associations in important export industries, in large measure to correct the deficiencies of the 1884 regulations, which contained weak enforcement mechanisms. Finally, the government passed a law relating to producers' cooperatives in 1900. In 1898 there were 351 such organizations nationwide, most of them taking the form of credit associations or cooperatives for collective sales. The 1900 law provided a legal foundation for these cooperatives.

Maeda and his supporters among the rural elite gained much from the legislation of the 1890's. A nationwide network of experiment stations, a system of agricultural societies, regulations for trade and industry associations and producers' cooperatives—these had been central demands of the movement. Some of the laws and regulations were weak, it is true. The 1899 law for agricultural societies included no stipulations for compulsory membership or dues. There were no provisions for a national agricultural association encompassing the organizations at the prefectural and local levels, just as there were no provisions for federations of producers' cooperatives. The regulations for cooperatives also did not allow them to engage in more than one activity: cooperatives established for collective sales, for example, could not extend credit, and credit associations could not engage in collective sales. Most of these deficiencies were corrected in the first decade of the twentieth century, after Maeda had left the movement and memories of his disloyalty to the bureaucracy had faded.[87]

There was much in the legislation, especially those regulations targeting the agricultural sector, that fell far short of what rural elites in Maeda's movement had envisioned. That agricultural societies received government subsidies and became organs of state policy was especially disturbing to his supporters. Local officials headed the societies in their areas. In the Gunma Prefecture Agricultural Society, formed in 1896, the top officers were bureaucrats. In Fukui the governor or prefectural secretary often headed the prefectural organization, while large landlords were appointed as officers. Local officials presided over the associations at the district, town, and village levels.[88]

In a very real sense, bureaucrats had no choice but to impose a different vision of how improvements were to be made at the local level. Times had changed. From the mid-Tokugawa through the mid-Meiji, farmers had experimented with new seeds, implements, and cultivation techniques and had recorded their results in diaries and treatises. By the 1890's there was in place a system of agricultural schools, where students learned the scientific principles behind farming. In effect, scientific advances and the spread of scientific knowledge had made obsolete the accumulated wisdom of improving farmers.

Equally important, despite the calls of rural elites for self-reliance, the fact of the matter is that by the 1890's large numbers of rural elites were abandoning direct cultivation of the land, moving from their villages, and living off the rents of their tenants. With the growth of modern industry, they also began to invest in spinning, railroads, local banks, and public bonds and all but abandoned concern for agricultural improvements. This was one very important factor behind the government's decision to build a nationwide structure for experiment stations and agricultural societies: the rural elite were no longer performing their traditional roles in society.[89]

The leasing of land by rural elites could be found in every village of Japan and had existed well before the Meiji period. As is clear from the work of Ann Waswo, until the mid-Meiji most landlords lived in the communities in which they rented out land and actively participated in village improvements and village affairs.[90] If their tenants suffered a crop failure, they would provide relief or reduce their rents. Most landlords continued to cultivate some of their lands themselves.

From the mid-Meiji, the landlords' roles underwent a significant transformation. One of the most visible signs of change was the landlords' abandonment of direct cultivation. Labor shortages and higher wages for agricultural labor meant that direct cultivation was no longer profitable, and agricultural improvements had made the leasing of land far less risky than in the past. Between 1883 and 1908, land cultivated by tenants increased from 36 to 45 percent of the nation's total arable land.[91] The reason there was only a slight increase thereafter was that the returns from investing in commerce and industry were far greater than investments in land. More and more landlords moved from their villages and became absentee landlords, no longer interested in undertaking local improvements.

It was not even clear in the 1890's whose interests the rural elite in the Diet were representing. To diffuse the Popular Rights Movement, the Meiji leaders announced in 1881 that a Constitution would be promulgated and a nationally elected assembly would be in place in 1890. As with the prefectural assemblies, steep minimum-tax requirements for the electorate and those eligible for election put control of the House of Representatives into the hands of the country's wealthiest citizens. Rural elites, many of whom had been active in prefectural assemblies, comprised half of the seats in the early years of the Diet. But it was hardly evident at times that these Diet members were in fact representing their communities. In 1893, for example, the Diet voted to abolish the tariff on seed cotton imports, to take effect in 1896, resulting in the precipitous decline of cotton cultivation. Moreover, although in the early years the Diet vigorously opposed all attempts to increase the land tax, by the end of the 1890's that opposition had considerably diminished, and an increase was passed in 1898.[92]

Not all landlords, of course, abandoned agriculture and moved from their communities. The large numbers of rural elites in Maeda's movement serve as ample proof of their continuing concern for local improvements. But to many the trend seemed to be in the opposite direction. Criticism of noncultivating landlords came from diverse sources. Agronomists and others with close ties to the Ministry of Agriculture and Commerce, such as Oda Matatarō and Yokoi Tokiyoshi, criticized landlords for lacking benevolence and living solely off the rents of their tenants, with no concern for the tenants' welfare or for making improvements on their lands. Yanagita Kunio, Ministry of Agriculture and Commerce bureaucrat and soon-to-be distinguished folklorist, rebuked those landlords who no longer engaged in productive activity and lived off tenancy fees. Writing in 1892, Maeda activist Ishikawa Rikinosuke of Akita labeled those investing in land solely to collect tenancy fees as the "criminals of agriculture." It was the duty of the landlord, he wrote, to periodically inspect his lands, to pay attention to the application of fertilizers, to lend money when necessary to his tenants, and to give rewards to the diligent.[93]

The *gōnō* engaged in an ambivalent relationship with political authorities throughout the protoindustrial period. By the mid-eighteenth century political authorities had largely acquiesced in the *gōnō*'s activities, such as land accumulation, interregional commerce, and manufacture, all of which had been frowned upon in the past. In exchange for loans and contributions, political authorities accorded them samurai status and stipends. They also incorporated rural elites in their monopolies and appointed a few to positions in domain administration. In the Meiji period the central government and its surrogates in prefectural administration provided entrepreneurial elites funds for local development projects, especially in the export-oriented sectors of the economy, and they appointed them to official positions, for example in areas relating to encouragement of industry.

In the final analysis, the benefits *gōnō* received from political authorities were small recompense for the burdens placed upon them. The incessant demands for loans and contributions in the Tokugawa forced many into bankruptcy or into reducing the scale of their business operations. Monopolies might have benefited a select few but they served as impediments to free trade. Initially, at least, the *gōnō* welcomed the policies of the new Meiji government, and they became active cheerleaders of and vehicles for encouragement-of-industry policies. By the late 1870's, however, they realized that the leadership had a different vision for Japan's economic and political transformation. Ignoring promises to bring "men of talent" into administration, the leaders largely excluded the *gōnō* from all but the most minor positions in the bureaucracy, and they plowed the bulk of government resources into the modern sector. Many *gōnō* raised their voices in protest, but it took quite some time for their message to be heard.

With the initiation of the first Diet session in 1890, the rural elite for the first time acquired real political power. In addition, many of their demands were realized in the 1890's with the passage of a host of regulations relating to the traditional sector. But by this time the *gōnō* had largely withdrawn from the concerns of rural society.

# 2

# The Transformation of
# Regional Production

THE MID-EIGHTEENTH CENTURY marks a critical divide in Japanese history. Dramatic increases in agricultural productivity and the transmission of manufacturing techniques and technologies to various parts of the country generated greater market activity. Many regions began to specialize in cash crops and manufactured products once largely monopolized by farmers and townspeople in the Kinai region, especially the cities of Osaka and Kyoto and surrounding towns and villages. By the Meiji period the sites and quantities of production had radically changed, with farmers across the country engaged in market-related activities. Even villagers in northeastern Japan, who had once been largely subsistence farmers, produced goods for consumption in domestic and international markets.

The rural elites—the gōnō—who emerged from the mid-eighteenth century initiated many of the changes that occurred in the Japanese economy. They introduced commodity production and new technologies into their communities, and they were in the forefront of technological advances which resulted in higher agricultural yields and improvements in manufacturing techniques. The commercialization of the economy, however, led to intense interregional competition for market share, and rural elites achieved little long-term stability through their economic endeavors. The purpose of this chapter is to illustrate how commodity production changed during the Tokugawa and Meiji eras, and how these changes created the foundation for the rise of the gōnō and influenced their economic activities. To highlight the transformation, let us look at regional production in the seventeenth century.

## Early Tokugawa Beginnings

Through much of the first half of the Tokugawa, the region in west-central Japan known as the Kinai monopolized the country's advanced agricultural and manufacturing sectors. All regions engaged in market production to one extent or another from the early Tokugawa, but none could rival the Kinai in levels of productivity. The Kinai also served as the preeminent center for commerce and finance.

Of Tokugawa Japan's three leading cities, Osaka and Kyoto were in the Kinai. Osaka became the leading market for the sale of surplus rice collected by the bakufu and domains in partial fulfilment of the land tax, especially that from the Kinai, western Japan, and regions along the Japan Sea to the northeast. Osaka also became the major center for the collection and shipment, and often the manufacture, of many of the country's major products, such as vegetable oils, soy sauce, sake, and cotton goods.[1] Kyoto occupied an undisputed position in the manufacture of labor- and technology-intensive luxury goods, including fans, lacquerware, gilt bronze work, and dyed goods. Its textile industry, in particular, was unparalleled. The Nishijin district, the center for Kyoto's weavers and cloth finishers, monopolized the techniques and technologies for producing luxury silks worn by the samurai and court elite.[2]

The third major Japanese city, Edo, depended heavily on imports from the Kinai. The Tokugawa bakufu set up its headquarters at Edo and initiated the system of alternate attendance (*sankin kōtai*), requiring daimyo to spend alternate years of residence in Edo and to permanently house their families there. By the early eighteenth century, Edo had an estimated one million people, half of whom were samurai. The surrounding region, however, was ill-equipped to meet the burgeoning consumer demand generated by rapid urbanization. For much of the early Tokugawa, Edo was dependent on the Kinai, in particular Osaka and Kyoto, for a number of necessities, especially those which needed processing, such as soy sauce, lamp and hair oils, ginned cotton, and staggering quantities of sake.[3]

High levels of agricultural productivity buttressed the Kinai's position within the early Tokugawa economic order. In addition to rice, farmers cultivated several major cash crops, including cotton, indigo, tobacco, and vegetables. As William Hauser has shown, cotton was especially vital to the Kinai rural economy. Not only was it used in the production of cloth and as a raw material for oils, but the scrap remaining after oil extraction was employed for fertilizer and feed.[4]

Other parts of the country were far behind the Kinai, but a number of factors converged in the seventeenth century to generate greater market activity. The bakufu and most domains ordered that a substantial portion of the annual land tax be paid in cash, obligating farmers to sell their crops or handicrafts to obtain specie. In addition, the removal of samurai from rural areas to castle towns from the late sixteenth to early seventeenth centuries required that there be a continuous supply of foodstuffs from rural areas to meet the needs of samurai and other town residents.

There were also important changes in rural society itself. Thomas Smith and numerous Japanese historians have extensively examined the background of the economic transformation in rural Japan. Land reclamation and irrigation projects, initiated over the course of the seventeenth century, resulted in major increases in production and yields. Improved seeds raised agricultural productivity, and new varieties of rice allowed for early, middle, and late harvests, enabling farmers to better allocate labor, fertilizers, and irrigation water. Farmers developed methods of seed selection to ensure the best yields, such as the soaking of seeds in water or brine prior to planting. Growing numbers around the country adopted the Kinai practice of applying cash fertilizers, such as dried sardines and oil cakes, which also resulted in increased yields. Inventive farmers developed new hoes suited to specific tasks and local soil conditions. A rake-like thresher, known as the *senbakōki*, developed in the early eighteenth century to strip rice and other grains from their stalks, had ten times the productivity of earlier devices.[5]

Also important to the transformation of Japan's regional production was the dismantling of patriarchal farming units.[6] Until the mid- to late seventeenth century, large numbers of farmers were in varying forms of servitude to powerful local families, many of whom claimed samurai lineage, having abandoned the sword and returned to full-time farming in the late sixteenth or early seventeenth century. As a result of productivity increases and the conscious policy of political authorities, most farmers acquired independence. The former patriarchs lost their dependents and some of their lands, but they were still largeholders and wielded considerable influence in their communities.

It was in the interests of such largeholders to encourage others in their communities to increase the productivity of their fields and to introduce commercial crops and handicrafts. They were no doubt motivated in part by a sense of paternalistic obligation to their former dependents, some of whom were related by blood. Although nominally independent and constituting small nuclear households, their former dependents cultivated minuscule parcels of land, often a half *chō* or less, and relied on their former patriarchs for loans and other forms of assistance in times of need. Self-interest was another compelling factor. It was hardly to the rural elites' benefit to have poorer farmers defaulting on their loans. Also, because political authorities assessed taxes on the productivity of the village as a whole, others in the community were forced to assume the tax share of impoverished farmers who abandoned their lands and left the village. Smallholders, too, now had an obvious incentive to increase their yields and to acquire additional income from pursuits outside agriculture. Their survival as farmers depended on it.

Despite unmistakable evidence of change in rural society, the Kinai continued to dominate the economic scene for much of the first half of the Tokugawa. This becomes especially clear from an examination of some of the country's most important products: textiles and their raw materials, tea, and sake.

By the early eighteenth century, some farmers in the Mikawa region of central Japan dedicated 50 percent or more of their dry fields to cotton, which they processed and shipped to the Edo market. Yields, however, were far below those of the Kinai. The anonymous author of the agricultural treatise *Hyakushō denki*, written in Mikawa in the 1680's, states that the cotton grown in the Kinai was the best in the country. Farmers from Mikawa wanting a superior crop would purchase seeds from the Kinai, as did farmers in western Honshū and Shikoku. We know from Sase Yojiemon's treatise *Aizu nōsho*, written in 1684, that even in northeastern Japan farmers cultivated small amounts of cotton. But the yield was far below that of other areas, about one-seventh the average yields of the Kinai.[7]

A number of regions outside the Kinai engaged in some aspect of the silk industry well before the Tokugawa. Farmers in western Japan and in regions contiguous to the Kinai engaged in sericulture and reeled raw silk from their cocoons. But until the late seventeenth century domestic production was insignificant. Massive quantities of raw silk still came from the China trade at Nagasaki. Several regions outside the Kinai produced silk textiles, but they produced monochrome plain-weaves and pongee, a coarse silk made from inferior cocoons. Even Kiryū in the Kantō, which was to become a center of rural silk textile production from the mid-Tokugawa, shipped much of its cloth to Kyoto for dyeing and final finishing.[8]

Every region of the country brewed sake in the first century of Tokugawa rule. A bakufu investigation, in fact, reported over 27,000 brewers in existence in 1698.[9] As in Mito domain, the largest brewers outside the

Kinai were in the castle towns, but numerous other, smaller, establishments could be found in towns and villages.[10] Sake produced by small brewers, though, was primarily for local consumption, and none could rival the quality of that produced in the Kinai. A contemporary observer, writing in 1695, considered the sake produced in the cities and towns of the Kinai—especially Nara, Itami, Kōnoike, Ikeda, and Tonda—to be of superior quality.[11]

Although many farmers across the country cultivated tea, it became an important product only from the late seventeenth century. Before this time, most tea sold in central markets was pulverized into powdered form and used in the tea ceremony. It was clearly a luxury product, consumed by samurai and court elites. Around the mid-seventeenth century, an early form of green tea—often produced by kettle-firing the tea leaves over a hearth—found a growing market. In 1679 there were only ten tea wholesalers in Osaka, but by the early 1710's sixty-four establishments there dealt in green tea alone. By the 1720's and 1730's Osaka wholesalers handled tea not only from the greater Kinai but from Hyūga, Tosa, Ise, Higo, Kumano, and Mino.[12]

No area, however, rivaled the quality of tea produced in the Uji area of the Kinai. The Uji powdered-tea industry was so important that it received bakufu protection, and farmers had to sell their tea through designated channels. Unlike farmers in other parts of the country, who cultivated tea on the footpaths between fields or on mountain slopes, Uji farmers grew their plants in groves. To produce a high-quality product, they latticed over their groves for superior grades of tea with straw or reed to protect the plants from the elements until the buds appeared. Uji farmers also excelled in the processing of green tea, especially as a result of innovations developed in the 1730's. Instead of kettle-firing, they steamed the leaves and then rolled and rubbed them over a hearth. This process produced a flavorful tea highly prized in central markets.[13]

There were thus several other sites of commodity production before 1700, but few could rival the Kinai. The Kinai enjoyed a virtual monopoly on the techniques and technologies for cultivating important cash crops and manufactured products.

## The Diffusion of Production and Technology

Although commodity production punctuated the farming economy outside the Kinai in the early Tokugawa, the mid-eighteenth century marks an important turning point in Japan's pattern of regional produc-

tion. Rural areas across the country began to introduce crops and agricultural techniques that had once been the preserve of the Kinai, as well as the
Kinai's manufacturing technologies, such as those for weaving luxury
silks, brewing refined sake, and tea processing.[14]

There were two primary groups behind the process of diffusion: political authorities—in particular, domains before 1868 and the new Meiji
government thereafter—and rural elites. As we saw in Chapter 1, financially pressed domains began to introduce new crops and technologies to
their territories from the mid-eighteenth century. The Meiji government,
too, played a major role in diffusing new and existing technologies. Far
more critical in the transformation of regional production were the activities of rural elites. Throughout the protoindustrial period, rural elites promoted the commercialization of agriculture and handicraft production by
introducing new crops and advanced agricultural and manufacturing
technologies. Indeed, a culture of "diffusionism" permeated the upper
ranks of rural society. Regions and their rural elites vied to introduce and
produce superior crops and products.

## THE DIFFUSION OF IMPROVED AGRICULTURAL TECHNIQUES

Agricultural treatises served as one very important means by which rural elites encouraged the diffusion of advanced technologies. The most
famous of the early treatises was Miyazaki Yasusada's Nōgyō zensho,
first published in 1697, which described crop varieties and agricultural
techniques in the Kinai and points west along the Seto Inland Sea. Miyazaki's work inspired village elites around the country to experiment with
the methods, seed varieties, and crops he described.[15] In many ways, they
were similar to the improving farmers of eighteenth-century England, always on the lookout for new seed varieties and better techniques.[16]

Authors of many later treatises described how local conditions differed
from those recorded by Miyazaki. Nagasaki Shichizaemon, a headman of
Nanokaichi village in Akita, wrote in his 1785 treatise Rōnō okimiyage
that many people in his region considered Miyazaki's work useless for
colder regions such as Akita. His task, he stated, was to adapt Miyazaki's
techniques to local conditions. Similar comments can be found in treatises
all over the country.[17]

The diffusion of improved agricultural techniques, seeds, and implements was a very gradual process, one that continued into the Meiji period
after 1868. In fact, many of the techniques advocated in the mid-Meiji had

been developed in the Tokugawa period or had improved upon Tokugawa practices. Agricultural discussion groups, seed exchange societies, and encouragement-of-industry associations continued the process of diffusion well after the collapse of the Tokugawa.[18]

## SERICULTURAL TECHNIQUES AND
## SILK-REELING TECHNOLOGY

Tokugawa Japan was a status society, and silk was the ultimate symbol of one's position in the upper echelons. With the end of internal warfare and the consolidation of Tokugawa rule, the demand for silk increased exponentially, and large quantities had to be imported from China to satisfy demand. So much was imported, in fact, that in 1685 and again in 1715 the bakufu ordered restrictions to reduce the outflow of specie, thus creating a tremendous demand for domestic raw silk.

Also of importance to the growth of the domestic silk industry were changes in fashion which made silk a more popular form of clothing. In the early seventeenth century, for example, samurai rarely wore silk apparel, but one hundred years later even village headmen could be found wearing it. With increased demand came greater market activity. This was most evident in Kyoto, where the number of wholesalers handling domestic raw silk jumped from nine in 1689 to thirty-four in 1734. The total quantity shipped to Kyoto increased from an estimated 88,000 *kin* in the 1640's to over 193,000 in 1715, and to 2.25 million *kin* by the early nineteenth century.[19]

Increased demand for domestic silk led to improvements in sericultural techniques. From the second half of the eighteenth century, farmers in some areas planted mulberry trees, the leaves of which they used to feed their voracious silkworms, in groves rather than on the footpaths between fields as had been common in the past. Sericulturists also devised a method for cutting the roots of the mulberry tree to improve its growth. By the end of the century the number of days needed for raising silkworms had been cut in half by the use of new heating methods and more closely regulated feeding schedules for the silkworms. This allowed some farmers to raise silkworms in both the summer and the fall. Improved rearing methods and new varieties of silkworms resulted in the doubling of the quantity of fibers per cocoon.[20]

Here, too, treatises facilitated the diffusion of improved techniques. Just as with agricultural treatises, works on sericulture reflected years of experimentation based on local conditions.[21] At least 100 sericultural treatises were published during the Tokugawa, the oldest dating to 1697 but the overwhelming majority only from the 1780's.[22] Many authors had a deep knowledge of conditions in other parts of the country. Uegaki Morikuni of Nishitani village in Tajima province, author of the 1802 treatise *Yōsan hiroku*, described sericultural and reeling methods in Ōshū (Iwashiro), the Kantō, Shinano, Tanba, Tango, and Ōmi.[23] At least six later treatises quoted or borrowed heavily from his work.[24]

In addition to studying and writing sericultural treatises and engaging in individual experimentation, improving farmers traveled to the advanced regions to learn the most up-to-date methods and to purchase high-quality mulberry seedlings and silkworm eggs. The best examples of such travel come from the Yūki region north of Edo, which had been the country's leading silkworm egg production region until a series of floods decimated the industry by 1742. The opening of Japan's ports to international trade in 1859 created a tremendous demand for silkworm eggs and raw silk, providing a golden opportunity for Yūki elites to improve their fortunes. To learn more about the silk industry, in 1858 Miyata Kunizaburō of Kanakubo village visited the Tajima household, a major sericultural family in Shima village in nearby Kōzuke province. In 1861 Sekine Minkichi of Naka village visited Tajima Tahei, also of Shima village. Yet another wealthy farmer from the Yūki region, Hiroe Kahei, visited Tajima Yahei in 1882 to learn everything he could about the sericulture industry. In later years, too, Hiroe traveled to various parts of the country to observe the latest techniques, so as to improve his current practices.[25]

The easiest means to produce superior raw silk was to purchase eggs from those regions producing well-known breeds. Uegaki Morikuni states in his treatise that he went to Ōshū at the age of eighteen to purchase egg cards, which he sold to villagers in western Japan. Even in the 1730's, he states, it was common for people to travel to regions that produced high-quality egg cards, such as Shinano, Yūki, and Ōshū.[26] The Satō family, a wealthy farm family in Fushiguro village in Shindatsu, sold egg cards to virtually every part of the country in the Tokugawa period—from distant northeast areas such as those around Aomori and Akita, to the Kantō, to areas along the Japan Sea (Etchū and Echizen), to Ōmi and Tango in the greater Kinai, and even to Satsuma domain on the island of Kyūshū.[27]

The reeling industry witnessed fewer technological advances from the second half of the eighteenth century. The most advanced reeling device was the *zaguri*, which doubled the speed of earlier devices through the use of belts or cogwheels,[28] but few reelers used it even in Ōshū and Kōzuke, the regions where two forms of this device had been developed. Because the fibers were not twisted when reeled, a process which gives elasticity and uniformity to the thread, domestic weavers considered *zaguri* raw silk inferior.[29]

The opening of the ports in 1859 and a silkworm blight in Europe created a tremendous demand for Japanese raw silk, and the *zaguri* assumed far greater importance in the production process. This was made possible by improvements to the *zaguri*, such as the inclusion of a mechanism to combine fibers from several cocoons into one thread. Especially important was the addition of a process known as re-reeling (*agekaeshi*): the *zaguri*-reeled raw silk was graded to standardize for luster and weight; reeled onto larger frames, with a device moving back and forth like a pendulum to evenly distribute the thread on the frame; and finally bundled in preparation for weaving.[30] In rapid succession, rural elites introduced the *zaguri* to their communities. Villagers in the Okaya area of Suwa district in Shinano, what was to become Japan's leading raw silk production region, introduced the *zaguri* from Kōzuke shortly after the opening of the ports. Masuzawa Seisuke of Koigawa village, also in the Suwa area, went to Yokohama in 1859 to observe export conditions. When he returned home, he decided to purchase five *zaguri* to produce raw silk for export. In 1861 he constructed 120 *zaguri*, which he sold both locally and to more distant regions. The *zaguri* came to Matsumoto in Shinano the same year; Irima district (Saitama) first used it in 1861; the Yao area (Toyama) of Etchū introduced it around 1866. Reelers in Yonezawa prefecture began to use the *zaguri* from 1887.[31]

WEAVING TECHNOLOGY

Of particular import in the transformation of regional production was the diffusion of weaving technology from the Nishijin district of Kyoto to rural areas. Kyoto textile houses had monopolized the technology for weaving and finishing high-quality silks, but from the 1720's this technology began to flow with alarming speed to rural areas. Large quantities of rural cloth began to be sold in the Kyoto market, quite to the shock of Nishijin's weavers.

Bakufu restrictions on foreign imports were an important incentive spurring the growth of the domestic silk textile industry. Until the mid-eighteenth century, however, rural weavers had used the *izari* or inclining loom, which was inefficient and incapable of producing complicated cloth patterns and designs. They thus had to ship their plain weaves to Nishijin for final finishing. The transmission of Nishijin technology dramatically changed the nature of rural production.

The first area to introduce Nishijin technology was Tango, a region to the north of Kyoto. Saheiji, a villager from the Mineyama region, went to work in Nishijin in 1719 and, upon his return the following year, introduced the technology for producing crepe. Soon he was making return visits to Kyoto, but this time to sell the cloth produced in his native area. In 1721 two local residents from the neighboring Kaya area, Shōemon from the town of Kaya and Sahei from Migochi village, went to Nishijin to serve as contract laborers (*hōkōnin*) and returned the following year with the technology for weaving crepe. By the early 1770's silk crepe weaving had became a major industry of the Tango region, with over 200 weavers in Kaya and Migochi alone.[32]

The rural town of Kiryū in the Kantō region was the next to introduce sophisticated Nishijin technology. In 1723 or 1724 a Kyoto cloth-fuller, Hariya Kyūkei, went to Kiryū to teach his skills to local residents. Soon after, Kiryū weaving establishments invited Nishijin experts in red cloth dyeing. In 1738 Kiryū weavers employed two Nishijin workers to learn their techniques, in particular that of the *takahata*, a draw loom for producing high-quality cloth. By 1741 there were over forty *takahata* in the Kiryū area; two years later they could be found all over the province of Kōzuke. Kiryū enjoyed two important advantages over Nishijin: its proximity to Edo, the country's largest consumer market, and its location in a major production area for raw silk.[33] The transmission of the *takahata* and other technology allowed Kiryū weavers to bypass Kyoto for final processing and to sell directly to central markets. What had once been a supply area for Nishijin had become one of its fiercest competitors.

As a result of this initial diffusion, Nishijin technology could now move from production region to production region, bypassing Nishijin altogether. In 1752 villagers near Nagahama in Hikone domain (Ōmi province) hired Tango merchants to teach them silk-crepe-weaving technology, which Tango farmers had acquired from Kyoto three decades before. Residents of Yonezawa domain in northeastern Japan introduced this technology from Tango in the early nineteenth century. From Kiryū, silk-weaving and silk-dyeing technology moved to nearby Ashikaga and to Hachiōji.[34]

The diffusion of the *takahata* was particularly pronounced, as depicted in Map 3. Not long after the diffusion of basic *takahata* technology, innovative rural weavers began to use the *takahata* for producing non-silk fabrics. Ashikaga weavers used the *takahata* to produce cottons and silk/cotton blends from the late eighteenth century and found that it substantially lowered production costs. The introduction of the *takahata* into the Echi-

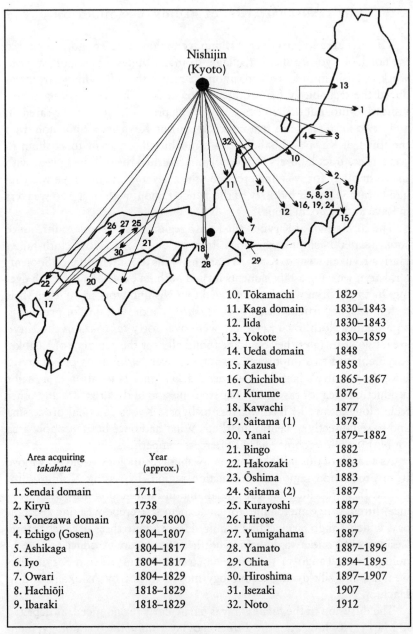

Nishijin
(Kyoto)

| Area acquiring takahata | Year (approx.) |
|---|---|
| 1. Sendai domain | 1711 |
| 2. Kiryū | 1738 |
| 3. Yonezawa domain | 1789–1800 |
| 4. Echigo (Gosen) | 1804–1807 |
| 5. Ashikaga | 1804–1817 |
| 6. Iyo | 1804–1817 |
| 7. Owari | 1804–1829 |
| 8. Hachiōji | 1818–1829 |
| 9. Ibaraki | 1818–1829 |
| 10. Tōkamachi | 1829 |
| 11. Kaga domain | 1830–1843 |
| 12. Iida | 1830–1843 |
| 13. Yokote | 1830–1859 |
| 14. Ueda domain | 1848 |
| 15. Kazusa | 1858 |
| 16. Chichibu | 1865–1867 |
| 17. Kurume | 1876 |
| 18. Kawachi | 1877 |
| 19. Saitama (1) | 1878 |
| 20. Yanai | 1879–1882 |
| 21. Bingo | 1882 |
| 22. Hakozaki | 1883 |
| 23. Ōshima | 1883 |
| 24. Saitama (2) | 1887 |
| 25. Kurayoshi | 1887 |
| 26. Hirose | 1887 |
| 27. Yumigahama | 1887 |
| 28. Yamato | 1887–1896 |
| 29. Chita | 1894–1895 |
| 30. Hiroshima | 1897–1907 |
| 31. Isezaki | 1907 |
| 32. Noto | 1912 |

Map 3. The Diffusion of Nishijin's *Takahata* Loom. (Adapted from Tsuno-yama, "Nihon no shokki," 290. When the source of diffusion is unknown, I have designated it as Nishijin. I have omitted Ōshima from the map because several areas share that name.)

go region in the early nineteenth century led to a tremendous increase in cotton cloth production. Kikuya Shinsuke of Iyo province made improvements on the *takahata* in the early nineteenth century to produce striped cotton and splashed-pattern cottons.[35]

## SAKE-BREWING TECHNOLOGY

All regions of Japan produced sake in the early Tokugawa, but brewers in Kinai towns dominated sales in central markets. Brewers in castle towns, mining towns, and other urban centers around the country produced sake primarily for local consumption, and there were countless family-run, rural, operations producing sake for the family itself or for the immediate area.[36] The greatest change to take place in this sector from the eighteenth century was the shift in production sites, away from the large cities and castle towns to rural villages.

The transformation was most dramatic in the Kinai, which produced the country's leading sake brands. Until the late eighteenth century, city and town brewers, such as those in Kyoto, Nara, Ikeda, Osaka, and Itami, had dominated sake production and had captured most of the Edo market. Thereafter, brewers in villages of the Nadame region, which had produced insignificant quantities in the past, seized the lead. Nadame brewers succeeded because they made two important advances in sake brewing: the use of the water wheel for polishing rice, which dramatically increased productivity; and the concentration of brewing in the winter season, which lengthened the brewing time but produced a higher quality sake. Almost all Nadame brewers started as largeholders and rural merchants, active both in coastal shipping and along overland trade routes in the region.[37]

Outside the Kinai as well, sake brewing moved from the cities (especially the castle towns) to villages. This was the case in Mito domain, where there were 119 sake houses in the castle town in the early Tokugawa. By the 1830's there were only fourteen, the others having sold their brewing licenses to farmers.[38]

Just as in other industries, those wanting to brew superior sake for sale in distant markets sought to import the necessary technology from the advanced regions. With sake, the most common pattern was to bring in brewing equipment and brewmasters (*tōji*) trained in superior techniques. The Nakamura Heizaemon family of the town of Shimodate in Hitachi province did this earlier than others. Nakamura sold some of his sake to the Edo market, so it was necessary to have the best technology to compete with shipments from the Kinai. In the early eighteenth century, Naka-mura ordered sake-brewing equipment from an Osaka merchant. His brewmaster responsible for overseeing the purchases, Tahei, also came from the Kinai. In 1836 the Satō family of Echigo invited a brewmaster and four brewery workers from Nadame to work for them. Not long af-ter, the family employed a brewmaster and brewery workers from Itami. The Watanabe Sazaemon family, also of Echigo, started sake-brewing op-erations from the 1670's, but only acquired the technology for brewing re-fined sake from the Osaka area around the mid-eighteenth century.[39]

Wealthy farmers in the Kantō often invited brewmasters from Echigo to run their sake operations. A number of brewmasters in Sawara village and in villages around Itsukaichi, both in the Kantō, came from the Echigo region. Some eventually launched brewing operations of their own. The Tanba region, just to the north of the Kinai, supplied brewmasters not only to Nadame but to other important production sites in the Kinai, in-cluding Nishinomiya, Fushimi, Ikeda, and Itami.[40]

Another means of improving brewing technology was to observe con-ditions in advanced regions. Hiroshima prefecture became the country's third largest sake-production region by the end of the Meiji largely through the efforts of brewers like Miura Senzaburō. Miura, who had started in brewing in 1878, traveled to the country's premier sake regions, including Nadame and Ise, and acquired information on the latest tech-niques. Through experimentation, he developed a distinctive-tasting sake that soon gained a nationwide reputation. With the growth of sake brew-ing in Hiroshima, brewmasters trained in Miura's production methods in-creasingly found employment in other parts of the country, including even such prominent production centers as Nadame and Fushimi.[41]

## TEA CULTIVATION AND TEA-PROCESSING TECHNOLOGY

To grow and process the best quality tea, wealthy farmers sought to emulate the cultivation and processing techniques used in the Uji area of the Kinai. Farmers in Shimōsa and Hitachi, for example, cultivated tea from at least the early seventeenth century and sold small quantities out-side the region.[42] In the early years, though, they employed somewhat primitive processing methods, such as sun-drying the tea leaves, which produced an inferior form of tea. With the commercialization of agricul-ture from the mid-eighteenth century, however, these farmers found that their tea could no longer compete in major markets with superior teas produced in other parts of the country.

To revive the local tea industry, rural elites in western Hitachi began to introduce superior techniques. In the early nineteenth century, Shichirōbei of Nagatsura village invited a tea specialist from Uji to learn the advanced methods used there. In rapid succession, others followed his lead. Nakayama Motonari of Heta village invited an Uji tea specialist to his village in 1834. So, too, did Nomura Saheiji of Yamazaki village, who introduced Uji tea-processing methods only a few years later. Not to be left behind, Sakurai Denzaburō of nearby Nagaido village invited an Uji tea specialist to his village in 1843.[43]

The Shizuoka area, including the provinces of Suruga and Tōtōmi, also cultivated tea from at least the early seventeenth century but produced only inferior, kettle-fired teas. Sakamoto Tōkichi of Ikumi village, Shida district, is credited with introducing Uji tea-processing methods to Shizuoka in 1836, when he learned the new methods from an Uji tea producer. The next year he invited an Uji tea specialist and several women tea pickers to his village.[44]

The production of superior tea became especially important with the opening of the ports in 1859, when tea became one of the country's leading export items. From 1859 to 1867 tea exports increased over eighteenfold, with more than 7 million pounds being exported in 1867 alone.[45] Farmers around the country began expanding their tea cultivation. In the western Shizuoka region, an 1883 survey found that 66 percent of the tea had been planted within only the last ten years. Over 45 percent of the tea acreage in Niigata prefecture in 1883 had come into existence within the previous decade.[46]

To compete with teas from other Asian countries, as well as from other production regions within Japan itself, farmers had to adopt the best cultivation and processing techniques. One after another, wealthy Shizuoka farmers invited Uji tea specialists to their communities or went on research trips to learn how to improve the quality of their teas. Some Shizuoka farmers purchased seeds from southern Ise, which at the time produced a superior tea, perhaps as a result of learning Uji tea cultivation and tea-processing methods earlier in the century. Kageyama Shirōbei of Iwamatsu village, Haibara district, learned Uji tea-processing methods from an instructor from nearby Musashi province. Sawano Seiichi of Sodeshi village, Ihara district, went on a tea inspection trip to the Kinai, Kyūshū, and Shikoku in the mid-1860's. As a result of such efforts, by the early to mid-Meiji Shizuoka had a core of specialists in Uji tea methods available for local hire and consultation.[47]

## Some Statistical Considerations

As a result of productivity increases and the diffusionist activities discussed above, rural areas witnessed extraordinary growth in cash crop production and manufacture. Although no countrywide aggregates of commodity production are available for the Tokugawa, data compiled in the early Meiji offer a general idea, though imprecise, both of those items that dominated the economy in its closing years and of the extent to which rural elites had contributed to the diffusion of cash crop production and manufacture.[48]

The *Meiji 7-nen fuken bussanhyō* (Tables of Prefectural and Metropolitan Area Products for 1874) provides data on the volume and value of goods in three categories: agricultural, manufactured, and primary products (forestry, fishing, mining, and livestock). As summarized in Appendix Tables 1–3, agricultural products dominated the economy, accounting for 61 percent of the total value, followed by manufactured products at 30 percent.[49] The extent to which agriculture dominated the economy is not surprising. Farmers constituted about 80 percent of the population in the early Meiji, and they engaged in manufacture, mostly handicrafts production, as a side industry.

The early Meiji data suggest the extent to which the economy as a whole had been commercialized. This is clear from the relatively high percentage (30 percent) of manufactured goods, including such items as sake, textiles, soy sauce, and raw silk. In the agricultural sector, too, "special-use agricultural products," e.g., such non-food items as cotton, rapeseed, and cocoons, were clearly commercial products. Even rice, much of which had been collected in partial fulfilment of tax obligations in the Tokugawa, had become an important commodity in many parts of the country. Working from the 1874 data, Yamaguchi Kazuo has estimated that 15 to 20 percent of the total harvest remained for sale after household consumption and payment of taxes.[50] The commodification of rice became all the more pronounced in later years, when the Meiji government revised the land tax and ordered all tax payments to be paid in specie.

The 1874 data also reflect the extent to which production had been diffused around the country. Appendix Tables 4–12 present data on the leading sites of production for cotton, sake, textiles and their raw and intermediate materials, and tea.

By the early Meiji the Kinai no longer dominated Japan's economic landscape. This is best reflected in the relative decline of cotton cultivation there. In 1874 farmers in every prefecture outside northeastern Japan and Hokkaidō grew cotton and engaged in its semiprocessing. Three areas in the Kinai—Kyoto, Osaka, and Sakai—are included among the top five, but together they accounted for only 27.1 percent of the national total. The leading cotton cultivation and cotton textile region in terms of the amount produced was Aichi, which was not part of the Kinai. Most of the leading tea cultivation and tea-processing regions, too, were in other parts of the country as of 1881. Even with silk textiles, Kyoto accounted for only about one-third of the national total in 1874, and its relative position declined further in later years.

Finally, the tables reveal a relative lack of regional concentrations of production, although some areas clearly produced more than others. Hyōgo, which includes the Nadame area, produced more sake than any other region but far from dominated national production. Kyoto and Tochigi (which at the time included not only Ashikaga but Kiryū, which soon became part of Gunma prefecture) were the leading producers of silks, but there were numerous other important sites of production. The five leading tea-processing regions produced only 41 percent of the national total in 1881. Kumagaya prefecture (which included present-day Gunma and Saitama) produced 17.4 percent of the country's raw silk, but the five leading regions produced only about 40 percent of the total. The major exception to this lack of regional concentration was silk/cotton blends, where Tochigi clearly dominated production.

The heaviest concentrations of manufactured goods were in the Kinki (or greater Kinai, including the outlying prefectures of Shiga, Wakayama, and Mie), followed by the Kantō. Together they accounted for 41.9 percent of the total value of "manufactured goods" nationwide. Although the Kinki and Kantō were the clear leaders, all other regions, with the exception of Hokkaidō, displayed clear signs of a well-developed protoindustrial economy, with manufactured goods accounting for 25 to 35 percent of the total value of production.[51]

Regional differences did not at all disappear by the early Meiji. The Kinai continued to produce more than other regions, even on a per capita basis.[52] Also, regional and prefectural data often obscure far more complex workings at the local level. As Kären Wigen reminds us, there were often sharp differences within regions, within prefectures and districts, and even within villages in the extent to which farmers participated in, or benefited from, the market economy.[53]

At the same time, the Japanese market economy in the early Meiji was of a far greater magnitude than in the early Tokugawa. Largely as a result of the efforts of diffusionist rural elites, important new sites of production emerged, and farmers across the country produced growing quantities of goods for sale in distant markets.

## Interregional Competition

By the early Meiji there had been a fairly high degree of diffusion of cash crops and manufacturing techniques. A significant feature of market production in the second half of the Tokugawa and into the Meiji, however, was its fluidity. Regions that dominated the market in a particular period might find themselves at the bottom of the heap in the next. The diffusion of cash crops and advanced techniques and technologies engendered intense interregional competition—between old and new production regions, among new production regions, and within regions. Regions, and their rural elites, had to struggle to maintain their market shares. Not all were successful.

### COTTON CULTIVATION

Fierce market competition was particularly evident in the cotton sector. Kinai cotton cultivators faced growing competition both from regions to the west, such as Hyōgo, Fukuyama, and Okayama, and to the east, especially Ise, Owari, Mikawa, and parts of the Kantō. These regions became major competitors in the eighteenth century. There were also newcomers to cotton cultivation, such as Tottori domain in western Honshū. Cotton was not a major crop there until the clearing of land around the Yumigahama peninsula in the first half of the eighteenth century. By 1877, however, Tottori prefecture accounted for 3.8 percent of all cotton cultivated nationwide.[54]

Kinai farmers faced stiff competition because their cultivating costs were high as a result of the application of expensive cash fertilizers, such as dried sardines. The Kinai's competitors, such as the Tōkai and Kantō regions, relied far less on cash fertilizers and thus fared much better. Cotton grown in Tottori required two to three times more seeds for sowing than the Kinai, and the harvest was 25 to 50 percent less bountiful, but instead of dried sardines farmers applied seaweed, giving them an important cost advantage over competitors.[55] As a result, many Kinai farmers reduced their cotton arable and switched to other crops. The Kinai was not alone in this fight for market share. Farmers in the domains of Fukuyama and Okayama found themselves unable to compete, especially from the early nineteenth century, because they too were heavily dependent on expensive cash fertilizers.[56]

Somewhat surprisingly, the opening of the ports in 1859 and the introduction of British cloth imports did not immediately depress the domestic cotton sector. Between 1874 and 1885, in fact, total harvests actually grew by 25 percent, largely as a result of greater domestic demand. Not all regions, of course, witnessed similar rates of growth. Total production in the Kinai province of Kawachi declined by over 43 percent between 1878 and 1884, and in 1884 production was only 38.9 percent of what it had been five decades earlier. But this was merely the continuation of a trend that appeared well before Japan's entry into international commerce.

Despite some initial growth in domestic cotton cultivation, conditions did not favor further expansion. Imported yarns were inexpensive, of higher quality, and more suitable to mechanized spinning and new forms of looms than domestic cotton, with its short, thick, fibers. When the Diet voted in 1893 to abolish the tariff on seed cotton imports, farmers found it necessary to abandon cotton cultivation and shift to more profitable crops.[57] In Hiroshima prefecture, the decline in cotton cultivation from the late 1880's devastated many villages and was an important contributing factor in the immigration of impoverished residents to Hawaii, the United States, and Canada. In Tottori prefecture, cotton cultivation declined after 1885, and farmers turned to sericulture and silk reeling in its place. The same precipitous decline occurred in Ibaraki prefecture, forcing farmers to switch to other marketable crops, such as mulberry trees and tobacco.[58]

COTTON TEXTILES

Cotton weaving could be found in virtually every prefecture by the early Meiji, but most regions were relative newcomers to the industry. Of twenty-one regions producing cotton cloth for sale in the Tokugawa, only five had their start before the mid-eighteenth century; the remainder appeared in later decades, especially the late eighteenth century.[59] Tottori, for example, had been a net importer of cotton cloth until this time. In 1797 farmers in Tottori produced about 167,000 *tan* of cotton cloth, 70 percent of which they shipped to Kinai markets. By 1874 total production had increased more than threefold over the 1797 level.[60]

Some regions could not withstand such competition. Many farmers in Yamashiro and Yamato, both in the Kinai, discontinued cotton weaving around the late eighteenth century. Farmers in Kii, Awaji, and Settsu gradually abandoned cotton weaving and instead specialized in some intermediate process, such as ginning or spinning.[61] Some areas witnessed vibrant intraregional competition. The bleached cotton cloth farmers produced in the Mooka area of Shimotsuke, for example, eventually found its way to outlying regions. By the nineteenth century, neighboring Hitachi produced more of this cloth than Shimotsuke. Similar intraregional competition took place in the Tōkai region. Nakajima Shichiemon of Okada village in the Chita region of Owari introduced the technology for bleaching cotton cloth from the nearby Ise region in the 1780's. By the first decades of the nineteenth century, the quantity of Chita bleached cotton had overtaken that produced in Ise.[62]

The opening of the ports had important consequences for the domestic cotton-weaving industry. British merchants shipped large quantities of cotton cloth to Japan, capturing 40 percent of the domestic market in 1874.[63] A few regions were forced to abandon cotton weaving as a result. Especially hard hit were those regions, such as Tottori, Wakayama, Mooka and Makabe in the Kantō, Hyōgo, and Hiroshima, manufacturing white cotton cloth.[64]

But cloth imports far from devastated domestic production. While imports deluged the market, there was a concomitant surge in domestic demand, perhaps as much as a threefold increase between 1875 and 1895 alone. As a result of declining prices, farmers began to purchase cotton fabrics for the first time, whereas in the past they had woven them in their homes or purchased used clothing.[65]

Domestic weavers withstood the competition from imports for two reasons. First, they produced a distinctive material. Throughout the prewar period traditional Japanese clothing and styles predominated. The narrow striped cotton fabrics, in particular, which had been popular among commoners since the Tokugawa, retained their popularity well after 1868.[66] Second, domestic producers lowered their prices by using the cheaper imported yarns, by using a combination of domestic and imported yarns, and by quickly adopting a far more efficient loom, the flying shuttle (*battan*). By significantly reducing prices, weavers created an even larger demand for their fabrics. Largely as a result of such innovations, the share of imports in the domestic cotton cloth market declined to only 15 percent in 1888.[67]

Even white cotton cloth, which had been initially devastated by British imports, soon enjoyed a resurgence in demand. Ehime prefecture, for example, had produced white cotton cloth since the late Tokugawa but only became a major producer in the Meiji period, especially from the 1890's.

Saitama and Nara became important white cotton cloth regions in the early Meiji by taking advantage of cheap yarn imports. In the Kinai, production stagnated or declined in Kawachi, but the southern half of Izumi, known as Sennan, witnessed tremendous growth. Sennan weavers survived, even thrived, because they adapted to new conditions. Around 1875 they began to use imported yarns as warp. And with the growth of the mechanized spinning industry, weavers switched to machine-spun yarns for both warp and weft. Around 1879 they adopted an improved version of the flying shuttle loom, which increased productivity over twice that of previous devices.[68]

Beginning in the late 1880's, cotton-weaving regions faced a new source of competition. Mechanized spinning mills, especially in Osaka and Aichi, engaged increasingly in weaving, capturing 22 percent of the market in 1905 and 41 percent in 1914. As a result, several regions—such as Yokote (Akita), Niikawa (Toyama), and areas in Tottori and Shimane prefectures—witnessed precipitous declines in production.[69]

### SERICULTURE AND RAW SILK

Sericulture and raw silk were major growth industries well before Japan's entry into the modern world economy in 1859. In the mid-Tokugawa, regions of northeastern and central Japan dominated production—especially the Shindatsu area of Ōshū, Kōzuke, and northern Shinano. Shindatsu's position in particular was unparalleled. In the mid-eighteenth century the area was the country's leading producer of silkworm egg cards, and it dominated the market in eastern Japan.[70] Shindatsu's dominance, however, did not remain undisputed. One source of competition was new production regions nearby. In Nihonmatsu and Miharu, for example, farmers produced inferior eggs but claimed they were of Shindatsu origin, thereby damaging Shindatsu's reputation in national markets.

Shindatsu's concerns were hardly unique. When a product gained a countrywide reputation, farmers in other regions would try to imitate that product, sometimes even affixing stamps that remarkably resembled those used on superior products. The Yūki region had faced the problem of egg card imitators as early as 1690.[71] Soy sauce producers in Tatsuno in Harima province faced the same problem in the late eighteenth century. Because Tatsuno produced a superior product and had captured a major share of the Kyoto market, rural producers outside Tatsuno tried to sell their soy sauce as a product of the Tatsuno region.[72]

Shindatsu also suffered when other regions began producing smaller cards, frequently one-fourth to one-half the size of standard cards. The smaller cards found a ready market among the increasing numbers of small farmers in eastern Japan who engaged in sericulture and silk reeling as a side industry. Shindatsu only began to produce the smaller cards after efforts to stop their production in other areas through bakufu intervention failed. Shindatsu production, which had reached its height of 182,000 cards in 1774, declined to 97,200 only three years later.[73] One of Shindatsu's greatest competitors was the Ueda region of Shinano, which had relied heavily on egg card purchases from Shindatsu until the early nineteenth century. Soon Ueda's egg card merchants were fiercely competing with merchants from Shindatsu, and by the 1830's Shinano egg card production surpassed that of Shindatsu.[74]

Shindatsu was also one of the country's leading areas for the production of raw silk. Narita Jūhei, author of an important treatise on sericulture, described conditions in the Fukushima area of Shindatsu as follows:

> In the Kyōho period [1716–35] I went every year to Ōshū with an Ōmi merchant living in my district, each carrying about 300 ryō, and bought raw silk in the Fukushima area. Around that time, sericulture was beginning to flourish around Fukushima. . . . Now, in the Bunka period [1804–17], it seems not at all unusual for one sericultural household to earn as much as 300 ryō in profits from raw silk or silk floss. The raw silk produced in Fukushima comes to over half of the countrywide total.[75]

Here, too, Shindatsu reelers faced competition from other areas, especially with the opening of the ports in 1859.

The opening of the ports was especially beneficial to Japan's sericultural regions. Because of a silkworm blight in Europe and the disruption in Chinese exports as a result of the Taiping Rebellion (1850–64), there was a tremendous demand in Western markets for Japanese egg cards and raw silk. Raw silk became Japan's leading export item, growing over sevenfold between 1868–72 and 1893–97, from 5.6 million yen to 40 million.[76]

The unprecedented demand for silkworm eggs and raw silk gave rise to new production regions. Wealthy farmers, merchants, and samurai in Ibaraki prefecture, for example, first launched into silk reeling on a substantive scale after the opening of the ports. In the early Meiji period Ibaraki still produced insignificant quantities, but the industry grew rapidly in subsequent years. From 1882 to 1892 production increased tenfold, and from 1892 to 1901 it doubled again. Residents of Aichi prefecture, a major cotton cultivation and cotton-weaving region, began silk reeling around 1872. By 1912 Aichi ranked second nationwide in raw silk production.[77]

Because of strong international demand, all the major raw silk regions of the late Tokugawa continued as major producers well into the Meiji. But the relative positions of each region changed greatly. The leading regions producing export raw silk in 1864 were those that dominated the market in the late Tokugawa: Ōshū (especially the Shindatsu region), Kōzuke (Gunma), and Shinano (Nagano), in that order; Ōshū produced twice that of Kōzuke.[78] By 1877 Kōzuke had become the largest producer of raw silk, followed by Shinano and Musashi; Iwashiro province, which included the Shindatsu area, was only in fifth position. By the end of the 1880's, Shinano had become the country's leading producer.[79] Within Shinano itself, the center of production moved from the northern half of the region, especially around Ueda, to the south, to Suwa district in particular.

Success in interregional competition after the opening of the ports depended in large measure on producers' willingness to adopt advanced reeling techniques. Those regions using improved versions of the *zaguri*, for example, fared better than those using more primitive reeling devices, because the *zaguri* produced a high-quality product in greater demand in export markets. Farmers in Gunma and Fukushima, where *zaguri*-reeling predominated, even competed quite effectively with raw silk reeled in the early filatures in Suwa. They were successful because they had many decades of experience and produced a superior product. Many of the early filatures, on the other hand, were more concerned with quantity than quality. It was only from the late 1880's that technological advances made machine reeling far more efficient than improved versions of the *zaguri*.[80]

Machine reeling became especially critical when, beginning in the 1880's, the silk-weaving industry in the United States increasingly adopted power looms.[81] Because of the greater speed involved, power looms demanded a far more uniform and higher-quality raw silk than the *zaguri* could produce. As a result, from 1894 machine-reeled raw silk surpassed that produced by the *zaguri*.[82]

Gunma and Shindatsu were very slow to make the transformation to machine reeling and, as a result, lost out in the competition to areas like Suwa. In 1879 there were 666 filatures in Japan employing more than ten reelers. Eighty-seven percent of the factories were in three prefectures: Nagano (especially the Suwa area), Gifu, and Yamanashi. All had been relatively minor sericulture and raw silk production regions when the ports were opened, especially when compared with Gunma, Shindatsu, and northern Nagano.[83]

SILK TEXTILES

The transmission of Nishijin weaving technology to rural areas resulted in intense interregional competition, both between Kyoto and the new production regions and among the new production regions themselves. Kiryū's adoption of the *takahata* in the 1740's enabled it to become Kyoto's strongest competitor, but it did not at all ensure its dominance in rural silk production. From Kiryū the *takahata* moved to a number of outlying areas, such as Ashikaga and Isezaki, and then on to Hachiōji.[84] Weavers in the Ashikaga area prospered because they produced more inexpensive textiles with mass appeal. Kiryū weavers, in contrast, largely targeted high-ranking samurai. As a consequence, from the late eighteenth century and particularly from the 1830's, the Ashikaga market thrived while the one in Kiryū suffered a serious, albeit temporary, decline.[85]

Japan's silk-weaving industry faced especially trying times with the opening of the ports. Merchants exported massive quantities of raw silk, and reelers began using the *zaguri*, which was poorly suited to weaving traditional silk fabrics.[86] Such raw silk as was available skyrocketed in price.[87] In addition, the tremendous disorder and confusion created by the opening of the ports and the overthrow of the Tokugawa bakufu depressed demand for expensive silk garments for almost three decades.[88]

To survive the difficult years after the opening of the ports, silk weavers had to change the nature of their operations. Some Kiryū weavers began to produce silk/cotton blends. By using imported cotton yarns, they were able to produce an inexpensive cloth that resembled silk. Weavers in nearby Ashikaga began using imported yarns as early as 1861.[89]

Other rural weavers sought new markets, both domestically and overseas. Okuzawa Shūhei of the Yūki area was instrumental in introducing the *kasuri* weave of pongee to his area in the 1870's, which he had learned about from trips to important production regions. The pongee Yūki weavers had produced before was a winter clothing. *Kasuri* could be worn in both summer and winter, so Yūki's market greatly expanded. Onozato Kizaemon III of Okuzawa village in the Kiryū area experimented with weaving various Western-style cloths not long after the opening of the ports, and his son was largely responsible for Japan's entry into the export of habutae silks, which led to a marked revival in Kiryū's fortunes.[90]

Kiryū's dominance in habutae production, however, was short-lived. In 1886 Fukui prefecture acquired habutae-weaving technology and soon usurped the market lead. One of the reasons for Fukui's success is that it quickly made the transition to mechanized production, while most Kiryū production was still under the putting-out system, making it more difficult to control for uniformity and quality.[91]

Other regions, too, became major centers of habutae production. Yasuda Riemon was responsible for the Kawamata area of Shindatsu launching into the habutae export trade. Motivated by the decline of the plain-silk–weaving industry in his area during the recession of the early 1880's, Yasuda discussed habutae production with export merchants in Kyoto and Yokohama in 1884. Not long after, local weavers established a training center for women to learn habutae production methods free of charge. By the late 1890's habutae had become a major product of the Kawamata area, far more important than the plain-weave silks of the past.[92]

SAKE

Until the late eighteenth century, competition in the sake-brewing industry took the form of rivalry among Kinai brewers, who dominated the markets in the major cities. Brewers outside the Kinai produced sake primarily for local consumption or for consumption in other rural areas. The fiercest competition in the Kinai was between brewers in Nadame villages and older establishments, such as those in Osaka, Nishinomiya, Ikeda, and Itami. In 1785, 82.5 percent of the sake entering the port of Edo came from the Kinai, but over 56 percent of this came from brewers in the Nadame area alone. Nadame's rise came at the expense of the established brewers. A 1784 report stated that 300 of Osaka's 700 sake brewers had suspended operations, the result of intense competition from new entrants to the business. Nishinomiya brewers witnessed a similar decline around the same time.[93]

Here, too, Nadame's position was far from secure. Between 1821 and 1866 Kinai sake sales to Edo declined by over one-third; Nadame's shipments declined by over 40 percent. One source of difficulty was growing competition from rural brewers in Owari province. In 1790 Owari brewers, most of whom were concentrated on the Chita peninsula, shipped 120,000 barrels of sake to Edo—about half of what Nadame and Imazu brewers shipped but still a significant source of rivalry for Nadame well into the early Meiji.[94]

Another problem was competition from brewers just outside the Nadame area, especially Imazu and Nishinomiya. While Nadame's sake shipments declined, those from Imazu increased almost threefold and those from Nishinomiya by 44 percent. Part of the reason for the success of Imazu and Nishinomiya was the discovery that well water from the area produced a better-tasting sake, one that quickly became the sake of choice in the Edo market.[95]

The opening of Japan to international trade had little effect on Japan's sake-brewing industry, but the political uncertainties accompanying the overthrow of the Tokugawa bakufu and the establishment of the new Meiji regime greatly constricted demand. Many brewing establishments, even the large firms in Nadame, fared poorly in the first decade of the Meiji. Much of the growth in the early Meiji sake industry came not in Nadame, but in relatively new production regions such as western Honshū, Shikoku, and Kyūshū. Nadame brewers had largely recovered and were again outperforming rivals by the late 1870's, increasing their share of the national market from 7.4 percent in 1874 to 14.9 percent in 1911. The scale of operations there was well over twice that of other areas, making it difficult for smaller brewers in other parts of the country to compete.[96]

All brewers, however, suffered in the 1880's. This was partly the result of the severe recession that gripped the nation stemming from the deflationary policies initiated by Finance Minister Matsukata Masayoshi. Especially important were the onerous taxes levied on brewers, as discussed in Chapter 1.

TEA

Surprisingly little is known about the quantity of tea sold to central markets before the opening of the ports.[97] Judging from the numerous examples of farmers seeking to learn Uji cultivation and processing techniques, however, we can assume that the Kinai dominated the market for superior teas.

The opening of the ports had a tremendous effect on Japan's tea industry. Many regions began to cultivate and process tea for the first time, and others greatly expanded the scale of their production. By the mid- to late Meiji, it became increasingly clear that Shizuoka prefecture, not the Kinai, was going to dominate the field. Those regions producing inferior teas were forced to abandon production. This was the fate of Niigata prefecture, which ranked twelfth nationally in tea production in 1881. Niigata farmers gradually abandoned tea production from the 1910's, when they switched over to mulberry cultivation. The Ise region (Mie prefecture), which had been far superior to Shizuoka earlier in the century in terms of the quality and quantity of its tea, gradually lost out in the competition and reduced its production.[98] As is clear from Appendix Table 11, similar declines in tea cultivation occurred in Gifu, Ibaraki, and the Kyoto area.

With tea processing, as well, Shizuoka had captured over 30 percent of the market by 1911. Shizuoka became so important, in fact, that when the port of Shimizu in Shizuoka opened to foreign trade in 1899 it soon became the major destination for Japan's export tea, overtaking Yokohama within a decade.[99] Part of the reason for Shizuoka's success was that its producers made the transition to mechanized tea processing from an early date, thus substantially reducing production costs. Those regions using traditional methods, such as western Hitachi, could not compete and were forced to abandon production.[100]

## Interregional Competition and the Rural Elite

The fluidity and volatility of regional production were sources of instability for the gōnō. One of their defining characteristics was the diversified nature of their operations. Not only were they farmers, tilling the soil using family and/or hired labor, but they were often active in several other pursuits—as merchants, landlords, moneylenders, or manufacturers. Commerce, in particular, was central to their business operations. They purchased goods smallholders in their localities produced, which they sold to distant markets. Loss of markets or market share was deleterious to not only the gōnō but to everyone in their localities. The gōnō fared better than most, precisely because their operations were diversified, but rural impoverishment could be disastrous for them as well. To be successful, the gōnō needed smallholders in their communities enmeshed in a vibrant protoindustrial economy.

To survive the competitive protoindustrial economy, the gōnō adopted several survival strategies. Clearly, they had to be continually attuned to market demand. They sought out new forms of commodity production and endeavored to improve the quality and quantity of products already produced. Yet another survival strategy was the move to mechanized forms of production, especially in export-oriented industries. Those regions whose weaving, reeling, and tea-processing industries survived into the late Meiji as major production sites were those that successfully made this transition.

The agricultural discussion societies and encouragement-of-industry associations of the Meiji period also served as important mechanisms through which rural elites worked to improve regional economic vitality and the quality of local products. Although these groups came under bureaucratic guidance and control from the 1890's, early Meiji societies were autonomous groupings, meeting the particular needs of localities.

Members discussed improved techniques for agriculture, sericulture, and egg card production, sometimes engaged in experimentation with new seeds and seedlings, and brought in improving farmers from other parts of the country.

Another important survival strategy, especially in the Meiji, was the formation of trade and industry associations (*dōgyō kumiai*) and producers' cooperatives (*sangyō kumiai*). Trade and industry associations were the successors to the guilds, or *nakama*, of the Tokugawa period. Like the guilds, they addressed issues of mutual concern to members. Their regulations frequently included provisions specifying where, when, and with whom goods were to be transacted and established standardized measures for weights and sizes. They also contained procedures for the inspection of goods, to prevent the sale of counterfeit products and goods of poor quality. All of these were important in the absence of codified commercial laws, and they served to facilitate trade nationwide.[101]

In the Tokugawa, guilds not only dominated commerce and manufacture in the large cities and castle towns but could be found in major rural sites of production as well, among weavers in the Kiryū and Ashikaga areas, for example, among Hachiōji textile merchants, or among soy sauce producers in the northern Kantō. Weavers in fifty-four villages in the Kiryū area, for instance, formed a guild to deal with competition from nearby Ashikaga. To prevent the outflow of technology, in 1781 the guild prohibited members and their contract laborers from working outside the domain. In the 1840's one prominent weaver even entertained the idea of petitioning for a ban on the use of the *takahata* outside their area.[102]

From 1884 the Meiji government devised regulations for trade and industry associations and actively encouraged their formation, but many had been in existence long before. They represented the spontaneous desires of rural elites to maintain regional economic vitality, especially through the implementation of inspection systems. Weavers and merchants in the Kiryū area established the Kiryū Kaisha (later renamed the Kiryū Textile Dōgyō Kumiai) in 1878 to improve the quality of local cloth; it inspected the cloth and affixed inspection stamps. Weavers in Isezaki formed a similar association in 1880, as did Ashikaga weavers in 1882.[103]

Producers' cooperatives resembled the trade and industry associations in that they were centered on producers and included product quality among their primary concerns. Unlike trade and industry associations, however, they were cooperatives, with members engaged in some joint economic activity, such as the extension of credit or collective sales. Collective credit activities had been common well before 1868, often taking the form of *mujinkō* or *tanomoshikō*, whereby villagers deposited funds in a type of village account and withdrew money on a rotating basis.[104] The Hōtoku (Repaying Virtue) movement in the late Tokugawa and Meiji also included credit among its most important functions. While urging farmers to practice diligence, thrift, and sincerity, Hōtoku members argued for extending credit to poorer farmers so that they could better their economic lot.[105] Cooperatives for collective sales, however, were primarily a product of the Meiji era.

In the early to mid-Meiji, sales cooperatives were especially common in export industries, such as raw silk, egg cards, and tea. In response to strong international demand, countless Japanese farmers began producing for export markets for the first time, but the resulting decline in quality drew the condemnation of Western merchants. Gunma egg card producers mixed rapeseed in with their silkworm eggs; Hitachi farmers laced tree and vine leaves, green vitriol, and dirt into their processed tea; farmers all over the country reeled raw silk with little concern for quality. Unless the major producers—the rural elite—established inspection systems, inferior products would be shipped out, at the expense of the entire region's reputation in export markets.

An early example of such an association is the Kangyō Kaisha, formed in Shima village in Gunma prefecture in 1872. Its purpose was to grade and inspect egg cards and to engage in collective sales to Yokohama export merchants, not production itself. The president of the company was yet another member of the Tajima clan, Tajima Buhei, who received encouragement from his relative, Shibusawa Eiichi, then working in the Ministry of Finance. Shibusawa arranged for Mitsui to lend the company 3,000 yen.[106]

Countless other producers' cooperatives came into existence in later years. Hoshino Chōtarō and Hagiwara Ryōtarō, both rural elites in Gunma prefecture, organized cooperatives for raw silk—for the purpose of re-reeling, improving quality, and collective sales—from the late 1870's. Producers in the Kawamata area of Shindatsu began organizing cooperatives in the mid-1880's with the growth of the export silk-weaving industry. They shared information on ways to improve the quality of their cloth, affixed inspection stamps to their cloth, and engaged in collective sales. Tea producers in Fuji district, Shizuoka prefecture, formed a producers' cooperative in 1882 to stem the production of inferior teas and to engage in collective sales.[107]

The ability of rural elites to unite smaller producers into such associations often determined the region's market fate. Tea producers in Ibaraki prefecture began organizing cooperatives from the late 1870's to improve the quality of their tea, which had declined with increased production. It proved difficult, however, to draw smaller producers into these associations because they produced insignificant quantities and viewed the inspection of their tea as a hindrance.[108] Partly as a result, total tea production there fell by over 23 percent between 1881 and 1897. From the late 1880's even large-scale tea producers had to reduce their operations or went out of business.[109] Here, too, we see the activities of gōnō and smallholders inextricably intertwined.

Finally, many rural elites were not at all averse to calling upon political authorities for assistance. Their petitions in the Tokugawa period for inspection systems are an early example of how rural elites believed political authorities could help bring about local improvements. Egg card producers in Shindatsu fell upon hard times in the 1770's when nearby regions started producing inferior imitations. To ensure Shindatsu's market position, producers petitioned for and received from the bakufu permission to use a trademark for egg cards from designated villages. Again in the 1860's, two wealthy Shindatsu egg card producers petitioned the bakufu for an inspection system to prevent the sale of inferior egg cards. This, too, represents an attempt to preserve the region's reputation, this time in international markets.[110]

Similar reliance on government assistance can be seen in the Meiji in requests for regulations for trade and industry associations.[111] By enforcing membership among all local producers, rural elites hoped for some institutional mechanism—backed by the enforcement powers of the state—through which to limit the production of inferior goods. Weavers and merchants in the Kiryū and Ashikaga areas had been pressing prefectural officials for approval for such organizations since the mid-1870's. Tea producers, meeting in Kobe in 1883, petitioned the government for a ban on the sale and production of inferior teas and for the formation of producers' associations.[112] The important role the government could play became clear when it enacted regulations in 1884 for trade and industry associations. Only two years later, there were 1,579 such associations nationwide. Similarly, the government issued regulations concerning tea producers' associations in 1884, and such organizations soon appeared in large numbers in the major production regions.[113]

The protoindustrial rural elite—the gōnō—who emerged from the mid-eighteenth century were the initiators and beneficiaries of the transformation of regional production. As the leaders of their villages, they intro-

duced new forms of commodity production. Some wrote agricultural treatises which reflected years of study and experimentation on improved
techniques and new crops. They traveled to other parts of the country to
learn advanced techniques and technologies; they purchased improved
seeds, seedlings, and silkworm eggs; and they hired workers and specialists from regions that had already acquired improved technologies.

By the early twentieth century, a network of bureaucratically controlled experiment stations and agricultural societies had largely obviated
the need for improving farmers. As a result of government policies
adopted in the 1890's, agricultural specialists—those who had graduated
from government schools and had a scientific understanding of agricultural matters—had taken on the responsibility for improvements in agriculture.[114]

The research institutes and training centers established by rural elites,
prefectural administrations, and the central government had much the
same effect. From the 1880's textile industry associations opened research
institutes to experiment with new weaving and dyeing techniques and
training centers for their diffusion.[115] National research centers experimented with ways to improve traditional industry. The Tokyo Industrial
Research Laboratory, established by the Ministry of Agriculture and
Commerce in 1900, analyzed the techniques of lacquer making, ceramics,
paper making, and textile dyeing. A government experiment station at Ōji
brought modern scientific methods to bear on the sericulture industry.
The Fermentation Laboratory (Jōzō Shikenjo), established by the Ministry of Finance in 1905, examined the techniques of sake production.[116]

But the full effects of such institutions were not felt until the early twentieth century. Until that time, gōnō competed actively for market share
and were themselves responsible for improving their region's competitive-
ness in national and international markets. They were in large measure responsible for the regional transformation of production but were sometimes also the victims of the very system they had been instrumental in
creating.

# 3

# Markets

WITH THE GROWTH of the market economy, many farmers launched into commerce for the first time, selling their region's products to distant parts of the country. Wealthy Shindatsu farmers sold raw silk to Kyoto and to merchants in rural weaving centers, such as Kiryū and Ōmi. Echigo farmers carried bundles of crepe to sell to the Edo market. Merchants from Ōmi trekked across much of the country, hawking their local products. Mikawa and Ise merchants sold cotton cloth to Edo wholesalers. Edo residents consumed massive quantities of sake shipped by Kinai brewers and consumed tea produced in Uji, Suruga, and Sashima. For many rural elites, the demand for local products seemed endless and the opportunities for profit vast.

But protoindustrial commerce itself underwent great metamorphosis. Japan's major cities accounted for much of the initial consumer demand, and the wholesaling establishments there dominated trade between regions. Some rural merchants profited enormously from the ties they established with urban centers, but they were also subject to the demands city merchants heaped upon them. The growth of the protoindustrial economy generated new opportunities for interrural and intrarural commerce, but the cities continued to exercise a powerful hold. Especially profound changes came with the opening of the ports in 1859. For those in the tea and raw silk trades, the prospects of enormous profits from exports were alluring, and numerous rural elites entered the export trade.

The changing nature of protoindustrial commerce required that rural merchants be able to continually adjust their methods of doing business. To meet the demands of city wholesalers, they had to find ways to lower their costs, and to purchase sufficient quantities of local goods, they had to outperform numerous competitors at the local level. The opening of the ports required that they shift the locus of their sales from domestic markets to international markets. Producers' cooperatives and modern factories presented far greater challenges because they signaled a complete reformulation of commercial practices. Few merchants survived for long in the competitive and extremely fluid economic environment. To better understand the changes unleashed in the protoindustrial era, let us first examine commerce in the seventeenth century.

## Early Tokugawa Commerce

By 1700, Osaka, Kyoto, and Edo—known collectively as the "three cities"—had become the country's leading urban centers. Edo had a population of about one million, and Osaka and Kyoto supported populations of over 350,000 each. They also occupied unrivaled positions in the country's commerce and manufacture. But before this time the "three cities" were in a process of great flux. Many rural town merchants engaged in interregional trade and were completely independent of merchants in the major cities. A few farmers engaged in this trade as well, but they were as yet insignificant participants.

Osaka became a major center for trade and manufacture only with the ascendancy of Tokugawa rule. Before 1600 there were several important cities in the Kinai region, many supporting thriving manufacturing industries and commercial establishments. When the bakufu decided that Osaka was to be the locus of Kinai commerce, however, large numbers of merchants from these other cities moved there, where there were greater possibilities for profit.[1]

Osaka's most important commercial activity was collecting and marketing rice and other products shipped from bakufu territories and domains. Many domains, especially those in western Japan, built warehouses (kurayashiki) in the city to store and sell their products, but with the growth of the Osaka market, they eventually ceded control over their warehouses to merchants. There also appeared large numbers of kuni don'ya, or wholesalers who handled products from particular domains or provinces. Most merchants were still unspecialized, handling a number of products from particular regions. They received goods on consignment and had no control over the production of these goods or the prices they received for them in the Osaka market.[2]

Osaka's role as an important manufacturing center, too, only came gradually. Rural towns in the Kinai engaged in various forms of manufacture, such as cotton ginning, cotton weaving, and oil extraction.[3] Town merchants often sent their goods to Osaka for shipment to their final destination, but the Osaka merchants handling them only acted as intermediaries between the buyers and sellers.

Kyoto had served as the administrative seat of Japan and the home of the imperial family for centuries and was far superior to Osaka in commerce in the first decades of the seventeenth century. But with the establishment of the Tokugawa bakufu at Edo, Kyoto's relative position in commerce and finance declined.[4] With the rise of Osaka as an important center for commerce and manufacture, most goods now bypassed Kyoto and went to Osaka, and Kyoto merchants moved there in growing numbers. Some of those running domain warehouses in Osaka, in fact, hailed from Kyoto.[5] Bakufu policies limiting imports of Chinese raw silk from 1685, too, worked to the detriment of Kyoto merchants active in foreign trade. The one area where Kyoto reigned supreme was the production of luxury goods, especially high-quality silks. In addition, there were a number of merchants there handling silks from other parts of the country.[6] Here, too, the wholesalers acted merely as consignment merchants, with no control over rural trade.

Edo in the seventeenth century lagged behind Osaka and Kyoto in commerce, finance, and manufacture, and the surrounding region was unable to meet the burgeoning consumer demand in the city. For much of the first half of the Tokugawa, Edo relied on massive shipments of goods from the Kinai to meet residents' needs. Like their counterparts in Kyoto and Osaka, early Edo merchants were largely unspecialized and acted as intermediaries in transactions between other parties.[7]

Far fewer records exist for interregional rural commerce in the seventeenth century than for later periods. The most active participants in long-distance trade were undoubtedly the legendary merchants from the towns and villages of Ōmi province. In the early Tokugawa they traveled across the country, especially to eastern Japan, selling Ōmi products and returning with goods for sale locally. Many later opened stores in the areas they had frequented.[8]

Outside Ōmi, rural town merchants dominated early interregional trade. Rural merchants in the Kantō and Tōhoku, for example, frequently did business with merchants in distant parts of the country. They sold such things as silk and tobacco to Edo, Kyoto, and Nagoya and purchased such goods as ginned cotton, cotton cloth, and tea. The merchant Nakamura Sakuemon of Makabe in the northern Kantō was probably fairly typical of rural town merchants at the time. To obtain ginned cotton, which he sold both locally and to merchants in the northeast, Nakamura placed orders with wholesalers in Kinai rural towns. The latter shipped the cotton to a merchant in Osaka, who then forwarded the consignment to an Edo merchant. The Edo merchant next routed the ginned cotton to Nakamura. The Osaka and Edo merchants acted as intermediaries, facilitating shipping and the transfer of payments. This was the typical pattern of early trade.[9]

Merchants in the "three cities" thus took a rather passive role in interregional commerce in the first century of Tokugawa rule. They handled goods from various parts of the country but few had control, financial or otherwise, over rural production or rural merchants. Rural merchants did business with other parts of the country in a remarkably free manner. In the seventeenth century, however, commerce was in its infancy. Market production itself was in a stage of gestation, and town merchants, not farmers, dominated long-distance trade.

## City Wholesalers and Rural Trade

The late seventeenth and early eighteenth century witnessed a remarkable transformation of Tokugawa commerce. Many of the old city merchants, who had close ties with political authorities, went bankrupt or lost their positions, and in their place a new merchant class came into being that changed the nature of commerce. These new merchants still maintained strong links with political authorities, but they were based on purely economic ties, and the bulk of their profits derived from ventures they themselves initiated. No longer content to act as intermediaries, they began to purchase directly from rural production regions, and they incorporated numerous village elites into their purchasing networks.

The most important manifestation of this transformation was the rise of a new type of city wholesaler. Unlike their predecessors the consignment merchants (*niuke don'ya*), the new wholesalers became increasingly specialized, handling a particular line of goods rather than several different products. The largest houses managed establishments in each of the "three cities" and appointed agents in the production regions.[10]

Especially important to the success of these new merchant houses was that they hailed from production regions, which accorded them intimate knowledge of local production and gave them an important competitive edge over the older city merchants. The major Edo cloth wholesalers in the eighteenth century, such as Mitsui, Hasegawa, Kawagita, Nagai, Tanaka, and Ozu, came from the Ise area in central Japan, a cotton cultivation region. Shirokiya, another major wholesaler, came from Ōmi; it operated lumber and sundries (*komamono*) stores in Kyoto before launching into the Edo market.[11]

From the late seventeenth century, the "three cities" consolidated their positions as the country's leading commercial and manufacturing centers. The extent of the change was first visible in Osaka. By the early 1710's there were well over 5,000 wholesalers there, over 65 percent of which were specialized by product. *Kuni don'ya* accounted for most of the remaining 35 percent, but thereafter their numbers gradually declined as they transformed themselves into specialized wholesalers.[12]

It was also from the late seventeenth century that Osaka strengthened its ties with the surrounding region. As we saw above, for much of the century Osaka merchants played only an intermediary role in the shipment of Kinai cotton to other parts of the country. In the eighteenth century, however, Osaka cotton merchants increasingly placed rural merchants under their control. This was the case in the nearby town of Hirano-gō. In the seventeenth century there were large numbers of independent merchants there dealing in cotton, but in the eighteenth century their numbers declined. They were replaced by rural merchants who were subordinate to Osaka cotton wholesalers. The Osaka wholesalers, not the rural merchants, now controlled the sale of cotton to other parts of the country. The same was true for the oil produced in the region.[13]

Kyoto's relative position in commerce had declined by the late seventeenth century, but it remained the major center for textiles and other luxury goods. Whereas cotton wholesalers were concentrated in the Osaka market, silk wholesalers established their main operations in Kyoto to facilitate their purchases of Nishijin silk. Although some of them maintained stores in Osaka, Edo was the primary destination of their Kyoto purchases.[14]

The transformation of Edo commerce was even more pronounced. Merchants who purchased directly from production regions (*shiire don'ya*) came to the fore, and they were no longer simply middlemen in trade. From about 1660 to 1720 the old and new merchants coexisted to an extent, but by the 1720's the consignment merchants had largely disappeared.[15]

By the early eighteenth century the "three cities" had thus consolidated their positions as the country's leading commercial centers. With a strong base in the production areas, they were well positioned to capture city markets. They now began to purchase their goods directly from producers. They could not do this on their own, however. For much of the Tokugawa and Meiji periods, farmers produced very small quantities of handicraft and manufactured items, invariably to supplement their income from farming. Especially in the textile industry, wholesalers needed networks of merchants in place at the local level, in particular those familiar with local markets, product quality, and prices.

The first step in this process was to appoint rural elites as their purchasing agents, either as *kaiyado* or as *kaitsugi*. Although the differences between the two are not always clear, *kaiyado* usually lived in local market towns in the center of important production regions. They lodged buyers sent by the city wholesalers and acted as their agents when making purchases in local markets. After the purchases had been made, the *kaiyado* consigned the goods to a shipper. In exchange for these services, the *kaiyado* received a commission on the total cost of the purchases.[16] *Kaiyado* also reported to city wholesalers on local conditions, especially the quality and prices of the goods to be purchased that year. Mitsui's *kaiyado* in the Kantō and Fukushima areas kept it informed about silk crop conditions and prices, which Mitsui then took into consideration when placing orders. Mitsui also frequently had the *kaiyado* send samples of local silk cloth so that it could judge the quality.[17]

*Kaitsugi*, most of whom resided in villages, themselves made purchases for city wholesalers, rather than acting as intermediaries for their buyers. The wholesalers sent purchase orders to their *kaitsugi*, stipulating the quantity and price of the goods they desired, and the *kaitsugi* then purchased and shipped the order. They, too, received a commission on total purchases. To enable the agents to purchase in bulk, the wholesalers provided them money in advance. All *kaitsugi* and *kaiyado* were powerful local personages, and the majority were also officials in the communities where they resided. But very few were capable of financing such a business on their own, at least not on the scale demanded by the wholesalers. The financial dependence of these rural agents was one means by which the city wholesalers controlled the flow of goods from the production regions.

Rural agents obtained the goods city wholesalers required from two sources. Purchases in local periodic markets were obviously important, but with production growth they increasingly relied on the services of small-scale merchant middlemen, known as jobbers (*nakagai*), who purchased directly from farm families. The weight of such purchases varied. Rural agents for raw silk obtained their supplies in both local markets and from area jobbers. In cotton regions the jobbers appear to have assumed a far more important role. In many areas, in fact, there were large numbers of small jobbers positioned between farm families and jobbers, and the jobbers themselves obtained most of their material from small jobbers.

The nature of city wholesalers' purchasing networks varied significantly by region and over time, but surely the most ordered pattern could be found in the Tōkai region of central Japan, a major center for cotton cultivation and cloth production.[18] Whereas the Osaka market received most of the cotton produced in the Kinai and areas in western Japan, that from the Tōkai went directly to Edo. By the end of the seventeenth century, Edo cotton wholesalers had united into two guilds, Ōdenmachō and Shiroko, so as to strengthen their control over the production regions. In 1696 the Ōdenmachō guild directed rural merchants in the provinces of Mikawa and Owari not to accept money for cotton cloth purchases outside Ōdenmachō and threatened to cut off money for purchases if they did. Similar orders followed in later years. In 1728 the Ōdenmachō guild informed the rural merchants that if they did business with outsiders, its members would appoint new agents in their place. The Shiroko guild, composed primarily of wholesalers specializing in silk fabrics but handling cotton, took similar measures.[19]

By the 1720's Edo cotton wholesalers had designated a number of these rural merchants as their agents and had placed them in regional groupings. The wholesalers also organized associations of jobbers who sold their cloth to particular agents. Each level of the hierarchy had clearly defined market spheres and sold directly to the next higher tier.[20] Very little Tōkai cotton went to areas other than Edo, so farmers in the region were dependent on sales to wholesalers in the Edo guilds. The purchasing hierarchy remained in place until well into the Meiji period. In western Mikawa, in fact, there were rural agents, jobbers, and small jobbers even in the 1880's.[21]

Silk cloth wholesalers established similar networks. Until the mid- to late eighteenth century, though, they obtained the overwhelming majority of their purchases from the Nishijin district of Kyoto. Most of the silks produced in rural areas, too, had to be shipped to Kyoto to undergo dyeing and finishing. With their headquarters in Kyoto, silk wholesalers were well positioned to control the sale of most of the country's silk cloth.[22] They had a firm grasp over the Kyoto market, so asserting control over the production regions was not a major concern. Wholesalers merely dispatched buyers to silk production regions, and they only gradually began to appoint agents.[23]

With the diffusion of Nishijin weaving and dyeing technology, however, city wholesalers had to take a far more aggressive role in the rural silk trade. With regions such as Kiryū and Ōmi now manufacturing high-quality finished silks ready for immediate sale in consumer markets, wholesalers had to ensure that these silks were sold to them alone. The wholesalers needed, in other words, a network of agents in the production regions. They were especially vigorous in appointing agents in the Kantō, where they had seventy-three in place by 1776.[24] The wholesalers' networks resembled those found in cotton regions, with rural agents and jobbers positioned to purchase at the local level. Also like the cotton textile regions, silk agents relied heavily on loans from city wholesalers to conduct their business.[25]

Raw silk wholesalers operated slightly differently. The larger silk cloth wholesalers, such as Mitsui, Ebisuya, and Daimonjiya, owned branch establishments in Kyoto that monopolized the sale of raw silk to jobbers, who supplied Nishijin's weavers. These raw silk wholesalers were similar to consignment merchants in that they acted as middlemen between rural merchants and Kyoto jobbers. They received a commission on the goods they handled—usually 1 percent from the rural merchants and 1 percent from the jobbers—and made additional profits by collecting various currency exchange surcharges from the rural merchants. Unlike earlier consignment merchants, however, Kyoto's raw silk wholesalers provided rural shippers with partial payment—usually 70 to 80 percent of total value—for the goods before being actually sold over to the jobbers. These payments were loans, on which the wholesalers earned interest, and were indispensable for rural merchants hoping to buy in quantity.[26] Thus raw silk agents were also heavily dependent on the funds city wholesalers advanced.

Tea wholesalers maintained purchasing networks, as well, though with less of the rigidity found in the textile trade. It was only in 1813 that twenty Edo tea wholesalers, now part of an officially licensed guild, designated particular Shizuoka wholesalers to handle all of the region's tea. The guild demanded that producers and other Shizuoka merchants sell their tea to the designated wholesalers alone.[27]

The large sake brewers of the Kinai were far more independent than producers and merchants in other trades. In the early Tokugawa they controlled the ships taking their sake to Edo, and many set up relatives or close associates as Edo sake wholesalers. But by the nineteenth century most Edo sake wholesalers were independent establishments, and they, too, sought to strengthen their control over the Edo market by ordering all shipments to go through them alone. Since Edo was the country's leading sake market, brewers had no choice but to comply with many of their requests.[28]

By the early to mid-eighteenth century, powerful wholesalers in the "three cities" had asserted a great deal of control over the country's most important production regions. The rural merchants they appointed as their agents had to sell to the wholesalers alone, and they were dependent on the wholesalers for loans for purchases. The major markets for the goods produced in rural areas were the "three cities," so the rural merchants became subordinate to the merchants controlling those markets. The pattern of autonomous trade between rural merchants in different parts of the country existing in the seventeenth century had largely disappeared.[29]

## The Erosion of City Wholesalers' Control

From the end of the eighteenth century, the city wholesalers' purchasing networks came under assault. The wholesalers aggressively competed among themselves for market share, and new city merchants appeared who purchased directly from rural merchants. The rural agents of city wholesalers, as well as growing numbers of new rural merchants, also began to sell to non-guild establishments, both inside and outside Edo. Of equal importance in the decline of city wholesalers' monopolies was the growth of the protoindustrial economy itself. With increased market-related activities in rural areas, raw and intermediate materials began to flow from rural area to rural area, bypassing the major cities, and eroding the wholesalers' ability to control local prices. The process of decline in the power of city wholesalers was at first most conspicuous in the Kinai, as shown in William Hauser's study of the cotton trade, but soon appeared in other major city markets, especially Edo.[30]

The first problem encountered by wholesalers was competition within the "three cities." Mitsui faced this problem from the 1750's. Its competitors, such as Ebisuya and Kameya, succeeded in attracting customers away, forcing Mitsui to lower its prices and to sell more on credit, a practice it had shunned in the past.[31] At the end of the nineteenth century, new wholesalers dominated major city markets. Of the ten leading Tokyo wholesalers selling luxury cloths at the end of the century, the top four had started around the 1850's, and only five had been in business since the seventeenth century. Of the largest ninety-one firms, only ten dated from the seventeenth century; all of the others for which information is available opened shop in the nineteenth. The same volatility could be found in the Kyoto and Osaka markets. Of fifty-seven Kyoto wholesalers, only three had started before 1700 and five in the next century. Of the thirty-seven of the top eighty-two Osaka cloth wholesalers for which information is available, thirty-two started in the Meiji and five in the Tokugawa.[32]

The newcomers hurt the established merchants because they increased

MARKETS                                87

competition for rural purchases. Mitsui faced this problem with purchases of Tottori cotton cloth. It started purchasing there in 1782 after it learned from Nishigami Sahei of Akasaki, its rural agent for Tottori safflower, that the region produced cotton cloth. No other major city wholesaler bought cotton there, so it could be obtained more cheaply than that from other production regions. It was so important, in fact, that Mitsui sold the cloth as a product of the Owari region, so as to keep competitors out of the Tottori trade. In 1793 Mitsui complained, however, that Osaka merchants were buying Tottori cotton cloth, leading to higher prices. In 1797 the western Tottori region, excluding the Yumigahama peninsula, produced 120,000 *tan* of cotton cloth, only 50,000 of which Mitsui purchased. Tottori merchants sold much of the remaining cloth either locally or to other merchants in Osaka and Kyoto.[33]

Many Edo retailers, who previously had been supplied by wholesalers, began to purchase directly from rural merchants. An 1817 investigation revealed that 208 Edo retailers bought silk valued at over 201,000 *ryō* from the production regions. Rural merchants, including even some agents of city wholesalers, increasingly bypassed guild wholesalers and sold to retailers and new wholesalers outside the guild organizations.[34]

The Edo wholesalers' response to this problem was to petition the bakufu to order the retailers to buy only from guild members. The bakufu frequently acceded to these requests because, as we saw in Chapter 1, it was in its interest to have well-ordered purchasing networks and guilds through which to monitor vexing price fluctuations. But often the Edo wholesalers won very tenuous victories when the bakufu interceded on their behalf. When wholesalers petitioned to block rural merchants from Ōmi, Echigo, and Hachiōji from traveling to Edo to sell their cloth, the bakufu simply ordered the rural merchants to pay a commission to the wholesalers' guild.[35]

Even when the bakufu prohibited rural merchants from selling to non-guild merchants, it did little to ensure enforcement. When the bakufu ordered Hachiōji area merchants not to sell directly to Edo, very little changed. The Hachiōji merchants continued going to the Edo market and selling to merchants outside the guilds. There were similar problems with peddlers from Echigo. In 1813 the bakufu limited their numbers to 115, accorded them licenses, and ordered that they pay a commission to the licensed Edo wholesalers on goods they sold, but many new unlicensed peddlers soon appeared. In 1835 wholesalers again asked the bakufu to ban unlicensed Echigo peddlers from the Edo market, but the bakufu instead increased their numbers from 115 to 195.[36]

Some rural merchants even launched into the Edo market in a far more direct way, by becoming Edo wholesalers. The best example is the Ōmi merchant house Chōjiya Gin'emon, or Chōgin, which became one of the most powerful cloth wholesalers in the Meiji period. Gin'emon, born in Kotagari village in 1777, began his career as a merchant by peddling Ōmi bleached hemp (sarashi). By the early nineteenth century, he had expanded his market base, selling to areas in eastern Japan, especially along the Tōkaidō road leading to Edo, and in 1830 the family opened a store in Edo. Chōgin was tremendously successful in commerce thereafter, because it took advantage of growing consumer demand for lower-priced textiles, such as silk/cotton blends, less ornate silks, and cotton fabrics.[37]

Not all rural merchants benefited from the erosion of the city wholesalers' purchasing networks. Many agents, in particular, suffered when unlicensed rural merchants appeared, selling local cloth freely to city markets. Rural agents in western Mikawa confronted this problem in the 1840's, when large numbers of new merchants started in the trade, intensifying competition for purchases at the local level. Conditions deteriorated in the 1850's, when the bakufu approved the formation of a new guild of Edo wholesalers, known as Kari, in addition to the existing Ōdenmachō and Shiroko organizations. Kari wholesalers did not begin to appoint rural agents in western Mikawa until the early 1860's, and until that time they purchased cotton cloth from a number of unlicensed area merchants.[38]

Increasing protoindustrialization also weakened city wholesalers' purchasing networks. In the early phase of protoindustrialization, most farmers carried out all stages of cloth production, from cultivation to weaving. To control prices at the local level, wholesalers only needed to monopolize the purchase of the final cloth. As the processes of cloth production became regionally differentiated, however, farmers and merchants sold the raw and intermediate materials either locally or to distant production regions, bypassing the wholesalers and weakening their control over prices. In addition, rural merchants began shipping even some of the finished cloth to distant rural markets, circumventing the major cities and their wholesalers.

The growth of interrural commerce was most evident in the cotton industry, where increasing numbers of farmers began to buy and sell raw and ginned cotton. Ise weavers, for example, relied in part on yarn purchases from neighboring Kii.[39] Farmers in a mountainous area of Chōshū domain purchased both raw, intermediate, and finished materials. Wealthy farmers purchased an average of 2 tan of cotton cloth a year, while middling farmers bought 0.9 *tan*. Wealthy farmers also purchased raw cotton, and middling farmers purchased not only raw cotton but used clothing, which became an increasingly important item in interrural trade. Poor farmers bought used clothing and raw cotton, but no cotton cloth. The area did not cultivate cotton, so residents imported the raw and ginned cotton from other areas.

Merchants in the Akita area of northeastern Japan, another region that did not cultivate cotton, imported on average 174,397 *tan* of cotton cloth per year from 1808 to 1810. They also purchased the cloth equivalent of 180,000 *tan* of ginned cotton, as well as 117,101 pieces of used clothing.[40] Interrural trade in the finished product heightened all the more in the Meiji period, especially during the inflationary years of the late 1870's. Rather than purchasing used clothing or ginned cotton for household weaving, farmers and townspeople bought new cotton clothing.[41]

Similar interrural trade, as well as a burgeoning intrarural trade, could be found even in the silk industry, which had far less specialization in the processes of production than the cotton industry. Merchants in Shindatsu sold their region's raw silk to weavers in Kiryū and Ōmi, for example. Kiryū weavers purchased their raw material from area merchants, who handled both locally produced raw silk and raw silk from other parts of the country. The weavers' reliance on the market was clear from a 1790 response from the Kiryū Silk Buyers Guild to a bakufu query concerning the mechanisms of price formation. The guild officials stated that the price of raw silk, volume of silk produced, and market demand determined the price for local textiles. The condition of the mulberry crop was also an important variable: the raw silk price would be high if the cost of the mulberry was high.[42] Farmers, in other words, cultivated mulberry for sale, not just to use in their own sericultural operations. Under such conditions, it proved impossible for merchants to control the price of the finished product.

City wholesalers also faced opposition from farmers and rural merchants opposed to their control over local trade. This was the case with tea producers in the Shizuoka area. When Edo wholesalers in 1813 designated particular Shizuoka merchants as the exclusive trans-shippers of the area's tea, village elites immediately launched a movement demanding a system of free trade. The bakufu ruled against them, but they initiated a new movement in the 1850's. Shizuoka producers had enjoyed a decade without trade restrictions from 1841, when the bakufu abolished the guild organizations. When the bakufu revived the guilds in 1851, the Edo wholesalers designated a few Shizuoka merchants as their agents, once again inspiring strong opposition from producers and other merchants. This time the bakufu ruled in their favor. They no longer had to sell their tea through designated production-region wholesalers.[43]

In the final decades of Tokugawa rule, city wholesalers were far weaker than their predecessors in the previous century. New market participants chipped away at the purchasing networks they had so assiduously created, and the bakufu oftentimes proved reluctant to uphold their monopolies. With growing intra- and interrural commerce, the wholesalers found it difficult to monopolize the purchase of the finished product and to hold down prices.

This should not be interpreted to signify, however, that the city wholesalers completely lost their influence over rural production. The "three cities" remained the country's most important consumer markets. With Shizuoka tea, for example, local merchants could, and did, sell their tea freely to areas outside the major cities, such as to Kōfu, Shinano, and the Kinai, and to areas in western and northeastern Japan.[44] But the major market until the opening of the ports was still Edo, and producers even in the Meiji period sold their tea to jobbers, and jobbers sold their tea to Shizuoka town and city merchants.[45] With textiles, the quality of the product often determined its market. Cotton cultivated in Hiroshima and Fukuyama, for example, was coarse and sold primarily to rural markets. The higher quality cotton produced in the Kinai, Tōkai, and Kantō went to the cities. Silk, crepe, and bleached cotton were all luxury cloths and sold primarily in the cities. Even those textiles sold to areas outside the "three cities," however, were handled by city wholesalers, especially the new entrants to the trade.[46]

City merchants exercised control over rural commerce in a number of ways. Rivalry for market share in the "three cities" forced wholesalers to seek production regions where products could be obtained more cheaply. This was one reason Mitsui cultivated strong ties with the Tottori region. Another strategy Mitsui adopted was to compare the prices for the cotton it obtained from various regions and to increase purchases from the low-cost regions. Both Ise and the Kantō, for example, produced a similar type of high-quality bleached cotton cloth, but that from the Kantō was more than twice as profitable.[47] Ise rural merchants obviously had to find ways to lower their prices.

City wholesalers also sometimes fostered competition among their rural agents in order to bring down prices. Mitsui did this on several occasions. Its Edo store Mukaidana had purchased much of its Ise cotton cloth from a related store in Matsuzaka, but from the early nineteenth century

Mukaidana began to purchase from other rural agents who supplied the product more cheaply. There were eleven rural agents in Matsuzaka at the time, and they fiercely competed with one another to buy the product as inexpensively as possible in order to increase their sales to the Edo wholesalers. It was in the interests of Mukaidana to foster this competition, even if it meant decreasing its purchases from the Matsuzaka store.[48] Mitsui adopted a similar tactic in other production regions as well. In Hachiōji, for example, it appointed two new rural agents for the explicit purpose of lowering prices through competition among them.[49]

The Ōdenmachō cotton wholesalers did the same with their rural agents in Mikawa. In 1832 officers of the Ōdenmachō guild summoned four agents to Edo and informed them that they would appoint an additional four or five other agents in the region to foster competition. In 1835 both the Ōdenmachō and Shiroko guilds notified their Mikawa agents that they would temporarily suspend purchases in the region until prices fell.[50] Hasegawa, one of the largest Edo cotton cloth wholesalers, went a step further in 1836 when it bought out a rural agent in Heisaka and directly entered the trade. It continued to use the previous agent's network of jobbers and small jobbers but, by eliminating the middleman, Hasegawa was able to enjoy an important competitive edge.[51]

Wholesalers sometimes forced rural merchants to sell at or below cost by setting a ceiling on the purchase price. The Maeki family of the Shindatsu region, a major raw silk merchant, faced this problem in the 1820's. One year Kyoto wholesalers indicated a price range of 220 to 225 *monme* of raw silk per one *ryō*. Prices in the Shindatsu region, however, were 225 to 240 *monme* and those in the neighboring Sendai region averaged 231 *monme*, so the family was barely able to make a profit after expenses. There were even some occasions when the local price exceeded that set by the Kyoto wholesalers. Although the family sold raw silk to other areas, such as Ōmi, Fukuchiyama, and Tango, most still went to Kyoto, leaving it heavily dependent on profits from the Kyoto trade. Other Shindatsu merchants faced the same problem, and Maeki himself soon abandoned the raw silk trade for silk floss, but here too he was subject to the dictates of city merchant capital.[52]

The machinations of city wholesalers were only one source of instability for rural agents in the textile trade. In the Kiryū area the opening of the ports and depressed demand for luxury silks forced many agents out of business. Only three agents active in the Tokugawa remained in the trade in the 1910's, Kakiage, Onozato, and Ishii. The Kakiage household had been in business the longest, since 1684. Onozato and Ishii dated from the early nineteenth century, and both only barely recovered from bankruptcy in the early 1890's. The Saba family, who had been by far Kiryū's most powerful merchant, went bankrupt in 1896.[53] Similar volatility could be found in the Kawamata area of Shindatsu. Most of the rural agents around 1900 were newcomers. The two oldest both started in 1831, but most of the others had only been in business since the 1880's and 1890's.[54] Of six rural agents in western Mikawa tied to the Ōdenmachō guild in 1856, four survived until 1871 and two until 1889.[55]

By the nineteenth century, city wholesalers were much weaker than their predecessors in the eighteenth. Old and new market participants eroded the purchasing networks they had created and nurtured, and the bakufu proved less willing to uphold their monopolies. City wholesalers also found themselves excluded when raw, intermediate, and finished materials began to flow from production region to production region, or were sold within their production regions. The wholesalers responded by forcing their agents to accept lower profit margins and to more actively compete among themselves for local purchases. Even the most powerful rural merchants found it difficult to continue their trade.

## The Opening of the Ports

The opening of the ports in 1859 heralded momentous changes to three key sectors of the Japanese economy: tea, raw silk, and silk textiles. Growing numbers of farmers produced tea and raw silk, many for the first time, to meet the enormous demand in international markets. The silk-weaving industry, on the other hand, was initially devastated. Merchants shipped much of their raw silk to Yokohama for export, and the little that remained jumped in price. The industry gradually recovered, especially from the late 1880's, when habutae silks became an important export item. Merchants in these industries had to respond quickly to these historic changes.

Village elites in the tea industry were little affected by the opening of the ports even though tea became Japan's second leading export item. This was because few had been significant participants in the interregional tea trade before 1859. At least in Shizuoka, merchants in the city of Sunpu, who had controlled shipments to Edo in the past, became active in the export trade.[56] Most tea cultivation at the time was carried out in remote villages in mountainous areas, where farmers were not extensively involved in production for the market, and upper-class farmers engaged in only minor forms of rural commerce.[57]

MARKETS                          93

There were two important exceptions to this general pattern: Nakayama Motonari of the Sashima area of Shimōsa and Ōtani Kahyōe of
Yano village in Ise. Nakayama entered the export trade for only a brief
period and will be discussed in Chapter 6. Ōtani went to work in Yokohama in 1862 for someone from a neighboring village who had become
an export merchant (urikomishō). He worked in various capacities, including employment as a buyer for Smith, Baker and Co., one of the
large Western merchant houses active in the city. Apparently with financial backing from this firm, he became an export merchant himself
in 1868, and he rose to become the leading figure in the Yokohama tea
export trade by 1890. Ōtani was one of the few who were successful:
there were thirty-two Yokohama tea export merchants in 1872, eighteen in 1898, and only thirteen in 1907.[58]

The commencement of foreign trade had a much more immediate effect
on rural elites in the raw silk trade. While countless new merchants entered the trade to capitalize on international demand, established merchants found it difficult to make the transition to an export-oriented
economy. Very few rural agents, in fact, successfully shifted from the domestic market, and most withdrew from the trade entirely. This was certainly the case with the Ōhashi Gizaemon household, examined in Chapter 5. The same was true with "three city" wholesalers. Mitsui, which operated a small raw silk business in Edo, began to handle export raw silk in
1860, but without success, and it left the trade in 1863.[59] Chōgin, a relative newcomer to the Edo market, fared much better, remaining in the
trade until the mid-Meiji.[60]

Rural elites, not city wholesalers, played the leading role in raw silk exports, but they were almost without exception newcomers to the trade.
There were two types of merchant in the export trade: shippers, who purchased raw silk from the production regions and sold it to Yokohama; and
Yokohama export merchants, who sold raw silk, purchased either directly
from the production regions or from shippers, to Western merchant
houses. A typical shipper was Ōtsuka Gorōkichi of Yarimizu village in the
Hachiōji area, who entered the trade as a petty merchant around the
1820's. He at first purchased raw silk from area farmers but soon started a
putting-out system, providing farmers with the cocoons necessary for
reeling. With the opening of the ports, Gorōkichi quickly turned to the export trade. There were probably hundreds of rural shippers like Gorōkichi
in each of the major production regions. In the early 1870's nine raw silk
merchants lived in Yarimizu village alone, five of them with sales of over
1,000 ryō. From 10/1871 to 9/1872 Gorōkichi sold raw silk valued at

21,519 *ryō*, and another member of the Ōtsuka clan sold well over twice that amount.[61]

A number of rural elites reached the pinnacle of the raw silk trade by becoming Yokohama export merchants.[62] Yoshida Kōhei was in many ways typical. His grandfather had operated a pawn house and engaged in sake brewing; he also served as headman of Arakawa village, near the town of Ōmama in Kōzuke. Kōhei's father, Wagorō, was set up in a new branch household in Ōmama, where he too ran a pawn business. A few years before the opening of the ports, Wagorō and his son Kōhei began dealing in raw silk and cocoons; they also engaged in the putting out of cocoons for reeling. With the opening of the ports, Kōhei moved to Yokohama to take advantage of the profits to be had in the export trade. He at first sold his raw silk to export merchants, but in 1862 he became an export merchant himself. In 1878 he handled the second largest quantity of export raw silk.[63]

Raw silk export merchants like Yoshida could make fabulous profits, but it was also the most volatile of occupations. Yoshida remained in the trade far longer than most, until 1879, when the family sold the business to a cousin of the Meiji industrialist Shibusawa Eiichi.[64] Few others were so fortunate. Of thirty-two raw silk export merchants in 1869, only two survived until 1888. A number of new merchants entered the trade, it is true, but of the estimated forty-eight newcomers, only eleven were still doing business in 1888.[65]

There were numerous sources of instability, both for local shippers and for export merchants. A most serious problem in the early years, especially for export merchants, was domains seeking to profit from foreign trade. Maebashi and Takazaki domains, both in Kōzuke, started in the export trade in 1869. Maebashi provided funds for merchants to purchase raw silk from producers, but those receiving such funds had to take their raw silk to the domain-operated store in Maebashi city, which then shipped the raw silk to the domain's Yokohama store for sale to Western merchants. Because financing was critical to the success of rural merchants, large and small, much of the area's raw silk ended up in the domain's Yokohama store, bypassing the export merchants. Ueda and Matsushiro domains in Shinano established similar systems around the same time. To survive, export merchants like Yoshida had to purchase as much as they could from other parts of the country.[66]

Volatility in raw silk prices also destabilized the trade. In the early years, merchants like Yoshida purchased their raw silk directly from the production regions, either through family connections or through local shippers, and their success depended on their ability to buy low and sell high. But Yokohama prices fluctuated greatly, and there was no guarantee that production region prices would always be lower than the Yokohama price. Wakao Ippei of Yamanashi, who had made massive amounts of money by shipping raw silk to Yokohama, felt this most keenly in 1875 when he lost half of his 250,000 ryō in assets as a result of a slump in Yokohama prices. He quickly recovered, but the problem he faced demonstrates just how unstable the export trade could be.[67] Conditions were especially poor during periods of international crises. When war broke out in Europe in 1870, for example, Western merchants stopped buying raw silk, forcing many export merchants out of the business.

There was similar volatility with currency exchange rates. The Yokohama export merchants received payment in the form of silver, which they then converted into Japanese currency. If the exchange rate was favorable, export merchants could make enormous profits, even when raw silk prices were unfavorable. But exchange rates were far from stable, and many merchants went bankrupt in their attempts to profit from currency exchange fluctuations. Those successful in the trade switched to consignment sales. By collecting a commission on raw silk sent to them by production region shippers, they were no longer so adversely affected by price fluctuations.[68]

Yet another serious problem confronting raw silk merchants was competition for purchases. Because the price differential between Yokohama and the production regions was often very small, export merchants had to sell in bulk. Family connections alone were insufficient, so they tried to secure as much raw silk as they could from production area shippers. The best way to do this was to provide them funds in advance for purchases. At first, the export merchants provided such funds at the time of the raw silk's arrival in Yokohama, but from the 1880's they increasingly loaned them money well in advance, before the raw silk was even produced. The shippers, in turn, provided loans to reelers to purchase cocoons.[69]

Finally, the laying of telegraph lines between Yokohama and the major production regions completely undercut the price-differential advantage rural merchants had enjoyed in the past. Producers and local merchants now could learn immediately the price on the Yokohama market and adjust their own prices accordingly. The laying of a telegraph line to Maebashi in 1877 was a critical factor in the downfall of some of the area's most powerful merchants, including the Shimomura family, one of the country's largest raw silk merchants. Other powerful Maebashi merchants abandoned the raw silk trade and instead launched into putting out. It proved far less risky to engage in production than export sales.[70]

Merchants and producers in the silk-weaving industry fared even worse. Because much of the country's raw silk was exported, little was available for domestic weavers, and what could be obtained had skyrocketed in price. In the Ashikaga area, raw silk prices jumped over fourfold between 1857 and 1865, making it almost impossible for weavers to sell their cloth. In the Kiryū area countless weavers had to suspend operations, especially those specializing in luxury silks.[71] In desperation, producers and merchants in the major silk textile regions, such as Kiryū and Hachiōji, petitioned the bakufu for an end to foreign trade.[72] The bakufu, however, made only a minor concession in response to domestic pressure. In 1860 it ordered that raw silk first pass through Edo wholesalers, who were to sell the raw silk domestically before shipping the remainder to Yokohama for export. The system remained in place until 1863, but it did precious little to stem exports.[73]

A few rural elites adapted to the changes, but they were the exception. One of the wealthiest families in the Ashikaga area, the Ōkawa household of Komata village, survived by operating a putting-out system: it supplied raw silk to households and paid them a piece-rate for weaving silks. The family profited by keeping piece-rates well below the rate of inflation. Despite a fourfold increase in prices for thread, silk cloth, and rice from 1858 to 1866, the average piece-rates for its weavers increased by only about 37 percent. But even Ōkawa found it difficult to survive the turmoil in the silk cloth industry, and he gradually turned his attention to other pursuits, especially landlord operations.[74] A rural elite active in the silk cloth and domestic raw silk trade, Fujiu Zenjūrō of Kirihara village endured, even prospered during, these difficult years by becoming an export merchant.[75]

Despite the opportunities international trade seemed to offer, few rural merchants profited in the long run. Conditions were especially unfavorable in the silk-weaving industry, where the export trade had a crippling effect on rural weavers and silk merchants. Countless numbers of new merchants emerged to take advantage of international demand for raw silk, but few survived for long in the trade, and for several it meant complete ruin.

## The Decline of the Protoindustrial Merchant Class

From the 1880's two important developments led to the decline of many once powerful rural merchants. To improve quality and become more competitive in international markets, producers established raw silk and tea cooperatives. Farmers took their raw silk and tea to the cooperatives, which inspected, graded, packaged, and shipped the products, completely circumventing established merchants in the production regions. Equally important, there were critical changes in the modes of production, in particular the advent of the factory system. As they expanded in scale, factories shipped their products directly to consumer markets and to Yokohama, bypassing local merchants.

Producers' cooperatives in the raw silk industry first appeared in Gunma prefecture in 1877, with the formation of Hoshino Chōtarō's Watarase-gumi. Several others followed in rapid succession. Area farmers took their raw silk to the cooperatives, which inspected, graded, re-reeled, and shipped it to Yokohama. Of the three largest Gunma cooperatives in 1893, the Usuisha and Kanrasha had thirty-nine branches (*kumi*) each and the Shimonida twenty-seven; in 1910 their numbers had increased to 162, 122, and 77, respectively. The Usuisha maintained branches not only in Gunma but in seven other prefectures. In 1902 over 46 percent of Gunma reeling households belonged to one of these cooperatives.[76]

The raw silk cooperatives thrived for two reasons. First, they dramatically improved raw silk quality through the process of grading and re-reeling, and thereby competed successfully with filature-spun silk from such areas as Suwa and Yamanashi. Second, the cooperatives served as financial institutions working for the direct benefit of producers. The Usuisha, for example, paid interest on deposits at about twice the bank rate, and it loaned money on favorable terms.[77] All these cooperatives engaged in collective sales to Yokohama, obviating the need for rural shippers in the export trade.

The cooperatives should not be viewed as economic levelers, because within each organization there were still large and small producers. Most producers utilized family labor alone. Two-thirds of all reelers in Gunma in 1902, in fact, were independent. The remaining one-third worked for others, either under the putting-out system or in small-scale manufacturing establishments.[78]

Producers in the tea industry also established cooperatives, though at a far slower pace. They first united for collective processing and sales in the late 1870's.[79] In 1884 there were fifteen tea associations in Shizuoka, composed of 40,073 producers, but they were weak and short-lived organizations.[80] It was only after the passage of a government law in 1900 relating to cooperatives that such organizations came into their own.[81] As with raw silk cooperatives, the tea cooperatives inspected and graded the tea for quality and then shipped it on to Yokohama.[82] Here, too, they bypassed established merchants in the trade.

There were a host of institutions in other industries that performed similar roles to the sales cooperatives. In the textile industry, for example, powerful weavers united into associations (*dōgyō kumiai*), which sometimes included collective sales among their primary functions. The Kawamata Silk Textile Industry Association, formed in 1896, engaged in joint production and sales. Such organizations also collectively purchased the raw material, thus bypassing the local market and its merchants.[83]

Particularly damaging to the activities of rural elites was the emergence and expansion of new modes of production, especially putting out and the factory system. In most areas, the putting-out system coexisted with traditional forms of commerce, but in western Mikawa the two groups were in intense competition. The new factories, especially those operating on a large scale, had a far greater effect nationwide, because they sold their goods directly to consumer markets. The effects of these changes were most keenly felt in the textile industry, but there were major differences in the speed of the transition to industrial modes of production.

Rural agents in western Mikawa fell upon hard times in the late 1880's, despite tremendous growth in the local cotton cloth industry. A convergence of factors contributed to their eventual withdrawal from the trade. First, the processes of spinning and weaving became increasingly specialized. Spinning companies, large (mechanized factories) and small (using the *garabō*, or rattling spindle), began to purchase much of the raw cotton produced in the area, while farmers began to specialize in weaving alone. Much of the weaving now took place under the putting-out system: merchants supplied farmers with the yarns they purchased from the new factories, as well as often the looms themselves, and paid them piece-rates for producing cloth. The specialization of production led to markedly increased productivity, especially with the growing use of the flying shuttle loom from the late 1880's.

Most merchants operating these putting-out systems were newcomers to the cotton cloth trade, and when selling their cloth they bypassed the rural agents. They also expanded their markets, shipping large quantities to regions other than Tokyo. Few rural agents made the transition to putting out, and the two or three who did were relatively new to the cotton cloth trade. Even many of those operating putting-out systems found their careers shortened with the advent of power-loom factories after the Russo-Japanese of 1904–5.[84] In general, intermediate-level merchants made the transition to factory modes of production far more easily than those at the pinnacle of the purchasing network, the rural agents. Eight jobbers who once sold cotton cloth to the agent Sugiura Mozaemon, for example, opened power-loom factories, while Sugiura himself, like other rural agents in western Mikawa, withdrew from the cotton trade entirely.[85]

The speed of the shift to factory production varied greatly from one region to the next. Power looms caught on quickly primarily in those regions producing monochrome cloths. The Osaka metropolitan area and Aichi (Mikawa) made the transition early, around the turn of the century, because they produced simple white cottons. In the silk industry, those regions producing habutae for export, such as Fukui, Ishikawa, and Fukushima, also shifted to mechanized production from an early date, because habutae did not entail exacting technical requirements. Those regions producing striped cotton, splashed-pattern cottons, crepes, and traditional silks, however, were slow to mechanize. The same was true of those regions with a long history in the silk industry, such as Kiryū, Ashikaga, and Kyoto.[86] As Sidney Pollard put it in explaining the situation in many European countries, "precisely because of its earlier success the specialist region will be among the last to let go of the old and adopt the new, by which time it may well be too late."[87]

In silk textile regions slow to mechanize, such as Kiryū and Ashikaga, the growth of the putting-out system and small-scale manufacture in the early Meiji did not lead to fundamental changes in the nature of commerce. Most rural elites operating putting-out systems or engaging in small-scale manufacture sold their finished cloth to rural merchants and purchased the raw material from them. Power looms only became dominant in the Kiryū area after World War I.[88]

The Kawamata area of Fukushima, which was quicker to mechanize, had a number of small-scale manufacturing operations before the advent of power looms. In 1889 the average number of looms per household in Kawamata itself was 3.8, and in nearby Kakeda it was 8.0. Merchants in local markets continued to perform vital roles, both in supplying the raw material and in purchasing the finished cloth. The establishment of power loom factories, especially after the Russo-Japanese War, however, not only decimated the household weaving industry and putting out, but completely changed the nature of rural commerce. The new factories bypassed local markets and the merchants operating there.[89]

Mechanization was especially rapid in the silk-reeling industry. It was most evident in the Suwa area, where small-scale filatures first opened in the early 1870's. Over the course of the Meiji there appeared a growing concentration in the Suwa reeling industry, and the region soon had the highest concentration of large-scale filatures in the country.[90] Areas like

Suwa made the transition to mechanized production in part because they had not been significant producers of raw silk in the past. The country's leading raw silk regions in the Tokugawa, such as Kōzuke (Gunma prefecture) and Shindatsu (Fukushima prefecture), on the other hand, were slow to mechanize. Both regions produced a superior product, and there was little incentive to establish factories and to abandon reeling within the household.[91] It was only in the early twentieth century, when technological advances had dramatically improved the quality of filature-spun silk, that Gunma and Fukushima began to launch into machine-reeling in a major way. Even Gunma's producers' cooperatives found it necessary to establish filatures. With the Usuisha, for example, filatures produced only 3 percent of its raw silk in 1903. In 1913, however, its filature-spun raw silk exceeded that produced by hand-operated devices.[92]

In a number of regions, there was no linearity in the transition from one mode of production to another. This was certainly the case in the Sennan area of the Kinai, a major cotton region. Putting out could be found in the area in the late Tokugawa, disappeared in the early Meiji, and reappeared from the late 1880's. One of the reasons for its re-emergence was the development of new types of looms, which produced a superior product critical to Sennan's survival in the competition with other production regions. In the past, farmers had constructed their own looms, even versions of the flying shuttle loom, but this was not possible with the newer forms.[93] Also, some once vibrant centers of protoindustrial activity did not make the transition to mechanized forms of production at all. This will become clear in my case studies of the northern Kantō bleached cotton region (Chapter 4) and the Sashima tea region (Chapter 6).

By the early twentieth century, producers' cooperatives and factories had largely obviated the need for the merchants who had been active in interregional trade in the past. The factories sold their goods directly to consumer markets or to the major export ports, displacing those who had traditionally handled these products. This did not at all signal the demise of the merchant class as a whole, however. The factories in particular sometimes created an even greater demand for merchants and new forms of protoindustry. They needed building materials and equipment, for example. The early spinning companies, especially those not yet involved in weaving, used large numbers of merchants to supply weavers with their yarns. The growth of a factory labor force created a demand for merchants and stores to sell them food and other necessities. But for traditional rural merchants—those who profited by handling in bulk and taking advantage of price differentials between production regions and consumer markets—the early twentieth century heralded few opportunities, and they were forced to refocus their energies in other areas.

A vibrant interregional trade characterized Japan's protoindustrial economy, but it was in a continual state of flux. Much initial commerce was predicated on demand in Japan's major cities, and city wholesalers sometimes exercised a great deal of control, over both rural production and rural merchants. Even in the nineteenth century, when new market participants seriously eroded their purchasing networks, the massive volume of goods flowing into the "three cities" assured them some power over both the flow of goods and prices.

Japan's entry into the modern world economy in 1859 augured still further changes in the nature of protoindustrial commerce, especially in export-oriented industries. Many existing merchants could not make the transition to an export economy, but countless new merchants readily stepped in to fill the void, in a process Pat Hudson has termed "waves of entrepreneurial renewal."[94] The same process occurred with the rise of modern factories, where few once powerful merchants made the transition.

Factors that made the *gōnō*'s business activities precarious were highlighted in earlier chapters. Political authorities' exactions and interregional competition, in particular, forced many rural elites into decline, or at least to take appropriate measures to respond. The challenges facing rural elites were nowhere so apparent as in commerce, where a bewildering array of changes presented obstacles often far too difficult for many to overcome.

# PART II

# Case Studies

# 4

# Rural Elites
# in Cotton Regions

Before the arrival of cotton, the nobility wore silks and stuffed them with silk floss to keep warm, but farmers and those of mean status were not allowed to wear such things. Also, because silk was expensive, common people inserted into their hemp garments a hemp floss [*owata*], which they produced by soaking and repeatedly beating the hemp waste. . . . Today, in its place, cotton is cultivated widely around the country and everyone wears cotton garments, even men and women in remote mountain villages and along the coasts.

Miyanaga Masakazu, *Shika nōgyōdan* (1789)

WITH THE CONSOLIDATION of the Tokugawa order, Japan witnessed a remarkable revolution in clothing.[1] Growing numbers of samurai began to wear expensive silks, many for the first time, and townspeople and farmers donned cotton garments, abandoning the coarser hempen clothing they had worn in the past. The popularity of cotton, in particular, is surprising, since it was a relatively new crop to Japan: it had been first introduced in the eighth century but then abandoned until the sixteenth century. By the mid-seventeenth century, it had become the country's leading clothing material.

Although villages and towns in the Kinai dominated early cotton cultivation and cloth manufacture, by the mid-eighteenth century numerous other sites of production had emerged, threatening the Kinai's position. To compete, many weavers began to produce distinctive textures and styles. In addition to several general fabric types, such as white cottons, bleached cottons, and striped cottons, there appeared a seemingly infinite range of weaves, often bearing the name of the region first producing it: Yūki striped cotton, Mooka bleached cotton, Kogura weave, Usuki floating weave, Sagara weave, Owari *santome* striped cotton, to name but a few.[2]

Wealthy farmers across the country became active in the cotton trade but, for a variety of reasons, with vastly differing results. To highlight the factors contributing to the emergence of a powerful class of rural elites, this chapter examines two quite different cotton regions: the Mooka area of the northern Kantō and western Mikawa in central Japan. Although the Kantō was a significant cotton cultivation region, accounting for almost 10 percent of the nationwide total in the early Meiji, farmers in the Mooka area, where much of the early cultivation was concentrated, were among the poorest in the country. Until the 1830's the nascent protoindustrial economy did little to improve their fortunes; indeed, it immersed them all the more in poverty and destitution. A powerful class of rural elites was slow to emerge. Rural elites in western Mikawa, on the other hand, thrived. They shipped massive quantities of cotton cloth and ginned cotton to Edo/Tokyo, and they extensively engaged in moneylending and land accumulation. But even they found little stability or permanence through their economic endeavors.

## Rural Elites and the Mooka Bleached Cotton Trade

Despite its proximity to Edo, the Mooka bleached cotton production area, encompassing the towns of Mooka in southern Shimotsuke (Tochigi prefecture) and Shimodate and Makabe in western Hitachi (Ibaraki prefecture), was one of the most economically depressed regions of the country for much of the Tokugawa. Over the period 1721 to 1834, the population of Shimotsuke province declined by almost 39 percent and that of Hitachi by 36 percent.[3] Some villages witnessed even more drastic declines, losing one half or more of their populations. Rural elites who were closely linked to market production appeared from the mid-eighteenth century, but they were a much weaker group than their counterparts elsewhere in the country. As poorer members of their communities defaulted on their debts and abandoned their fields, rural elites faced seemingly insurmountable difficulties.

Villagers in the northern Kantō cultivated cotton and produced cotton cloth before the mid-Tokugawa. Judging from the types of town business establishments in operation, cotton was one of the most important products of the region. In 1670 eight Mooka establishments engaged in dyeing, and three handled seed cotton and *shinomaki*.[4] In Makabe there were thirteen striped cotton wholesalers in 1696, with a total sales volume of over 7,000 *ryō*. There were many more small merchants who sold local cloth to the wholesalers, and five merchants selling ginned cotton.[5]

But until the mid-eighteenth century cotton cultivation was in an early stage of development. In 1697 Isasa villagers dedicated about 1.5 *chō* to cotton cultivation, or only about 10 percent of their dry field acreage. Similar conditions obtained in Shimo-Obata, where villagers planted 3 *chō* of cotton, or about 15.6 percent of their dry fields.[6] Farmers often had to purchase ginned cotton in local markets to supplement their crop. Two powerful town merchants, Nakamura Sakuemon of Makabe and Nakamura Heizaemon of Shimodate, bought ginned cotton from the Kinai, which they sold not only to towns in northeastern Japan, such as Sendai and Fukushima, but to local residents.[7]

The northern Kantō's farmers were in many ways self-sufficient. The major crops of Isasa and Shimo-Obata in the 1690's were rice and barley. Much of the farmers' rice went toward tax payments on their paddies, which political authorities in the region collected in kind. They grew several other crops, such as crowfoot millet (*hie*), soybeans, wheat, cotton, "fall vegetables," and Japanese radishes (*daikon*), but in very small quantities, suggesting that they were primarily for household consumption.[8] Villagers, of course, did utilize local markets. Political authorities dictated that taxes on dry fields be paid in specie, obligating farmers to sell some of their crops. Farmers often sold their surplus rice, using their barley as their primary food staple, and their striped cotton cloth, which farm women wove.

From the mid-eighteenth century, farmers dedicated more and more of their fields to cotton cultivation and produced growing quantities of cloth. This was certainly the case in Higashinuma village. Forty-seven of fifty-one families cultivated cotton in 1833 and on far more acreage than most other dry field crops. Thirty-three households wove cotton cloth.[9] The importance of cotton is also clear from the activities of town merchants. They continued to import ginned cotton from the Kinai but in smaller quantities. They purchased growing quantities of ginned cotton and *shinomaki* produced in the region itself, which they sold locally and to merchants in the northeast. By the nineteenth century many of these merchants began to sell locally ginned cotton to the Edo market. In 1851 there were twelve such merchants in Shimodate alone.[10]

The diffusion of bleached cotton cloth production significantly contributed to the growth of the cotton industry.[11] Unlike the striped cottons and white cottons produced in the past, which were sold primarily to towns in the northeast, bleached cotton was a luxury item, highly prized in the Edo market. With increased market demand, more and more town merchants launched into the bleached cotton trade and became rural agents (*kaitsugi*) to Edo wholesalers. The sphere of production also expanded. In the early years, the center of bleached cloth production was the region encompassing the town of Mooka, and throughout the Tokugawa the material was known as "Mooka cotton cloth." By the second half of the eighteenth century, outlying areas, in particular Makabe, Shimodate, and Utsunomiya, assumed a growing share of production.[12]

Rural agents, all of whom resided in the major towns, were at the center of the bleached cotton trade in the northern Kantō. They purchased the unfinished cloth woven by farm women and subcontracted the bleaching out to households who specialized in this arduous task. Unlike rural agents in other regions, who attempted to free themselves of the tight control of city wholesalers, agents in the northern Kantō continued to ship only to Edo wholesalers, even after the bakufu ordered their guilds dissolved in 1841. Since bleached cotton was a luxury item, Edo remained the primary market for its sale.[13]

Until the early nineteenth century, farm families sold their cloth to the agents operating out of the local market towns. If farmers did not like the price a merchant offered, they would go to another merchant and, if still dissatisfied, take their cloth to another market in the area.[14] With increased production in the nineteenth century, growing numbers of jobbers appeared. The jobbers, many of whom were farmers themselves, purchased cloth directly from farm families, then sold it to the agents in the towns. In the closing years of the Tokugawa, almost 100 cloth jobbers could be found in villages across the northern Kantō.[15] There were also large numbers of village jobbers handling ginned cotton.[16]

Village jobbers became so important in regional trade that they posed a threat to the livelihoods of merchants operating out of the towns. This was certainly the case in Makabe. Town merchants complained to the local bakufu intendant in 1794 that their market was in decline, with many establishments going bankrupt. With the growth of the bleached cotton industry, they stated, merchants from other areas, who had purchased striped cottons there in the past, no longer frequented the market. Farmers did not come either. Village merchants purchased their products, and farmers could buy whatever they needed from village merchants or from small village stores. Farmers, the Makabe merchants reasoned, should only be concerned with farming, so village commerce should be prohibited. Having failed to win concessions from the intendant, Makabe merchants petitioned again in 1805. Conditions, they wrote, had only deteriorated. There were now over twenty stores in surrounding villages; they sold not only clothing and sundries (*komamono*), but such food dishes as *udon* and *soba*.[17]

We know very little about rural jobbers, but few appear to have specialized in cotton cloth alone; rice and other grains were far more important in their trade. Nomura Toyofusa of Tomiya village might have been typical of wealthier jobbers. According to a journal he kept of his business activities from 1783 to 1791, Nomura handled only small quantities of cloth, but he was hardly a petty merchant. He included in his journal a detailed account of price movements in local markets (such as Makabe and Shimodate) and in the major cities (especially Edo and Osaka) for such items as ginned cotton, rice, soybeans, and wheat. By keeping continually informed of price fluctuations, he was able to shift the focus of his sales to earn the greatest profits. Nomura was also well aware of the reasons behind price shifts, such as Sendai domain's flooding of the Osaka market with rice, crop conditions in the Kinai and other parts of the country, and the volcanic eruption of Mt. Asama in Kōzuke.[18]

Despite the growth of village merchants, even at the end of the Tokugawa those who bought the semi-finished cloth, had it bleached, and shipped the finished material to Edo were all wealthy town merchants. The dominance of town merchants stemmed in part from the expense of producing the cloth. It required considerable sums to purchase the unfinished cloth and to provide loans in advance to bleachers, who processed the cloth over a period of from sixty to one-hundred days, and only wealthier, better established town merchants had the necessary capital.[19]

But this was not the case with the bleached cotton industry on the Chita peninsula in central Japan, which supported a number of powerful rural elites. In the mid-eighteenth century, Edo wholesalers maintained six rural agents on the peninsula, all of whom resided in villages. Many of the jobbers, too, were of considerable means. Five of twenty-four jobbers sold the rural agent Takeuchi over 1,000 *tan* of cloth in 1833. In 1843 sixteen of thirty-four jobbers sold the family over 1,000 *tan*. Most had surnames or store names, suggesting that they conducted business on a fairly large scale.[20] The weakness of the rural elite in the northern Kantō can be seen in other trades as well. With sake, for example, the Tsuji family of Mooka at times completely monopolized its sale in a few villages in the area. Many of the village pawn houses that appeared in growing numbers in the nineteenth century were also under the control of town pawn houses.[21] This was quite unlike the situation in other regions, where village elites themselves had long since become active in these trades.

Serious population decline contributed in no small measure to the relative weakness of the northern Kantō's rural elite. Large numbers of farmers reduced the size of their households or left the region entirely, which resulted both in a labor shortage on the lands of the wealthy and in a dwindling market for the goods the wealthy handled. Every village in the region witnessed severe declines in population, especially from the mid-eighteenth century. The population of Isasa village, near Makabe, dwindled from 244 in 1697, to 226 in 1749, and to 160 in 1789. The population of Shimo-Obata, also near Makabe, increased from 234 in 1698 to 345 in 1761, then precipitously declined. There were only 145 remaining in the village in 1790, almost 10 *chō* of fields had been abandoned, and seventeen residents had to seek work (as *hōkōnin*) outside the village.[22]

Historians of early modern Japan have been confronted with the vexing question of why Japan's population remained fairly static from the 1720's to 1850, at around 26 million. If there was indeed marked growth in the economy, and if the western European case serves as any type of demographic model, Japan's population should have increased to at least 35 million. In recent years, historians and demographers have attributed the stagnation to deliberate family-size limitation through the practice of infanticide; farmers limited the size of their households in order to maximize their standards of living.[23] The veracity of such claims is beyond the concerns of this study, and no doubt demographic components varied widely from one village to the next. Even in western Europe there seem to have been a variety of demographic responses to protoindustrialization, and not all regions witnessed population growth.[24] What is clear from the northern Kantō is that few farmers enjoyed the luxury of worrying about ways to maximize their profits. Survival was a far more pressing concern.

Epidemics were one source of the region's population decline. As Ann Jannetta has shown, epidemics played only a minor role in Tokugawa Japan's overall population stagnation.[25] This was probably also true of the northern Kantō, but when combined with other factors their effects could be devastating. The epidemic that struck Shimo-Obata in 1761 killed off 155 people, or about 45 percent of the village, and an epidemic the following year left another forty-five dead. Similarly, the enteric disease, coupled with crop failures, that struck Kameyama village from the 1760's to 1780's led to many deaths and widespread impoverishment.[26]

Infanticide also contributed to population decline. Judging from sex ratios, female infanticide was widespread and intensified from the mid-eighteenth century. Males outnumbered females in Isasa village by 14 percent in 1697 and by 21 percent in 1789. In Shimo-Obata, males outnumbered females by 9 percent in 1698 and by 20 percent in 1788.[27] Out-migration of women may have contributed to their decline, though available records do not yet warrant such a conclusion. It is a fact, however, that area farmers, in the grips of increasingly depressed conditions, widely practiced infanticide, and countless documents attest to its pervasiveness. As Kameyama's headman explained the problem:

> When people were fortunate enough to leave as contract laborers in other areas or to become scattered [risan tsukamatsuri sōrō], parents and children and brothers became separated. They completely lost their spirit, and morals were pushed to the wayside. Even if people gave birth, they detested raising the children. As a result, they killed their babies at birth, [in a practice] known as weeding out [mabiki], and the population gradually declined.[28]

The hapless farmers sketched in Nagatsuka Takashi's novel The Soil, set in a region not far to the south in the early twentieth century, would no doubt have been horrified by the conditions in their region one hundred years before.[29] Despite the deplorable conditions surrounding their lives and continuing evidence of infanticide, the characters were at least able to survive as a family.

A far more important source of population decline, however, was out-migration. Unable to earn a livelihood from the soil and sinking further into poverty, many farmers abandoned their fields in search of a better life. The low productivity of the land contributed to this trend. In Haga district, which encompasses the Mooka area, the rice yield per tan was only 0.92 koku in 1877, quite low compared with that of other parts of the country. In advanced regions, such as along the Seto Inland Sea, tenants paid more than twice that amount in tenancy fees alone, and their yields were probably well over 3 koku. The low productivity of the northern Kantō's lands is also reflected in the land valuations set as a result of the Meiji land reform of the 1870's. The land price of paddies was 36.6 yen per tan in Haga, compared with 62.1 yen in Ashikaga district to the south, another area of relatively low land productivity.[30] Productivity had increased by the 1870's, so we can assume that conditions a century before were even more severe.

The market economy itself contributed to poor farmers' problems. Because they had to pay a large portion of their annual tax in specie, many smallholders switched to cash crops and cleared new fields. To get the most from their fields, they purchased fertilizers from village and town elites. But because smallholders did not witness significant productivity gains on their lands, they became increasingly indebted, until eventually they were forced into bankruptcy.[31]

High tax rates and other exactions compounded smallholders' difficulties in earning a livelihood from the land. Representatives of six villages in the Mooka area blamed their difficulties in part on a change in the way the domain collected the tax on their rice paddies. The daimyo in 1718 ordered farmers to pay using a higher grade of rice, which amounted to a significant new financial burden. Greater exactions, though, were only one of several factors contributing to village decline. Heavy winds, rain, and flooding the same year washed away their fields, homes, and belongings. In later years, too, farmers suffered from crop failures, and an epidemic killed many in the area.[32]

Farmers in Isezaki village in Haga district faced similar problems with onerous exactions. In response to a bakufu intendant's inquiry in 1761, village officials placed much of the responsibility for abandoned lands and "broken farmers" (*tsubure hyakushō*, meaning impoverished farmers) on the shoulders of political authorities. Thirty-two years before, they said, villagers had been called upon to supply labor and horses for a samurai procession to Nikkō, an exaction that forced them to neglect their fields and to pay large sums of money out of their own pockets. The following year, the villagers "without exception went under" and had to hire themselves out as laborers. Wind and rain damage to their crops compounded their difficulties, but the bakufu intendant did nothing; he actually increased their tax burden that year. In 1734 the intendant ordered village officials to reclaim the land that had been abandoned in 1730; if they did not, he told them, he would confiscate their residences and banish them from the village. When village taxes went into arrears in 1742, the intendant summoned two village officials, Sennosuke and Kichibei, to Edo and placed them in custody. Kichibei became ill while imprisoned, and once he was home, his family had to nurse him and purchase medicines. They were forced to abandon some of their fields and serve as contract laborers. The same year Sennosuke, whose family had served as headman for generations, became a "broken farmer." Expenses associated with another procession to Nikkō in 1752 impoverished villagers all the more.[33]

A tenacious and pernicious form of status discrimination further aggravated the smallholders' plight. In the early seventeenth century, powerful families reigned over many of the country's villages, and the same was true in the northern Kantō. Many such families had samurai lineage, having remained on the land after the Tokugawa house confiscated their daimyo's territories or moved the daimyo to another part of the country. These powerful families resided in large compounds, sometimes surrounded by moats, owned much of the village land, and had large numbers of farmers in various degrees of servitude to them. With about 86 *koku* of land in 1683, Ichimura Gorōemon of Shitayakai village near

Makabe was not at all unusual. Eighty-six people were in some degree dependent on the family. In addition to nineteen servants (*genin*) hired annually, six families (nineteen people) and four other people were hereditary servants (*fudai*) and lived within the family compound; nine families (forty-four people) of weaker dependency status, known as *yashikisha*, lived outside the compound but provided labor at critical times in the agricultural cycle.[34]

Over the course of the seventeenth century, most such estates broke apart, giving rise to a large class of smallholders. The same process occurred in the northern Kantō, though at a much slower pace. The number of Ichimura's dependent farmers declined primarily from the eighteenth century, and in 1800 the family controlled only four *yashikisha*. In the village as a whole, the number of *yashikisha* fell from 154 in 1702 to only 47 in 1800. Newly independent farmers were among the first to leave their communities. With only small holdings and unable to sustain their families from the soil, they departed in search of a better life elsewhere.

Many may also have left because they realized that they could never become fully free of their former masters while remaining in the village. This became painfully clear to the *yashikisha* Tsunesuke, who had been a dependent of Ichirōemon, a village elder (*toshiyori*). The Ichirōemon household collapsed in 1826, leaving Tsunesuke masterless. When the Ichirōemon household was revived in 1868, Tsunesuke's successor once again became the family's *yashikisha*, all of forty-two years after Tsunesuke became masterless. Jūzō of Motoki village faced a similar problem in 1802. Although his family had gained independence fifty years earlier with the collapse of its master's household, his former master's relative Danroku continued to discriminate against him, treating him as an hereditary servant and refusing him permission to cultivate lands Danroku had received from the former master.[35] Many of the details surrounding these examples are unclear, but they do reflect the tenacity of status discrimination in the area. If farmers wanted to be truly independent, they had to completely escape the clutches of their former masters and village opprobrium.

The village elite faced a far different set of concerns. The Katsuta Rinzō family of Motoki village well illustrates this point. Katsuta Kiemon, the head of the clan, had returned to farming in the early seventeenth century, after having served as a retainer to Lord Makabe. Kiemon owned around 300 *koku* of land and controlled eleven households of dependent farmers. Over the next two centuries, the Katsuta family granted independence and lands to many of its dependents. It owned about 100 *koku* of land and had six households of dependent farmers in 1745, when a catastrophe befell the family. Katsuta Kiemon VII became embroiled in a conflict with another powerful household, Mazaki Shichirōzaemon, presumably over control of nearby mountain forests. The daimyo, finding both at fault, ordered that Shichirōzaemon's lands and property be confiscated and that Kiemon VII commit suicide.[36]

Katsuta Rinzō, Kiemon VII's younger brother, saved the family from total collapse. Before serving as interim head of the main family until the heir came of age, Rinzō had acquired experience in commerce in the market town of Kugeta and later, under the powerful merchant Nakamura Sakuemon, in the town of Makabe. As interim head, Rinzō began sake brewing and sold firewood to villagers, who then made charcoal for sale in the market. Rinzō also traded in cotton, lumber, grains, and soybeans. Largely through the pawn business, he increased Kiemon's lands from 62.4 *koku* in 1772 to over 100 *koku* in 1783. When Kiemon VIII established Rinzō in a branch household in 1783, he gave him over 44 *koku* of land and ownership of these various operations. Rinzō, now independent, owned over 80 *koku* of land in 1793 and served as financial purveyor (*goyōtashi*) to Kasama domain. In 1803 he added soy sauce brewing to his other activities.

But not long after, Rinzō's business operations faced tremendous obstacles. In 1813 Rinzō had reduced his landholdings to around 40 *koku*, he had abandoned many of his commercial and manufacturing operations, and he had released all his employees. Unrecoverable loans to Kasama domain exacerbated Rinzō's problems. In the 1780's and 1790's he had loaned Kasama over 520 *ryō*, little of which had been repaid.

Other Motoki largeholders met a similar fate. Katsuta Ichirōji, another branch household of the Kiemon clan, owned over 60 *koku* of land from the 1740's to 1810's. He once had employed large numbers of contract laborers to work his fields but from the 1780's suffered a labor shortage, and in 1813 he had no laborers at all. The Shimada family, which had owned the most land in the village in the 1750's, was listed as "broken" in 1773, and ten years later the head of the household and his son hired themselves out as contract laborers.[37]

The major reason for Rinzō's and other largeholders' difficulties was a precipitous population decline, beginning in the 1750's. From 1747 to 1833 the number of households in Motoki decreased by almost half, from 133 to 68, and the population fell from 723 to 345. The decline resulted primarily from the departure of smallholders, especially those with under 5 *koku* of land: in 1745 there were thirty-five such smallholders in the village, but only ten in 1793. They had previously been classified as landless (*mizonomi*) or as hereditary servants (*kadonomae*) to the village elite, such as to Katsuta Kiemon.[38]

Together with low levels of agricultural productivity and high tax rates, Rinzō's commercial and moneylending activities promoted the bankruptcy of smallholders, especially those with less than 5 *koku* of land. Having lost their holdings, poor farmers were unable to earn a livelihood from tenancy or side industry and therefore left the village. Population decline in the region thus not only led to the disappearance of large numbers of smallholders, but to the downfall of many village elites.

From the late 1830's, however, many northern Kantō villages began to recover from the devastation of the previous century. After the poorer members of their communities departed, middling farmers, some of whom had once been largeholders, worked to increase their yields and intensified their cultivation of cash crops. The Matsumoto family of Wakatabi village had been doing this since the 1780's. It kept detailed agricultural diaries that recorded the weather, tasks completed each day, and allocation of labor for various tasks. The Suzuki family of Kameyama village did much the same. Beginning in the 1850's, the head maintained an agricultural diary, noting the weather, agricultural tasks completed, and the names of those engaged in farm tasks. He also composed a brief treatise recording the appropriate times of the year for agricultural tasks, crop-rotation methods, and sowing amounts. Such activities undoubtedly facilitated the family's rise to economic prominence. Rising from middling farmers in the mid-eighteenth century, by the closing years of the Tokugawa the family had attained the position of major landlord, as well as that of headman.[39] More important, the agricultural methods and seeds they had so painstakingly experimented with both increased productivity and provided farmers in their areas with new resources to enable them to survive as farmers.

As productivity increased, so too the population of the northern Kantō began to increase. The population of Hitachi province grew by 29.8 percent between 1840 and 1872, and that of Shimotsuke by 35.6 percent. There were still fewer people in both provinces than in 1721, but notable strides had been made in recovery. The number of families in Motoki village increased from sixty-eight in 1833 to eighty-seven in 1870. The population increase resulted not only from the return of once "broken farmers" but from in-migration from other parts of the country and the establishment of new branch households by those who had remained in the village.

The residents were in a much stronger financial position than those living in the village one hundred years before. In Motoki there now existed a strong nucleus of middling farmers with 5–15 *koku* of land, comprising half the village population. There were still smallholders in the village—nineteen families owned less than 5 *koku* in 1870—but they were able to survive as farmers by tenanting the land of others, by producing more for the market, and by engaging in miscellaneous occupations, especially petty commerce. Although the Rinzō family never fully recovered from the blow earlier in the century, the Katsuta Kiemon household steadily increased its landholdings, reaching 96.7 *koku* in 1859. In addition to its landlord operations, it engaged in moneylending and commerce, especially fertilizer sales.[40]

A new village elite came into being as a result of these changes. In the Makabe area, village merchants once again threatened the position of town merchants. In an attempt to stem village merchants' activities, sixty-three town merchants united in 1857 to successfully lobby Kasama domain officials to accord them a monopoly on all transactions in grains and cotton cloth. It proved impossible to stem village commerce, however, and village merchants' vigorous protests forced the domain to reverse its decision.[41]

Cotton continued to be an important product of the northern Kantō through the mid-Meiji. Cotton cultivation in Ibaraki prefecture, in fact, grew by 25 percent between 1883 and 1887.[42] But bleached cotton declined in importance, with white cottons and striped cottons only partially taking its place. From a peak of about 380,000 *tan* around the 1820's and 1830's, bleached cotton production fell to 40,000 *tan* in 1875 and to only 10,000 *tan* in 1881.[43] Hardest hit was the Mooka area, once the center of such production. Even the town of Mooka itself saw a slump in its fortunes. Unlike town residents in other parts of the country, who increasingly moved from agriculture into commerce and industry, Mooka residents remained predominantly farmers, and even those in industry and commerce engaged in farming on the side.[44] In 1890, in fact, 61 percent of the town's families were still farmers. In surrounding villages, too, farmers engaged in far fewer side industries in the early Meiji than earlier in the century. Kameyama and Aotani villagers, for example, emphasized staple agricultural crops, especially rice and barley, and they produced few other commercial goods.[45]

Despite the growth of cotton cultivation, especially in the Ibaraki area, the northern Kantō's rural elites still engaged in diffuse commercial activities. In addition to handling small quantities of cotton cloth and selling fertilizers, they purchased farmers' surplus crops, especially grains and soybeans. Part of the explanation for these diffuse activities is that area farmers continued to weave only small quantities even in the Meiji, and they produced no cloth at all when prices for their rice and other grains were more favorable. This is clearly reflected in the cotton cloth production statistics for Makabe district: residents wove 19,361 *tan* in 1897, 106,000 in 1899, 8,330 in 1901, 120,000 in 1909, and 32,990 in 1911.[46] The tremendous fluidity of production would have made it difficult for merchants to handle cotton cloth alone.

With the growth of yarn imports from the 1870's, the rural elites' role in the local cotton trade declined all the more. The towns' rural agents, in addition to handling the region's cotton cloth, imported Western yarns, which they sold to local farmers for weaving. Farmers took their cloth to the agents and used part of the money they received to purchase yarns for later weaving.[47]

Some rural elites in the northern Kantō worked to introduce and diffuse new forms of side industry to their areas. Nozawa Taijirō in the Mooka area engaged in sericulture on a fairly large scale in the 1870's but soon turned his attention back to cotton. Hoping to revive the Mooka cotton industry, he initiated plans to construct a number of looms. When he heard about the Meiji government's plans to sell ten 2,000-spindle spinning machines, purchased from England, he immediately petitioned to purchase one of the facilities. The government's decision to grant Nozawa's request was largely fortuitous. Mooka was no longer an important cotton region, and Shimodate would have been a far better choice, but Nozawa's ties with an influential government official sealed the deal.

Likewise, Taniguchi Yasōji of Sakurai village in the Makabe area became active in silk reeling. Not long after assuming the family headship in 1866, he began to engage in sericulture, and he opened a mulberry field and purchased egg cards from Shima village in Gunma prefecture. To assist him in *zaguri* reeling, which he started in 1875, he hired five women reelers from Tomioka in Gunma. Despite successive years of losses, he refused to abandon reeling. Indeed, in 1881 Yasōji opened a mechanized filature, seeking to profit from economies of scale. Through the efforts of rural elites like Taniguchi, Ibaraki prefecture gradually became a more important production region for cocoons and raw silk, and by the early 1890's the value of the cocoons its residents produced surpassed that of raw cotton.[48]

But throughout the Meiji period, Ibaraki remained overwhelmingly agricultural. In 1874, industrial products accounted for 20.8 percent of total production in Ibaraki, as compared with 30.3 percent nationwide. Processed agricultural products, including raw silk, cotton yarn, textiles, oil, and paper, accounted for 11.2 percent of nationwide production but only 4.5 percent in Ibaraki. Most Ibaraki farmers were largely self-sufficient, producing far more grains than other crops. Even into the late Meiji period, they continued in the occupations of their ancestors; Ibaraki's percentage of farmers was 77.6 percent in 1910, as compared with 54.7 percent nationwide.[49] And despite the tremendous increase in cocoons, half of total production supplied silk-reeling facilities in other prefectures, not Ibaraki itself.[50]

The region's rural elites, too, were far more involved in landlord operations than commerce and manufacture. In the early twentieth century, Haga district, encompassing the Mooka area, had several families owning over 50 *chō*. One landlord family in Naka village only began acquiring land on a large scale in the deflationary 1880's, when many area farmers were deeply in debt. Reflecting the new emphasis on income from tenancy fees, the family abandoned its pawn business and trade in firewood and charcoal. By the turn of the century, it was using a growing portion of its income to purchase stocks in a local bank.[51] Although landlords like the one in Naka village offered monetary inducements to their tenants to produce high-quality rice, bureaucrats rather than landlords themselves increasingly assumed responsibility for encouraging and enforcing agricultural improvements.[52]

Rural elites in the bleached cotton production area of the Kantō were very different from their counterparts in other parts of the country. Although many engaged in commerce and manufacture from the mid-eighteenth century, the low productivity of the soil and the absence of viable sources of income from side industry precluded significant growth. Their activities served merely to further impoverish smallholders, spurring the mass exodus of poorer farmers. This in turn weakened the foundation of the village elite's operations, forcing many to drastically curtail the scale of their businesses. It was not until around the 1830's that conditions improved in the region. Rural elites once again became active as merchants, manufacturers, and moneylenders. Unlike many other parts of the country, however, the region supported few vibrant side industries, and farmers emphasized the cultivation of grains. A few rural elites established modern industries, but the northern Kantō as a whole remained overwhelmingly agricultural.

## The Fukami Clan and the
## Western Mikawa Cotton Trade

Western Mikawa was second only to the Kinai in cotton cultivation and cotton weaving, both in the Tokugawa and in the Meiji. And unlike the northern Kantō, the region supported a vibrant rural elite. Village merchants traded actively with major Edo/Tokyo wholesalers, engaged in extensive moneylending activities, and accumulated large landholdings. Here we will examine the activities of two members of the Fukami clan of Niibori village, Fukami Sahei and Fukami Kihei. Niibori is currently part of Okazaki city in Aichi prefecture.

Although no records are available for Niibori itself, cotton cultivation and cloth production in western Mikawa as a whole had early roots. Farmers cultivated cotton from at least the sixteenth century and sold small amounts of cotton cloth to the Kyoto market. In the seventeenth century western Mikawa witnessed tremendous growth in cotton cultivation, despite its inferior position vis-à-vis the Kinai. As is clear from *Hyakushō denki*, an agricultural treatise written in western Mikawa in the 1680's, Kinai farmers cultivated a superior cotton. Yields in western Mikawa, too, were about one-half those of the Kinai.[53] Even in the nineteenth century, they continued to lag behind.[54]

Western Mikawa farmers successfully competed with the Kinai in part because they relied far less on expensive cash fertilizers. One wealthy Mikawa farmer applied on average 0.46 *koku* per *tan* of dried sardines, one of the most important cash fertilizers of the period, as compared with about 2 *koku* per *tan* applied by farmers in the Kinai. He supplemented dried sardines with large quantities of natural fertilizers, especially night soil and grasses. Although his yields were below those obtained by most Kinai farmers, he also did not suffer as greatly when dried sardine prices rose from the late eighteenth century.[55]

The percentage of dry fields in western Mikawa dedicated to cotton ranged from 35 to 60 percent in the early eighteenth century, far higher than in the northern Kantō. Cultivation rates on paddies were somewhat less but became more important over time.[56] The early eighteenth century appears to have marked a peak in cotton cultivation, and rates thereafter. slightly declined.[57] We can only surmise the reasons. Perhaps in a rush to profit from cotton cultivation, farmers planted as much as their fields could bear. With growing levels of cultivation, they curtailed production to conform to market demand and the constraints of the soil. From the early to mid-eighteenth century, however, there was no further decline in total production, and western Mikawa maintained its position as one of the country's leading cotton cultivation regions until the 1890's.

High levels of taxation undoubtedly contributed to cotton's popularity. As in other parts of the country, domains in western Mikawa increased tax rates in the late seventeenth to early eighteenth century. Tax rates in Sasame village in Kariya domain, which had averaged around 30 to 40 percent from 1649 to 1661, increased to over 50 percent in later years. Okazaki domain elevated taxes on paddies in Yamazaki village from 42 percent in 1667 to 81 percent the following year. Many other villages in Okazaki had tax rates of over 90 percent of the assessed valuation.[58]

Despite onerous taxes, western Mikawa's farmers faced few of the difficulties of their counterparts in the northern Kantō. They benefited, in particular, from the growing gap between political authorities' assessed valuations of land productivity and actual yields. Since most political authorities conducted no new land surveys after the late seventeenth century, farmers profited from subsequent productivity gains. In Enokimae village, landlords in 1792 collected tenancy fees of 1.05 *koku/tan* on upper-grade paddy lands, which had been assessed at 1.4 *koku/tan*. We have no data on real productivity, but we can safely assume that it was much higher than 1.4 *koku*, perhaps as high as 2 *koku*: income of 0.35 *koku* per *tan* would have been insufficient for tenants to earn a living, especially after outlays for seeds and fertilizers.[59]

Western Mikawa farmers also supplemented their agricultural incomes through side industries. Cotton ginning and weaving were especially important by-employments.[60] In addition to using some of the raw cotton to weave cloth for household use and for sale, farmers often sold their excess.[61] A number of area merchants shipped substantial quantities of raw and ginned cotton and cotton yarn to Edo, especially from the nineteenth century. In addition, numerous establishments in the castle towns and rural towns handled raw cotton and pressed cottonseed into oil.[62]

Large numbers of farmers, rich and poor alike, also engaged in commerce. In 1842 there were sixty-two merchants in twenty-four of the forty-two villages in the Higashi Sanchū Tenaga area of western Mikawa; at least forty-eight had started business in the nineteenth century, and only one had been in business since the seventeenth. Twelve villages centering around Komō village along the eastern bank of the Yahagi had sixty-eight merchants in 1862; Komō village alone supported twenty-two merchants. Another group of twenty-four villages in the plains area along the western bank of the Yahagi had 145 merchants in 1864, and only one of the villages had no merchants at all. Most merchants in these clusters of villages operated on a small scale, handling such items as *sushi, soba,* sake, tobacco, confections, and paper, but some engaged in trades that we can assume required more capital, such as the sale of cotton and grains.[63]

While there was clearly significant economic growth, demographic data appear to contradict assumptions concerning the beneficial effects of market growth on western Mikawa's farmers. As in other parts of the country, the population of western Mikawa stagnated. In Okazaki domain, in fact, the non-samurai population declined slightly, from 48,767 people in 1784 to 47,467 in 1833. A full understanding of demographic trends requires extensive analysis of temple registration and death records, but two points seem clear. First, female infanticide did not contribute significantly to population decline or stagnation as it did in the northern Kantō. Females actually outnumbered males in Okazaki domain by over 7 percent, and there was an even higher percentage of females in those villages where cotton was a major side industry. Also, population stagnation or decline stemmed at least in part from families' having fewer children. In Higashi-achiwa village, from 1795 to 1869 the population decreased from 208 to 160, a decline of over 23 percent, while the number of families remained relatively stable. The average number of children per family declined from 4.3 to 3.3.[64]

The reasons for Tokugawa Japan's demographic stagnation are beyond the concerns of this study, but we must note that early protoindustrial development resulted in few opportunities for population growth. Economic change took place within the confines of Japan's small farming system, in such a way that population growth was restricted, not stimulated, before the 1850's.

Another important characteristic of western Mikawa villages was a wide disparity in fortunes. In Kamiyada village, Sugiura Mozaemon owned 35.2 *koku* of land in 1857, but 33.6 percent of the residents owned less than 1 *koku*, and 44.5 percent owned between 1 and 5 *koku*. These poorer farmers had to supplement their income through side industry, by renting the land of the village rich, or by hiring themselves out as contract laborers.[65] A few became petty merchants, but these were invariably short-term occupations. This was certainly the case in the Komō village vicinity, where twenty-eight merchants had suspended their business at some point in the recent past.[66]

Many poorer farmers found themselves saddled with enormous debts. A survey conducted by Nishio domain in 1838 revealed that Kamiyada farmers owed 382 *ryō* in unpaid taxes, and thirty people were recorded as "hardship cases."[67] In Hora village a 1859 survey listed six households of "broken farmers," with debts totaling over 728 *ryō*. Of the remaining forty-eight families, twenty were impoverished, with debts of over 428 *ryō* and most owning less than 3 *koku* of land. Over half of the total households survived in part through wage work, including occupations outside the village.[68] Admittedly, both surveys were conducted during difficult times—the period of the Tenpō crop failures and the inflationary years around the time of the opening of the ports—but they do suggest the tenuous nature of farmers' lives. They were already living at the margin, and a serious crop failure, or even a succession of minor ones, could force them into debt and threaten their very survival as farmers.

A small group of wealthy villagers were at the other end of the class spectrum. Some, like Uchida Jin'emon of Higashi-achiwa village, acquired much of their wealth through the cultivation of rice and other cash crops, especially cotton. Owning only a minuscule plot of land in the 1670's, the family had become the largest landowner in the village by the 1760's. Early in the nineteenth century, it invested in a water wheel facility, which polished rice and pressed cottonseed into oil. The fortunes of the Ishikawa Shinpachi family of Hashime village followed a similar trajectory. Established as a branch household in 1744, the family owned over 36 *koku* in 1812. In the 1840's it had over twenty tenants cultivating some of its fields.[69]

Despite the relatively high productivity of the soil, few farmers of means in western Mikawa appear to have amassed considerable wealth through landlord operations alone. For one thing, the tremendous fluctuations in crop yields might have been a powerful inducement not to do so. Uchida Jin'emon's total cotton harvests, for example, varied by as much as 600 percent between 1781 and 1891.[70] His rice yields fared no better. From 1781 to 1871 total rice harvests increased steadily, but yearly fluctuations were great. In 1786, a time of countrywide crop failures and famine, Uchida's rice harvest fell by over 70 percent; the late 1820's, the 1830's, and the decade bracketing the Meiji Restoration of 1868 showed equally pronounced variations.[71]

Poorer farmers suffered far more from crop failures, so that landlords like Ishikawa Shinpachi had to annually adjust the fees their tenants paid.[72] Sugiura Mozaemon of Kamiyada did the same. He took in 395 bags of rice in tenancy fees in 1858, 175 in 1860, 353 in 1863, and 111 in 1866. In addition to lowering the fees his tenants paid in times of crop failure, Sugiura frequently provided food relief to poorer members of his community.[73] In many ways, rural elites' income from tenancy fees served to supplement, not supplant, income from other sources, such as the sale of crops they cultivated themselves. Large-scale landlord operations did not appear in the region until the mid- to late Meiji period.

Because of the importance of cotton to the western Mikawa economy, rural elites found the cotton trade an especially alluring activity. The Fukami clan of Niibori village produced two rural agents (*kaitsugi*) and one jobber: Fukami Tarōemon served as a ginned cotton agent; Fukami Sahei as an agent for cotton cloth; and Fukami Kihei as a cotton cloth jobber. Having three families in the same clan involved in commerce was mutually advantageous. They frequently borrowed from and loaned to one another to facilitate their various activities. Here we will examine the activities of the Sahei and Kihei households.

Very little is known of the Fukami clan before the late eighteenth century, but there is much evidence to suggest that Sahei and Tarōemon had substantial assets. Lord Mizuno of Numazu domain, who had acquired control over Niibori only a few years before, appointed Sahei in 1775 as one of his financial purveyors (*goyōtashi*).[74] Since domains strictly limited these positions, at least until around the 1830's, we can assume that Sahei had considerable wealth. Also, when he became a rural agent in 1791, he put up 200 *koku* of his land as security to the Edo guild.[75] The productivity of Niibori village as a whole, it should be noted, was only about 430 *koku*, and most western Mikawa farmers owned less than 5 *koku*. That Tarōemon appears with a surname in documents from the 1790's suggests that he, too, had considerable wealth. For five years after Sahei became an agent, in fact, Tarōemon was his partner. In 1796 Tarōemon sold his share of the business to Sahei for 331 *ryō*; within a few years, Tarōemon had turned his attention to the sale of ginned cotton.[76] Both, no doubt, had had long experience well before the 1790's as jobbers in the cotton cloth trade. Edo wholesalers restricted the number of rural agents, and only those well established in the trade could hope to receive such an appointment.

Fukami Sahei was one of the area's most powerful merchants. Unfortunately, no records survive concerning the family's assets or the volume of its cloth trade, but since Sahei was one of only four to six rural agents in western Mikawa, the volume of his Edo sales must have been massive. Even one of Edo's largest cotton cloth wholesalers, Masuya, borrowed money from the family on occasion.[77]

Despite the scale of his business, even Sahei eventually experienced difficulties. His debts totaled over 5,500 *ryō* in 1845, forcing him to draw up a repayment schedule for his creditors.[78] In the absence of direct evidence, the reasons for Sahei's difficulties can only be surmised. Instability in headship probably contributed to the family's problems. In 1835 the head (for convenience's sake, Sahei II), who had run the family business from 1804 until his retirement in 1824, passed away. One month later, his eldest son (Sahei III), decided to retire, leaving a nephew as the new head (Sahei IV). The nephew died the following year, leaving Sahei III's brother, young and no doubt inexperienced, as the heir (Sahei V).[79]

At the same time, there appears to have been a lack of attention to the family business. Sahei II had a passion for composing *kyōka*, or comic tanka verse, and all his children became enthusiastic patrons of the arts. Sahei III apparently found his fondness for flower arranging (*kadō*) and the art of bonsai more satisfying than commerce and decided to retire, though the next in line as head was only a child.[80]

Contributing to the family's difficulties, Numazu domain began to demand more and more loans. It requested 1,250 *ryō* in 1819, 233 *ryō* in 1825, 350 *ryō* in 1838, and 1,000 *ryō* in 1843, and the family provided countless smaller amounts and gifts to the daimyo and his officials in intervening years. In gratitude, the domain granted the family the right to use a surname and wear a sword; it also granted a stipend and numerous tokens of appreciation, including ceremonial garb, sake, and fish.[81] The status increases and favors Sahei received from Numazu, no doubt, became less and less valuable over time. As the domains in western Mikawa struggled to meet their annual expenditures, they turned to the village elite for assistance, granting them status increases with reckless abandon. Nishio had only thirty-nine financial purveyors (*goyōtashi*) in the domain itself in 1834, but by 1864 there were ninety-four, as well as 138 with statuses below *goyōtashi*.[82] Okazaki domain, too, turned to its wealthy residents for assistance in reducing its debt. An 1860 record lists over 330 financial purveyors of various ranks, about two-thirds of whom resided in villages.[83] By the last decade of the Tokugawa the "symbolic capital" associated with status increases had considerably diminished. Almost every person of wealth in this region had some tie with political authority.

The abolition of the Edo wholesalers guilds in 1841 was especially crippling to Sahei's trade. Any merchant could now sell directly to Edo wholesalers, completely bypassing the established rural agents. When the bakufu revived the guilds a decade later, it allowed these new entrants to continue in the trade, as long as they received licenses from the Edo wholesalers. The Edo wholesalers revived their purchasing network, with small jobbers selling to jobbers and jobbers selling to their rural agents. But these measures did little to stem the entry of merchant newcomers, and the Edo wholesalers themselves sometimes purchased cotton cloth from unlicensed rural merchants.

Sahei even faced steep competition from relatives in Niibori village itself. Fukami Tōjū, for example, who branched from the Tarōemon family, became a rural agent for cotton cloth around the 1840's or 1850's. Another member of the Fukami clan, Kiichirō, was a cloth jobber but sold directly to the Edo market, even though he was not licensed as a rural agent. Undoubtedly as a result of these various problems, the Sahei family sold its rural agent's license in 1871 and left the cotton cloth trade entirely.[84]

The Kihei branch of the Fukami family amassed its fortune through a different combination of economic pursuits. Fukami Kihei branched from the Tarōemon family in 1827 and, with the 700 ryō he received, immediately became a moneylender and entered the cotton cloth trade. His assets grew steadily in later years, reaching 1,569 ryō in 1836 and 4,924 ryō in 1882. Profits from moneylending were especially important in the early years after branching.[85]

The pattern of Kihei's moneylending activities was similar to the one Ronald Toby found among rural elites in Mino province.[86] In the absence of credit institutions, rural elites loaned money to and borrowed from one another to finance their various activities. This is clear from the size of Kihei's loans: in 1849 he provided thirteen loans of from 100 to 300 ryō and nineteen loans of over 300 ryō. Many of the large loans went to the same people, invariably other rural elites, including Fukami Sahei. Kihei also borrowed money from other elites, including stem family Tarōemon and the Ōta family, a large-scale miso producer in the region. He returned almost all the amounts he borrowed within one to three months.

Moneylending was usually linked to land accumulation, but Fukami Kihei did not begin to accumulate land until the Meiji. His land within Niibori village, in fact, only amounted to 0.42 chō at the end of the Tokugawa.[87] This was not the typical pattern among western Mikawa's rural elites. The cloth jobber Sugiura Mozaemon of Kamiyada village, for example, owned over 31 chō of land in twenty-six villages in 1873. He had accumulated most of his land from the mid-eighteenth century by taking in unredeemed pawned land and by investing in newly reclaimed land along the coast.[88] The reason Kihei accumulated little land was the nature of his moneylending operations: he loaned primarily to people of wealth rather than to the poor, so he did not acquire much land as a result of people's defaulting on their debts.

Fukami Kihei also provided loans and contributions to Numazu domain. Most such outlays, though, were small—50 *ryō* in 1843 and another 50 *ryō* in 1844, for example—especially when compared with Sahei's. In return, the domain allowed him to wear the crested kimono worn by samurai. It also accorded him the rank of *godeiri*, the lowest of three financial purveyor ranks, below *goyōtashi* and *goyōtashinami*. Sahei and Tarōemon held the rank of *goyōtashi*, in recognition of their far greater financial position in the domain.[89]

Kihei's moneylending activities became less important in the final decade of Tokugawa rule. From a peak of 12,040 *ryō* in 1849, his loans declined to 5,221 *ryō* in 1869. The political and economic uncertainty of the time undoubtedly contributed to this decline. Many rural elites encountered difficulties in their businesses, so they were unable to loan as much money to one another as in the past.

Kihei also engaged in the cotton cloth trade as a jobber. As noted in Chapter 3, rural agents rarely purchased directly from farm families. Because textile production was a side industry to farming, agents needed large numbers of jobbers at the subregional level to supply them with cloth. Jobbers, too, oftentimes relied on large numbers of small jobbers who purchased directly from farm families.[90]

No data are available on the number of jobbers and small jobbers, but they were undoubtedly numerous. In the early nineteenth century, Nishio domain set the number of jobbers' licenses in its territory at 100.[91] If the other eleven groupings of jobbers in existence at the time were of similar size, there may have been over one thousand jobbers and small jobbers in western Mikawa. Komō village alone had seventeen jobbers. The cluster of twenty-four villages along the western bank of the Yahagi River had twenty-five jobbers and another five people who handled cotton in addition to other items.[92]

Kihei's cloth sales increased from 125 *ryō* in 1836 to 2,317 *ryō* in 1882, and the family remained in business for an unusually long time, until 1896. His business was no doubt facilitated by his connections to Tarōemon and Sahei. Having two powerful families already in the trade provided Kihei's business partners some assurance that powerful relatives would come to his assistance to pay off debts, should the need arise.

Kihei purchased both directly from producers and from smaller jobbers, and he sold his cotton cloth in more or less equal lots to rural agents in western Mikawa, including Sahei. He did not have particularly strong ties with any single agent.[93] By the time Kihei entered the cloth trade, the rigid lines of the purchasing hierarchy had greatly blurred.

Despite the steady rise in Kihei's assets and sales volume, his business was hardly stable. His assets reached a peak in 1869, with 5,099 *ryō*, but thereafter they stagnated and eventually declined. This was clearly not the result of a decline in production, because in 1899 western Mikawa cloth production was almost eight times greater than in 1878.[94] But the volume of cloth handled by individual merchants fluctuated greatly. The value of cloth Kihei sold and had in stock, for example, amounted to 531 *ryō* in 1846, 180 *ryō* in 1856, and 1,002 *ryō* in 1866. In the Meiji, too, his sales volume suffered violent swings: 9,132 *tan* in 1879, 3,721 *tan* in 1882, 5,600 *tan* in 1884, 8,935 *tan* in 1891, and 551 *tan* in 1892.

There were several reasons for this instability. Western Mikawa farmers, like farmers elsewhere, produced cotton cloth as a side industry—most of Kihei's purchases were concentrated in the slack season, beginning in December and peaking in May—and the quantity available for sale was a function of climatic and economic conditions. When cotton yields were poor, farmers produced less cloth. The deflationary years of the early 1880's were especially difficult times, both for producers and for merchants. The amount of cloth shipped out of the major Mikawa ports was 3.12 million *tan* in 1882, 0.6 million in 1883, 1.11 million in 1884, and 1.15 million in 1885.[95] High rice prices had much the same effect. Farmers emphasized rice cultivation over cotton cultivation when rice prices rose, and returned to cotton when they fell.[96]

Rural merchants also suffered when prices on the Edo/Tokyo market were unfavorable, an all too common occurrence. No price data are available for Mikawa cloth, but a comparison of local cotton cloth prices and *average* cotton cloth prices on the Edo/Tokyo market reveals that local prices were higher in seventeen of the twenty-one years between 1859 and 1879. Mikawa cloth, which enjoyed a good reputation, no doubt brought higher than average prices on the Edo/Tokyo market, making conclusions hazardous. Mikawa merchants, though, did have to compete vigorously with cloth merchants from numerous other sites of production. If Mikawa prices were high, city wholesalers increased their purchases from other parts of the country.

Increased competition also affected the profitability of Kihei's purchases. Newcomers to the cotton trade always had been a concern, but far more important was the threat posed by new modes of production, especially putting out. The putting-out system could be found in some parts of Mikawa from at least the 1830's but only became a dominant mode of production from the 1880's. With the growth of raw cotton imports and the decline of domestic cotton cultivation, weavers relied on merchants to supply them with the raw material.[97]

Putting out had a number of advantages over direct purchases. It allowed merchants to maintain a fairly constant supply of cotton cloth. Although there was great fluidity among those engaged in ginning and weaving for wages, there was always a surfeit of farmers who needed outside income and who had no immediate access to the raw material. Putting out also enabled merchants to better control the quality of the finished cloth. This became especially important from the 1850's, when Edo/Tokyo wholesalers increasingly lodged complaints against the deteriorating quality of local cloth. Rural agents tried to control the problem but apparently with little success; one rural agent, in fact, came under particularly harsh attack for shipping substandard cloth and was forced to leave the trade altogether.[98] Lastly, because farmers specialized in weaving alone, their productivity increased. Two technological innovations contributed to this growing specialization: the diffusion of the rattling spindle (garabō) for cotton spinning and the flying shuttle loom (battan), both of which dramatically increased productivity over earlier devices.[99]

Putting out itself was only a transitional mode of production and declined with the advent of power loom factories, especially after the Russo-Japanese War of 1904–5. The growth of the silk industry, too, contributed to its demise. Because of cotton's dominance in the area economy, and despite prefectural encouragement, sericulture did not become an important industry of western Mikawa until the late 1880's. With the growth of imports of raw cotton, however, farmers abandoned cotton cultivation and turned their fields over to mulberry cultivation. In 1902 cotton harvests in Aichi prefecture were only 3 percent of what they had been in 1884; mulberry acreage, on the other hand, increased from near zero in 1884 to almost 9,440 chō in 1902, and more than doubled over the next decade. The appearance of several large-scale filatures in western Mikawa spurred the growth of the local sericulture industry all the more.[100]

Western Mikawa's rural elites faced a dizzying array of changes in the final decades of Tokugawa rule. For much of the Tokugawa and the early Meiji, farmers cultivated cotton and produced cotton cloth, which they sold rather freely to local merchants. The two branches of the Fukami family initially prospered from these activities, but they encountered difficulties the longer they persisted in the trade. Fukami Sahei, who sold his agent's license in 1871, left the trade for probably a host of reasons, but certainly greater competition for cotton purchases was an important factor in his decision. From the mid-Meiji, the putting-out system began to dominate the area economy, only to be replaced by a system of modern factories in the early twentieth century. It proved difficult for established elites to make the transition from the older modes of production to the newer, and many abandoned the trade entirely. Kihei persisted far longer than most, until 1896, but he had been experiencing difficulties in the trade for quite some time before this.

The rural elites leaving the cotton trade did not go bankrupt but had to channel their energies into other activities. We know little about Sahei's and Kihei's subsequent activities, but they hardly descended into destitution. Sahei was included in an 1895 directory listing powerful merchants nationwide.[101] Other families of means accumulated land. The Kihei household did this on a far smaller scale than most; it owned only 4.12 *chō* in 1894.[102] The third Fukami household, Tarōemon, was noted as a "large landlord" in an 1898 publication listing powerful people in commerce and industry in Japan.[103] The cloth jobber Sugiura Mozaemon, who owned over 31 *chō* in 1873, purchased another 26 *chō* between 1879 and 1888.[104] As with so many rural elites, the survival of these western Mikawa cotton merchants and moneylenders depended on their ability to adapt to changing markets and opportunities.

## Conclusion

The *gōnō* and their communities were in a symbiotic relationship. Rural elites needed farmers with the means to survive as farmers and the ability to produce for the market. As we saw with the Mooka region, *gōnō* growth was impossible without a viable economic foundation underpinning their communities. Their activities merely led to the further impoverishment of villagers. Likewise, the trade activities of the rural elite in Mikawa presupposed the existence of a broad mass of petty commodity producers from whom they could purchase their goods.

Rural elites in the northern Kantō and western Mikawa were involved in diverse activities. Most engaged in farming, using a combination of household and hired labor, and they also rented land to others. But commerce was an especially important component of their economic undertakings. As they introduced commodity production into their communities, elites became the merchants who collected and sold villagers' goods. As in the northern Kantō, they also supplied farmers with the cash fertilizers necessary for their new crops. Their role as merchants was necessitated by Japan's small farming system. Farmers engaged in side industry in the slack season and produced only in small quantities. An intricate hierarchy of merchants was needed to get their goods to market.

Commerce, like farming, was far from a stable occupation. Most village merchants were in petty forms of trade, such as selling food and drink, and few survived for long. Many acquired large sums through the cotton trade, as the Fukami Sahei and Fukami Kihei families did, but here too there was tremendous instability. The nature of cotton cloth production itself was a contributing factor: it was a side industry and total output varied greatly from one year to the next. Cotton merchants also faced intense competition from newcomers to the trade, especially from the 1840's. With the growth of the putting-out system and the advent of factories from the mid- to late Meiji, most elites abandoned the cotton trade completely and refocused their ambitions in other areas.

# 5

# Rural Elites in Silk Regions

Ancient simplicity is gone. With the growth of pretence the people of today are satisfied with nothing but finery, with nothing but what is beyond their station or purse. You have only to look at the way our citizens' wives and daughters dress. . . . [O]f recent years, ever since some ingenious Kyōto creatures started the fashion, every variety of splendid material has been used for men's and women's clothes, and the drapers' sample-books have blossomed in a riot of colour.

Ihara Saikaku, *The Japanese Family Storehouse* (1688)

[I]n recent years, thanks to the advance in sophistication, even ladies of prominent family have grown tired of ordinary underthings: each step . . . reveals a glimpse of red silk gaiter. To protect their collars in the back, they use pale blue pongee wraps; to keep the dust from their oil-stiff, pinned coiffures, they order waterproof hats in the style worn by nobles at Court. One supposes that they dress for a solitary trip to the country as if going to hear the oracle at Kashima.

Ejima Kiseki, *Characters of Worldly Young Women* (1717)

S AIKAKU'S AND KISEKI'S fictional accounts, set in the flamboyant Genroku era (1688–1703), depict a world intoxicated with the luxuries and extravagances of urban life. Sightseeing, picnics, flower-viewing, kabuki performances, visits to the pleasure quarters, elegant lacquerware and screens, exquisitely dyed and embroidered silk crepes, damasks, and satins—these are but a few of the scenes and stage props in their stories. This was not the world bakufu officials had envisioned. Through a host of sumptuary edicts, officials attempted to uphold status distinctions by closely regulating what people consumed, how they entertained themselves, and the types of fabrics they wore.

Bakufu officials were concerned particularly about ostentatious silk garments worn by social inferiors, because this disrupted social hierarchy and had a corrosive effect on the morale of the country's leaders, the samurai. Townspeople were to wear monochrome silks, pongee, cotton, or ramie; village officials could wear monochrome silks and pongee; and common farmers were restricted to cotton and ramie fabrics. To maintain "distinctions between lord and vassal, superior and inferior," even samurai were to observe the regulations and conventions of dress.[1] But it proved impossible to enforce clothing styles. Townspeople found ways to circumvent the bakufu's proscriptions, and officials invariably relaxed their vigilance within a few years. City merchants, rural elites, and farmers scrambled to meet the seemingly insatiable demand of townspeople for luxury silks.

This chapter examines Japan's silk industry through the lens of two powerful rural merchants, Ōhashi Gizaemon of the Shindatsu region of Ōshū province (Iwashiro) in the northeast and Nakano Kyūjirō of the Hachiōji area in Musashi province west of Edo. Shindatsu and Hachiōji were typical of the country's rural silk production regions. Both had early roots in sericulture and raw silk production but became major production centers only from the mid-eighteenth century.[2] Shindatsu became the country's leading production region for silkworm egg cards and raw silk, and rural elites around the country sought to emulate its superior production techniques. Hachiōji supported a vibrant silk textile industry and could be counted among the country's leading rural silk-weaving centers. Ōhashi Gizaemon and Nakano Kyūjirō became powerful merchants with the growth of the silk industry in their regions.

## Ōhashi Gizaemon and Shindatsu Raw Silk

Ōhashi Gizaemon was typical of the rural elites who rose to positions of economic prominence in the protoindustrial period. Although from a poor farming village, he became one of the country's leading rural raw silk merchants. The family developed a purchasing network which extended over much of northeastern Japan, and it sold massive quantities to Kyoto wholesalers and to merchants in the new rural sites of silk cloth production. And like other rural elites, successive Ōhashi heads maintained close ties with their political overlord, Shirakawa domain.

Currently part of the town of Ryōzen, Ōishi was a large mountain village in Shindatsu's Date district. Ōishi had an assessed productivity of 2,075 koku and a population of 1,031, quite large by Tokugawa village standards.[3] Because of its size, for much of the Tokugawa Ōishi was divided into two administrative sections, Shimo-Ōishi and Kami-Ōishi, each with distinct village officials. The Ōhashi Gizaemon family resided in Kami-Ōishi.

Shindatsu, like the Kantō and the Kinai regions, was an area of highly fragmented rule. The bakufu and several domains controlled territory there, and there were frequent changes in political jurisdiction. Yonezawa domain controlled Ōishi village until 1664, when it became bakufu territory. Except for two brief periods when it was ruled by Fukushima domain, Ōishi remained under bakufu control until 1742, when it was incorporated in Shirakawa domain.[4] Shirakawa ruled Ōishi, both directly or as custodian (as *azukarichi*), until the Meiji Restoration of 1868. Because its main territory was to the south, Shirakawa ruled its villages in Shindatsu through an administrative office (*jinya*) in the town of Hobara, about six miles from Ōishi.

Ōishi villagers produced for the market from an early date. Political authorities in the region collected half the annual land tax in specie, obligating farmers to sell many of their crops and other products in local markets. High levels of taxation also encouraged greater production for the market, especially of non-food items, where it was easier to evade taxation. Between 1662 and 1742, taxes on Ōishi's fields more than doubled.[5] In 1831 tax rates on assessed productivity alone averaged over 40 percent, and there were several additional levies (*komononari*) on side industry, such as raw silk, persimmon trees, pheasants, safflower, and sake.[6]

Small landholdings also compelled farmers to seek additional sources of income outside agriculture. In 1672 over 71 percent of Shimo-Ōishi households cultivated under ten *koku* of land, insufficient to support a family from farming alone.[7] Many such smallholders had once been in servitude to powerful local families, in the form of either *nago* (families with separate residences but owing various services to a powerful family) or *genin* (individuals in total servitude, usually living in the household of their master).[8] As a result of growing land productivity and the deliberate policy of political authorities, these farmers had acquired independence in the middle decades of the seventeenth century, but their lands were of insufficient size to support their families from farming alone. Side industry became essential to their survival as farmers.

Although villagers engaged in sericulture and reeled raw silk from the early Tokugawa, the late eighteenth to early nineteenth century marks a turning point in the scale of such production. Until that time, farmers combined sericulture and raw silk production with other, equally important forms of side industry and cash-crop production: safflower cultivation and lacquer production were especially vital to the village economy.[9] Even in 1743, when other Shindatsu villagers had become immersed in sericulture production, Ōishi farmers were not significant producers.

They raised some silkworms, feeding them with mulberry planted in the village, but they channeled much of their labor into other tasks. This was particularly true of the women, who traditionally constituted the bulk of the labor force in all processes of the silk industry. Ōishi women threshed rice and grains after the harvest, and they wove cotton cloth for household use. Their participation in the silk industry was limited.[10]

Largely through the efforts of rural elites such as Satō Tomonobu of neighboring Kakeda village and Satō Yosōzaemon of Fushiguro village, Shindatsu witnessed a remarkable transformation of its economy in the middle decades of the eighteenth century. Tomonobu's family had been keeping records of its sericultural operations since the early eighteenth century, and Tomonobu himself penned a widely acclaimed sericultural treatise in 1766. Yosōzaemon began keeping sericultural diaries and records of experimentation in 1743, and later generations continued the practice for over a century.[11] The gradual improvements in sericultural technology that such families initiated enabled Shindatsu to become the country's leading egg card and raw silk production region.

By 1805 production in Ōishi had markedly changed, with the raising of silkworms and cultivation of mulberry trees now dominating the village economy. Women's labor, in particular, became thoroughly consumed in the silk industry: they raised silkworms in the spring, reeled raw silk from their cocoons, and produced silk floss.[12] That there is no mention of women weaving cotton cloth suggests that they now purchased their clothing in local markets. Because of the growing specialization of production, villagers no longer produced lacquer and safflower, both important products in the past.

Some Ōishi women were incorporated in a putting-out system: they received wages for reeling raw silk and for producing silk floss, most likely from cocoons supplied by wealthy villagers. But putting out in Ōishi was only a temporary phenomenon, and later records contain no mention of such work.[13] As the industry developed and farmers acquired additional income from this side employment, putting out would have become unnecessary. Farm families produced much of their raw silk from cocoons they raised themselves and fed the silkworms the leaves of the mulberry trees planted on their fields.

The growing importance of Ōishi's sericulture and raw silk industries led to important demographic changes. Villagers in Tokugawa Japan adopted various means to bring population into balance with their income from the soil and side industry. As we saw in the Mooka region of the northern Kantō, many people left their villages and practiced infanticide. Ōishi families appear to have widely practiced female infanticide.

In 1743, before sericulture and reeling became important village industries, Ōishi males outnumbered females by 38 percent. Since there is no evidence of women taking employment in other parts of the country, and nearby villages displayed similar ratios, we can assume that farm families "weeded out" (*mabiki*), as the euphemism went, many of their newborn girls. Because of the small size of landholdings and the relative lack of profitable forms of side industry, females were probably of little economic value to farm families. They were simply additional mouths to feed, which most families could ill afford.

The growth of the silk industry unquestionably elevated women's importance within the farm household. In 1807 males still outnumbered females but by only 20 percent; in 1823 the figure had declined to 5 percent.[14] The new importance of female children is evident, too, in the age composition of villagers. In 1834 there were 377 males and 343 females between the ages of fifteen and sixty, while there were 182 males and 190 females under the age of fifteen.[15] As with the cloth industry of western Mikawa, the silk industry provided farm families a greater incentive to retain their female offspring, whose labor power was so vital to these side industries.

By the 1830's and 1840's sericulture and raw silk production had done much to improve the fortunes of Ōishi residents. Appendix Table 13 shows the distribution of landholdings for Shimo-Ōishi in 1820 and for the village as a whole in 1846. Although the number of households with fewer than 10 *koku* of land remained the same (73 percent of total households), the number of families with less than 1 *koku* markedly declined. In 1846 there existed a strong nucleus of middling farmers (over 57 percent of total households) with from 5 to 15 *koku* of land. Since the population remained relatively stable, we can assume that many smallholders acquired enough income, undoubtedly from the silk industry, to purchase land from their wealthier neighbors.

Despite beneficial changes to the village economy, many residents faced a precarious existence, constantly at the mercy of nature. Because Ōishi was a mountain village, natural disasters were a frequent occurrence. Almost every year, in fact, Shirakawa domain reduced the tax farmers had to pay, often by 10 percent or more of assessed productivity, because of damage to or loss of village fields.[16] A number of serious crop failures also bankrupted many people. In response to a domain inquiry in 1790 asking

why its population had declined since the previous year, officials in Ōishi
responded that because the village was sandwiched between two mountain ranges, it was susceptible to floods, and some parts of it received insufficient sunshine. In the past there had been damaging droughts and
frost, and even in good years villagers had difficulty earning a livelihood
from the soil. As a result of a major crop failure in 1755, farmers abandoned over 300 *koku* of land; and crop failures in the 1780's forced more
villagers to leave their lands.[17] From around 1799 there was another series
of poor crops, forcing thirty-two people to seek employment in other areas; the village petitioned the domain for 200 *koku* in tax reductions and
85 *ryō* in relief loans.[18]

The growth of the silk industry did little to end the extreme volatility in
farmers' fortunes. This became especially evident in the 1830's, when successive years of crop failures impoverished smallholders and resulted in
widespread starvation. In 1831 Shimo-Ōishi officials petitioned Shirakawa domain for a loan of 87 *ryō* in relief to twenty-nine "starving"
farmers whose lands had been washed away by floods and landslides. In
1836, and yet again in 1837, the village faced more disastrous crop losses,
resulting in a major famine.[19] Sericulture had done much to improve the
fortunes of the village, but farmers were still subject to the misfortunes of
climate. A succession of poor crops could easily force many into poverty,
wiping out any gains they had made in years of bounty.

As Ōishi's most powerful household, the Ōhashi Gizaemon family easily weathered such crises. Few records exist for the family before the mid-
Tokugawa. Local lore, unsupported by documentary evidence, maintains
that the Gizaemon household descended from the main Ōhashi clan who
controlled much of the village in the late sixteenth century.[20] Considering
that Gizaemon established ties (as *kaitsugi*, or rural agent) with Kyoto
raw silk wholesalers in the mid-1740's, we can assume that he had substantial assets and was a major landholder. Wholesalers in the major cities
only did business with powerful local personages, those who had sizable
landholdings to put up as collateral for funds they advanced for local purchases.

Despite Ōhashi's early ties with Kyoto wholesalers, the first decades of
the nineteenth century were the period of greatest growth in the family's
raw silk trade. With the emergence of new rural sites of silk textile production, such as Kiryū, Ashikaga, and Ōmi, demand for raw silk greatly increased countrywide. In 1810 Ōhashi's son Gizaemon II[21] sold raw silk to
over 100 establishments. Included were sixteen Kyoto raw silk wholesalers, but the remainder were merchants and producers from rural produc-

tion sites, such as Ōmi and Kōzuke.[22] The magnitude of Gizaemon II's sales is astounding. In the second half of 1833 alone he sold raw silk valued at over 22,000 *ryō*; the weight of his shipments totaled over 5,000 *kanme*, or more than 43,000 pounds.[23]

To purchase in such massive quantities, Gizaemon II maintained a very broad purchasing network. Within the Shindatsu area itself, he bought large quantities in several periodic markets, where farmers brought their raw silk for sale.[24] He also purchased small quantities directly from smallholders, often those who were financially in debt to him. This was a common practice. Poorer farmers frequently borrowed money from local elites, with payment taking the form of the finished product, either from their fields or from side industry. Finally, Gizaemon II dispatched employees and other merchants to areas northeast of Shindatsu, such as Sendai and Morioka, and he used merchants in other production regions as intermediaries in purchases for the family.[25] To run a profitable enterprise, Ōhashi monitored prices in the major raw silk production regions and sales prices in the country's weaving centers. For that purpose, he communicated extensively with merchants throughout the northeast and in the major cities.[26]

Family connections were important to the Ōhashi business. While Gizaemon II supervised the overall family operations and dealt with Kyoto wholesalers and raw silk merchants from other parts of the country, he delegated responsibility for purchases to others. Gisuke (Gizaemon III), his eldest son and heir, assumed responsibility for purchases in the Shindatsu region when he came of age in the 1820's; Gisuke also dealt with merchants with close ties to the family, such as Ōhashi Jūhei, who purchased raw silk in Sendai domain and areas to the north of Sendai. Gisuke's younger brother Gihei assisted him in his dealings.[27]

Like Fukami Tarōemon of western Mikawa, Ōhashi Gizaemon headed a patrilineal kinship group, or *dōzokudan*. At least three families were included in the Gizaemon *dōzokudan*: the Giemon household, Ōhashi Jūhei, and Ōhashi Gihei. Both Giemon and Ōhashi Jūhei sometimes provided labor to the Gizaemon household at critical points in the agricultural cycle. Ōhashi Jūhei also worked for Gizaemon in his raw silk trade. The same was true for Ōhashi Gihei, Gisuke's younger brother. Upon assuming the family headship in 1837, Gisuke (Gizaemon III) established Gihei as a branch household. But the ties between the Gizaemon stem household and its branches existed only in a very attenuated form. The branch households all maintained separate residences, and their relationship with the stem household was based largely on contractual obligations. When, for example, branch households received loans from Gi-zaemon, the repayment terms were clearly elucidated in documents be-tween the two parties. In most ways Gizaemon treated his branch families no differently than other employees.[28]

We know far less about other activities in which the Ōhashi family en-gaged. Some Ōhashi heads served as village headmen, but not for signifi-cant periods of time. This was not at all unusual. Although the family was of substantial means and no doubt descended from distinguished lineage, the position of headman could prove to be a tremendous burden. There were seemingly endless communications and requests for information from political overlords. When poorer farmers defaulted on their tax payments, the burden often fell into the lap of the headman, who was re-sponsible for shipping the village's tax obligations to the domain.

The Gizaemon household also engaged in farming, silk reeling, and co-coon production. Two brief agricultural diaries that remain among the family's papers suggest that the cultivation of non-rice food crops—such as red beans and barley—was a relatively minor pursuit; the same was true of reeling. Far more important were the family's rice harvest and mulberry trees. When its own mulberry crop was insufficient, it purchased addi-tional leaves; when there was a surplus, it sold leaves to others in the vil-lage. The family also extensively engaged in cocoon production, selling the cocoons to merchants and farmers in the area. To assist in these agri-cultural tasks, the family employed outside labor and sometimes enlisted the services of members of its kinship group (as *tetsudai*).[29]

Few records survive pertaining to family landholdings. An 1846 docu-ment listing landholdings contains no mention of a "Gizaemon." If the "Ichibei" listed is indeed Ōhashi Ichibei, Gizaemon III's eldest son, then the family owned only about ten *koku* of land, less than many others in the village. But this was a period of decline for the family, and only a few years before it had given Gihei land to establish a branch household.[30] Judging from the large number of land-sales documents among its papers, the family was undoubtedly a significant landholder earlier in the century; it frequently purchased land from smallholders unable to pay their debts.[31]

Ōhashi heads also engaged in extensive moneylending. Many of their loans were related to the raw silk trade: they extended funds to dozens of merchants to purchase for them in other areas. Through such loans, the family provided purchasing power to numerous small merchants, who otherwise would have lacked sufficient capital. This was a critical factor in the family's success in commerce, enabling it to buy in bulk over a broad region.[32] Ōhashi also extended small loans to residents of Ōishi and other villages. In 1822, for example, Ōishi farmers owed the family 492 *ryō* in "old loans"; farmers in other villages owed 1,930 *ryō* in "old loans."[33] The magnitude of loans outside the village suggests that many of these, too, were related to the family's raw silk trade.

The family's various ventures were enormously profitable. According to a ledger for 1808–35, the family's assets increased almost fourfold: from 6,612 *ryō* in 1808 to 18,640 *ryō* in 1832, and to 23,145 *ryō* in 1835. At the end of the ledger, Gizaemon II noted the "felicitous continuation" of growth in family assets and "prayed [that this growth] would be perpetuated into the future."[34] The family's prosperity was a source of tremendous pride, enhancing its reputation both in the village and among its peers. Gizaemon II, who wrote this ledger at the age of seventy-five, one year before his death, was also sending an unmistakable message to his heir: continue the prosperity of the household.[35]

But from the late 1830's a number of factors propelled the family into decline. The first was the instability of the headship. Gisuke (Gizaemon III) assumed the headship in 1837, but he soon became seriously ill and had to entrust household management to others.[36] Who occupied the position of family head in later years is not clear. In 1841 Gisuke brought into his family (as *mukoiri*, or adopted son-in-law) a merchant's son from the nearby town of Koori to serve as interim head until his own son came of age.[37] The merchant's son, however, does not appear in a temple registration document composed the following year.[38] The same document contains no mention of Gisuke's daughter having a husband, suggesting that he returned to his house of birth. Another document notes the death of a "Gizaemon"—perhaps Gisuke—in 1846.[39] The success of *gōnō* operations depended on the enterprising spirit, perspicacity, and diligence of the family head and the proper training of successors, so the instability in headship dealt a serious blow to the Ōhashi business.

Especially harmful was a series of onerous exactions imposed upon the family by Shirakawa domain. In 1834 Shirakawa officials asked Gizaemon II, who had been appointed financial purveyor (*goyōtashi*), to provide over 4,500 *ryō* in loans.[40] Gizaemon lent another 4,400 *ryō* in 1836, 3,099 *ryō* in 1837, and 1,220 *ryō* in 1838.[41] Such massive outlays of capital could prove disastrous to merchants in the raw silk trade. Because of the seasonal nature of the business, Ōhashi needed a constant flow of capital over a concentrated period to purchase raw silk. And despite assets of over 20,000 *ryō* in 1833, only a portion was available for immediate use. In 1828, for example, Gizaemon II recorded assets of over 17,000 *ryō*, but only 6,470 was "on hand"; he had invested the remainder in purchases of raw silk and in the form of loans to other parties.[42] These "on-hand" funds had to be continually reinvested in new purchases.

In return for his loans, Shirakawa accorded successive Ōhashi family heads rural samurai (*gōshi*) status, the right to wear a sword and to use a surname, and a stipend.[43] Domain officials also bestowed upon Gizaemon a number of gifts, such as rice, fans, and fabrics.[44] They loaned him money from time to time, including 50 *ryō* in 1816, 180 *ryō* in 1817, 200 *ryō* in 1818, and 130 *ryō* in 1821.[45] The extension of massive loans to the domain, however, proved a tremendous strain on Gizaemon's business, forcing him to considerably reduce his transactions in raw silk.

A series of crop failures throughout the 1830's compounded the family's financial woes. The raw silk trade could be one of the most profitable of pursuits, but it could prove disastrous in times of crop failures, bringing misfortune upon all classes of farmers. Poorer farmers suffered, and often-times defaulted on their annual tax, because of crop losses; they also had to suspend activities in sericulture and reeling as a result of damage to their mulberry trees. Small merchants, most of whom were smallholders themselves, could not repay loans from wealthier villagers, like Ōhashi, for purchases of raw silk. Wealthier villagers naturally fared better than poorer farmers in their communities, because they could live off assets accumulated during years of prosperity. But they, too, faced difficult times when crop conditions were poor: poor farmers defaulted on their loans; there was less raw silk available for purchase and sale; and domains, facing increasing deficits because of declining revenue, redoubled efforts to obtain contributions and forced loans.

As a result of the crop failures, the Ōhashi family faced serious problems in recovering many of its loans. This is apparent in a petition an employee, Kazō, sent to the domain office at Hobara in 1839. Kazō pleaded for help in recovering over 1,100 *ryō* in loans due Gizaemon III, who was ill and on the verge of bankruptcy. Many were small loans of about 1 to 3 *ryō*, but others were more substantial, ranging from 25 to 250 *ryō*. Most of the borrowers were merchants, in all probability those who purchased raw silk for the family. Kazō noted that it was difficult to earn a livelihood in the village in good years, but a succession of poor harvests over the last decade had made matters worse.[46]

In addition, Ōhashi's raw silk trade was a far less profitable endeavor by the late 1830's. The trade was always a somewhat risky venture. Kyoto wholesalers maintained agents in the production regions who reported on crop conditions, production volume, and local prices. When sending purchase orders to their rural agents, like Ōhashi, the wholesalers stipulated not only the quantity but the price they would pay for the raw silk. Kadoya and Aburaya, both fairly large raw silk agents in the region, had to suspend their operations around 1824 because of debts they could not immediately repay. Maeki Kyūhei of Naka village abandoned the raw silk trade around the same time. As in years past, he received purchase orders from Kyoto wholesalers that stipulated prices below local market rates.[47]

Ōhashi Gizaemon fared better at first than other Shindatsu merchants, perhaps because of the massive volume of his purchases and the loans he provided others to purchase for him. But in the late 1830's, he, too, faced similar problems. Total costs in 12/1838 for his raw silk purchases and related expenses came to about 1,712 ryō, while income from their sale amounted to 1,719 ryō, leaving a net profit of only 7 ryō. In 12/1839 total expenses came to about 2,700 ryō, while income amounted to 2,725 ryō, resulting in a net profit of 25 ryō. And again in 8/1846 net profits came to only 5.3 ryō on purchases of about 1,269 ryō.[48]

With such low profit margins, few rural merchants could remain in business for long. For merchants such as Ōhashi, though, moving out of the raw silk business was not an easy matter, because there were numerous merchants under him whose livelihoods depended on the family trade. This was why Kazō petitioned officials in 1839 for help in recovering loans due the Ōhashi family. It also explains why six Ōhashi employees wrote to domain officials in 1837. The domain's onerous loans, they remarked, forced the Ōhashi family to suspend its dealings in raw silk. The loans they received from the family provided them the capital to purchase raw silk, on which they earned a commission. This enabled them to make ends meet in a situation where they could not earn a living from agriculture alone. They pleaded with the domain to allow Ōhashi to continue his trade, free of the impediments of the past.[49] The petitioners risked a great deal in sending such an appeal, but they had little choice. The downfall of such a powerful family had repercussions far beyond the family itself.

The Ōhashi family continued in the raw silk trade but soon faced more impediments in the final years of Tokugawa rule, including Shirakawa domain's unending scavenging for funds. None of the forced loans or contributions were of the magnitude of those of the 1830's—few were over 100 ryō—but they came with annoying frequency. Most payments to the domain now took the form of contributions rather than loans: 80 ryō in 1855 and 45 ryō in 1856 for military-related equipment to meet the growing foreign menace; 15 ryō in 1855, when there was a major earthquake in Edo; 25 ryō in 1858 for construction of the daimyo's Edo residence; and 90 ryō in 1864, when the daimyo was appointed to a new position in bakufu administration. These were but a few of Shirakawa's all-too-familiar demands.[50]

In the years before the Restoration, Shirakawa's incessant impositions exasperated the family. In an 1867 ledger listing all loans and contributions to the domain since 1836, Ōhashi noted that on several occasions Shirakawa officials had unilaterally converted loans into outright contributions; at other times, they had ignored his pleas of inability to pay. Most suggestive is a notation for the domain's outstanding debts due the family, in the amount of 278,862 *ryō*. This staggering sum stemmed from a series of loans totaling about 8,770 *ryō* over the period 1836–38, only 300 *ryō* of which had been repaid. The remainder was accumulated interest—at about 12 percent—and on which no further payments had been made.[51] That Ōhashi refused to wipe off the books loans from thirty years before is telling of his frame of mind. Shirakawa's exactions had been a major source of the family's difficulties, and there was no reason to be magnanimous about it.

Another serious blow came to the family in 1866, when participants in a major uprising across the region attacked his house and destroyed many of his personal belongings. The proximate cause of the Shindatsu uprising was the bakufu's imposition of a new inspection system and tax on raw silk and egg cards. Farmers resented the new tax, which they could ill afford. They also resented the manner in which two wealthy Shindatsu farmers had colluded with officials to get the inspection system and tax implemented. Equally serious, an inflationary spiral, unleashed with the opening of the ports and exacerbated by bakufu currency reminting policies, forced rice prices to soar, threatening poorer farmers' survival. While poorer farmers suffered, wealthy farmers hoarded rice, waiting for prices to rise even further, and they increased their interest rates on loans.[52]

There is no evidence that the Ōhashi household hoarded rice or increased its interest rates on loans, nor is there evidence to the contrary. But it is not difficult to imagine why its residence was included among those attacked. The family continued to give the impression of wealth, despite evidence to the contrary in its ledgers. It resided in a large compound, containing about a dozen structures, on a hill overlooking the rest of the village. It also appeared to be in league with political authorities, like the two wealthy farmers who had been responsible for the inspection system and tax. Gizaemon continued to receive various gifts and honors from domain officials. He worked for a time in Shirakawa's administrative office (*jinya*) in Hobara, and in 1860 the domain appointed him as one of three officers in charge of a domain monopoly office for raw silk, cloth, and floss.[53]

Especially crippling to the Ōhashi business were the structural changes in trade brought on by the opening of the ports in 1859. Merchants immediately began to ship Japan's raw silk to Yokohama for export, completely bypassing existing trading networks. Ōhashi made an attempt to enter the export trade, but with little success. The reasons for the failure are not entirely clear, but certainly the family's poor finances weakened its ability to take advantage of the export trade. Shipments to Yokohama also involved considerable risk, at least in the first few years after 1859. Masterless samurai (rōnin), many undoubtedly from the not-so-distant Mito domain, sometimes stopped and destroyed raw silk shipments destined for Yokohama.[54]

More important, the opening of the ports intensified competition for raw silk purchases. Large numbers of small merchants began to buy raw silk for the first time, seriously eroding Ōhashi's purchasing network. One such merchant was Ōhashi Jinbei, also of Ōishi village but unrelated to the Gizaemon clan. Jinbei launched into the raw silk trade with the opening of the ports and soon developed a broad purchasing network extending over precisely those areas where the Gizaemon household had been active in the past.[55] Ikeda Tomokichi of Awano village increased his raw silk sales around the same time; between 1859 and 1866 his cash outlays for raw silk increased almost fivefold.[56] Many of these new merchants sold their raw silk to establishments in the town of Fukushima, who had ties with Yokohama export merchants. Ōhashi Gizaemon and other once-powerful Shindatsu merchants were forced out of the raw silk trade entirely.[57]

In the early Meiji the Ōhashi household was in decline. In an 1871 petition to Yanagawadate prefecture, which now had jurisdiction over Ōishi, Gizaemon asked to be relieved of his position as financial purveyor. The Shindatsu uprising, he stated, had led to the destruction of his home and many of his belongings. The previous daimyo, Lord Tanagura, who had taken over the area with the Meiji Restoration, had made frequent requests for loans but had repaid nothing, forcing Ōhashi to borrow money from others. Since the uprising, he had been unable to make a living from the silk trade and had returned to agriculture alone.[58]

There was no doubt some hyperbole in Gizaemon's entreaty. We know little about the family's activities in the Meiji period, but it was hardly impoverished. In 1882 its lands were valued at over 1,076 yen, the fourth largest in the village, while the lands of almost 63 percent of other Ōishi villagers were assessed at under 200 yen; and he was the fourth largest egg card producer in 1881.[59] Gizaemon also served as village headman (nanushi) from 1870 to 1871, as assistant headman (fukukochō) in 1873, and as mayor (*sonchō*) of the reconstituted Ryōzen village from 1901 to 1905.[60] A 1912 report on sericultural conditions in Date district described Gizaemon as a "man of high repute" and "person of wealth," who "examined ways to produce only the best, immunized, silkworm eggs." Every year he invited two talented students from the local sericultural school and put them in charge of raising the eggs.[61]

And yet we are left with the nagging feeling that Gizaemon II would have been disappointed and dismayed. Despite his injunction to his heir in 1837, the family's prosperity had considerably diminished. Indeed, the family had faced near-ruin on at least two occasions since his death. But there was much that he could not foresee. He could not predict the illness of his heir and the subsequent instability in headship. He had no way of knowing that Shirakawa domain would sink ever further into debt and be forced to scour for still further sources of income. And certainly he could not have foreseen the changes unleashed by the opening of the ports. The ties he had so assiduously forged with wholesalers in the silk textile production regions were destroyed almost overnight.

## *Nakano Kyūjirō and the Hachiōji Textile Trade*

Like Ōhashi Gizaemon, Nakano Kyūjirō of Nakagami village became one of his area's most powerful rural merchants with the growth of the local silk industry. He purchased large quantities of silks throughout the region, selling them to Edo wholesalers and to merchants in other parts of the country. He also became heavily involved in moneylending and accumulated sizable landholdings.

Nakagami, currently part of Akishima city, was a farming village in Musashi province in the Kantō, about five miles from the Hachiōji town market and twenty-five miles west of Edo. Like Shindatsu, Musashi was an area of fragmented rule, with countless small territories controlled by the bakufu, its bannermen (*hatamoto*), and small domains. In the seventeenth century, Nakagami was under bakufu rule, but thereafter two bannermen controlled different parts of the village.[62]

As in Ōishi, a confluence of factors forced Nakagami villagers to turn to the market from an early date. Political authorities in the area collected taxes on dry fields in specie, so farmers had to sell many of their crops in local markets. Growing tax burdens had the same effect. Although no data are available for Nakagami, taxes in neighboring Kamikawahara village jumped by over 50 percent from 1692 to 1721. Similar increases occurred in villages throughout the area.[63]

Small landholdings also dictated that farmers seek sources of income outside agriculture. Pages are missing from a 1667 Nakagami land register but, of the forty-eight people listed, thirty-three (66.7 percent) owned under 0.5 *chō*, far less than necessary to support their families from agriculture alone. Small farm sizes also encouraged farmers to purchase fertilizers, such as rice bran and night soil, to get the highest yields from their crops. Cash fertilizers became especially important from the 1720's as a result of bakufu policies that encouraged the clearing of village commons. Not only did this deprive residents of an important source of natural fertilizers, but the poor quality of the reclaimed land required large applications of cash fertilizers to make cultivation profitable.[64]

To supplement their incomes from agriculture, farmers in the Hachiōji area engaged in several forms of side industry. In 1689 the periodic markets in the town of Hachiōji handled a number of goods produced in the surrounding region, such as pongee, cotton cloth, and firewood. The growth of the market economy from the mid-eighteenth century generated new forms of side industry and in far greater quantities than in the past. Although farmers continued to weave cotton fabrics and pongee, silks and silk/cotton blends became especially important to the area economy. Again no information is available for Nakagami, but clear changes in side industry can be seen in records from nearby Kamikawahara. In 1720 village women engaged in sericulture on a small scale, and men went to the mountainous areas, especially to the Itsukaichi market, to purchase firewood and charcoal, which they took to Edo for sale. The men also engaged in packhorse work along major roads in the area. According to a 1746 record, the men's sideline pursuits remained the same. Kamikawahara women continued to raise silkworms, but now they also wove small amounts of pongee, which they produced from their cocoons, and cotton cloth, for which they obtained the raw material in local markets. One farmer sold silk in the Edo market. By the end of the century sericulture and weaving had assumed far greater importance. In addition to sericulture, women produced Ōme cloth, a silk and cotton blend.[65]

Most area farmers sold their fabrics to merchants operating out of periodic markets, where they also purchased a number of necessities. In addition to Hachiōji, there were several such markets in the area, including Hirai, Haijima, Ina, Itsukaichi, and Ōme. By the late eighteenth century Hachiōji had come to dominate transactions in fabrics, forcing a few other such markets to shut down. That many Hachiōji merchants had established ties with Edo wholesalers no doubt contributed to the market's position.[66] In the past, sales to Edo had been largely intermittent; merchants sold their cloth to Edo wholesale and retail establishments, who made their purchasing decisions based on current demand. As the region's silk industry developed, Edo establishments purchased area fabrics far more regularly, and they appointed agents (*kaiyado* or *kaitsugi*) in its major market, Hachiōji. It was only natural, then, that farmers would take their cloth to Hachiōji, where there was a constant demand.

Among those purchasing silk in the Hachiōji market were merchants living in the town itself and merchants commuting from area villages. There were many types of rural merchant, but most operated on a small scale. They sold their cloth freely to both large and small Edo wholesalers and retailers. A few rural merchants did not operate out of the Hachiōji market at all; they bought cloth from farm families, which they sold directly to consumers or to itinerant merchants.[67]

With the growth of the market economy, competition arose country-wide between town merchants, many of whom had been granted monopolistic commercial rights by political authorities, and rural merchants, who increasingly usurped trade from the towns. The same pattern could be found in Hachiōji, where three major disputes erupted between the two groups. The first dispute arose in 1757. The Hachiōji merchant Mikawaya Yogobei, in collaboration with other town merchants, devised a plan to limit rural merchants' participation in the market. Rural merchants immediately protested and, together with farm households in the region, initiated a market boycott. Later the same year, farmers from "several tens of villages" attacked and destroyed the houses and belongings of a number of Hachiōji town merchants. The Hachiōji merchants were forced to abandon their scheme.[68]

Another major dispute flared in 1794, for much the same reason. The local bakufu intendant, probably at the urging of Hachiōji merchants, ordered merchants operating in the market to appoint a representative (*sewanin*) who would issue them licenses. Rural merchants, most still small in scale, immediately objected. They opposed the licensing system, because they would have had to pay fees for the licenses. They also feared that the representative would be selected from among town merchants, who would limit rural participation. In response, rural merchants launched a well-organized campaign against the new system, which led the intendant to rescind his previous directives.[69]

Again in 1818, town merchants unilaterally decided that the Hachiōji silk market was to open at seven in the morning, with seating based on time of arrival, and that all merchants needed licenses to operate in the market. Both directives disadvantaged village merchants, who lived some distance from Hachiōji and objected to the financial burdens of a licensing system. They thereupon initiated a boycott among area farmers of the entire Hachiōji market, forcing Hachiōji merchants to back down.[70] Many of the events surrounding these conflicts are obscure, but it is clear that Hachiōji town merchants perceived rural merchants as a threat to their livelihoods. Almost all rural merchants operated on a very small scale, which explains their opposition to the licensing system. They were also a highly fluid group. Of 164 rural cloth merchants in the greater Hachiōji area from 1794 to 1874, 102 (62 percent of the total) were in business for fewer than five years, and 140 (85 percent) remained active for under ten years. Most rural merchants were poor farmers themselves, not rural elites, which explains the strong mutuality of interests between rural merchants and area farmers in each of the above disputes. The problem was that there were too many rural merchants, far outnumbering the Hachiōji town merchants. From 1794 to 1874 the number of rural cloth merchants in the greater Hachiōji area fluctuated between twenty-four and fifty, as compared with fifteen to twenty-two town merchants.[71]

Where did Nakano Kyūjirō stand in these disputes? The family is not named in records relating to the 1757 dispute; it was probably not yet involved in the silk trade. The family archives include a document relating to the 1794 conflict, so we can assume that Nakano collaborated with other rural merchants in forcing the abandonment of the licensing system.[72] In the 1818 dispute Nakano Kyūjirō VII was one of two representatives of the rural merchants first notified concerning the new regulations. He was heavily involved in the initial stages of the opposition movement but soon withdrew. The reasons are not clear, but perhaps Nakano by this time had far more in common with Hachiōji town merchants than with his fellow rural merchants. He had been active in the trade for a long time, at least since 1766. He also handled large quantities, unlike most rural merchants, and had developed close ties with Edo wholesalers. It was thus to his advantage to limit other rural merchants' participation in the market.[73]

How did Nakano attain this prominent position in the silk trade? Little is known about the early history of the family, but several documents suggest that it had acquired some degree of wealth well before the mid-eighteenth century. A 1665 document records a land sale: a poorer farmer, unable to pay his annual tax, sold his land to the family.[74] A 1685 death record notes that the deceased Saburōbei (Kyūjirō I) had been the first generation of the family.[75] Since only households with substantial landholdings could afford to establish younger sons as branch households, we can assume that Saburōbei was born into a family of means. Village officials also turned to Nakano in 1724 and again in 1739 to meet demands from their political overlord, the bannerman Tsubouchi Hanzaburō, for advance payment of the annual tax. In 1789 Tsubouchi asked Nakano for a seventeen-year repayment schedule on advance tax payments amounting to 120 ryō, with yearly payments to be deducted from the annual tax.⁷⁶ The Nakano family made these payments despite the fact that no member of the household occupied positions in village administration until the 1810's.⁷⁷

Until the early nineteenth century, the scale of the Nakano family business was relatively small. From 1754 to 1764 Kyūjirō V and his heir Bun'emon (Kyūjirō VI) operated a store in Haijima, a nearby market town, but they entrusted management to Shōemon, who owned the property where the store was located. The store had an inventory of only 350 ryō: in-stock goods accounted for about 60 ryō, while the remainder consisted of loans, pawned land, and pawned articles.⁷⁸ According to a 1766 ledger, the total receipts from various family businesses came to about 368 ryō, but the family suffered a net loss of 25 ryō after deducting expenditures. Its cloth business occupied a large share of receipts—about 175 ryō —but it was hardly on a major scale. The local silk industry was still in a process of gestation, and rural merchants like Nakano handled only small quantities. In addition to the cloth trade, the family engaged in the pawn business and, for a short time, sake production and sales.⁷⁹

The first decades of the nineteenth century were a time of tremendous growth in the family's prosperity. In 1831 family assets totaled over 4,500 ryō, and they continued to increase in subsequent years, reaching over 7,500 ryō in 1844.⁸⁰ The family accumulated profits through four primary activities: sales from its store, the silk trade, moneylending, and income from its lands. Store sales occupied a relatively minor position. The family operated its store in Haijima for about a decade in the mid-eighteenth century. At some point it also opened a general store in Nakagami itself, which remained in operation until the family's bankruptcy in 1874. This store handled goods to meet the needs of farmers in the immediate area, such as rice, soy sauce, salt, oil, coal, and various wooden products, with rice being the most important item. In 1835 the inventory was valued at only about 200 ryō, hardly sufficient to make the family prosperous.⁸¹

The silk trade was far more instrumental in the family's rise. The family obtained most of its silks and other fabrics from the Hachiōji market. In 1832 alone Nakano or his assistants—he employed fifteen workers (hōkō-nin) to assist in his cloth trade that year—made fifty-six trips to Hachiōji and twenty-four to the market in Ōme. Nakano also used merchants as intermediaries to purchase for him in other areas, such as the Gunnai area to the west.[82]

In the early years Nakano sold his fabrics primarily to Edo. When dealing with large Edo wholesalers, Kyūjirō VII at first used a Hachiōji agent (*kaiyado*) as an intermediary. As the scale of his trade increased, he established direct ties. In 1799 he petitioned Mitsui to be allowed to ship directly, in the capacity of rural agent (*kaitsugi*).[83] There is no record of a response, but it is reasonable to assume that Nakano now operated on a much greater scale than in the past; as we saw with the Ōhashi family, only merchants with substantial assets and trading networks could expect to be appointed to such a position. Over the next two decades, Kyūjirō VII further expanded his links with Edo wholesalers, primarily through the purchase of rural-agent licenses from bankrupt merchants.[84]

No information is available on the family's sales volume, but it was obviously large. In the last decades of the Tokugawa, the family operated "stores"—perhaps storage facilities for its cloth—in Edo and Hachiōji. The extent of his sales in 1832 is suggested by the thirty-seven trips Nakano or his assistants made to Edo to deliver cloth. The same year, the family had cloth, mostly silks, in its inventory valued at over 550 *ryō* and was expecting payment of over 1,560 *ryō* for recent sales.[85]

Despite close ties to Edo wholesalers, Nakano also sold silks to other parts of the country, including Osaka, Ōmi, Shinano, and Echigo.[86] Edo wholesalers ordered their Hachiōji agents in 1813 to sell only to the licensed wholesalers, but there was little they could do to stop the trade. Hachiōji merchants, including Nakano, continued much as they had done in the past, selling their silks all over the country.[87] Because of a growing demand for styles popular in the Edo market, Kinai cities became an especially important destination for Hachiōji silks.[88]

In addition to operating its general store and trading in silk, the Nakano family engaged extensively in moneylending. In the early years of its rise to prominence, the pawn business was especially important. As we saw above, one of the primary activities of the Haijima store was to take in farmers' land and goods as pawn, in exchange for interest-bearing loans. In 1831 Nakano Kyūjirō VII owned two pawn businesses. He operated one within the family compound itself, entrusting the management of the second to someone by the name of Hasegawa. Together they held pawned articles and pawned land valued at about 442 *ryō*, on which Kyūjirō VII earned interest of about 30 *ryō*. Around 1835, however, Kyūjirō VII drastically curtailed both pawn operations, and by 1839 they no longer appeared in the family ledgers.[89]

While gradually withdrawing from the pawn business, the Nakano family increased its moneylending activities, which assumed an important position within the overall family operations. Between 1831 and 1844 loans owed the family more than tripled, from 1,107 *ryō* to 3,365 *ryō*. By the mid-1830's the family's moneylending activities began to outstrip its silk transactions.[90]

Problems in the silk trade no doubt prompted the shift away from silk transactions. Cold weather in 1833, repeated in 1835 and 1836, destroyed crops, including farmers' mulberry trees, resulting in a decline in silk production. Depressed economic conditions countrywide and bakufu sumptuary edicts on silk garments greatly reduced demand. There were also problems with the quality of Hachiōji silks. Many farmers added starch to their silks to increase their weight, thus damaging Hachiōji's reputation in outside markets. In 1836 town and rural merchants united to combat the problem, but apparently with little effect. Regulations banning such fabrics had to be reissued in 1840.[91]

Nakano Kyūjirō was of course a farmer, and in the early years profits earned from the sale of cash crops at least partly facilitated his commercial activities. But with the growth of the market economy and side industry, the family gradually placed less emphasis on the lands it cultivated. In the 1720's the family owned about 5 *chō* of land, most of which it cultivated itself with the help of hired laborers. In the 1790's it owned about 10 *chō*, most of which it rented out. On the land reserved for itself, the family continued to employ hired labor to assist in cultivation, but most of its crops were for household consumption, not for sale in the market.[92]

Appendix Table 14 shows landholdings in Nakagami village in 1872. The two largest landholders, the Nakano and Genmo families, owned 40 percent of village arable, while fifty-two people, or 50 percent of the population, owned only 4 percent. The Nakano family had sold off some of its land by this point, so the polarization of holdings in the last decades of the Tokugawa was probably even more acute. In 1850, even after having granted some of its lands to a new branch household eight years before, the family owned 23 *chō*, or 30 percent of village lands.[93]

The Nakano family acquired many of its fields from poorer farmers in the region. Like Ōishi residents, villagers in the Hachiōji area were often at the mercy of nature. From the 1750's to 1780's, a flood or a drought occurred about once every three or four years.[94] The famine years of 1835–37 were especially difficult times. Repeated crop failures forced small farmers to sell their lands and to turn to wealthier farmers for loans. In 1865 Nakano Kyūjirō XI had 104 tenants: seventy-five in Nakagami and twenty-nine in other villages. They were a very unstable class: of forty-seven tenants cultivating Nakano's paddies in 1865, eleven rented more land the following year, fifteen rented less, nine were no longer his tenants, and twelve kept the same amount of land. Those who were no longer Nakano tenants in 1866 were among the poorest farmers: they had rented an average of 1.4 *koku* in 1865, and they all owned less than 0.25 *koku* of land in 1872.[95]

The family provided relief funds during times of hardship, to farmers in both Nakagami and nearby villages. In 1784, for example, it loaned 4 *ryō* without interest to farmers suffering from famine in Miyazawa village and another 2 *ryō* to farmers in Nakagami.[96] The Tenpō famine years required far greater outlays. The family provided 100 *ryō* of relief to Nakagami villagers in both 1835 and 1837. In 1836 it contributed 100 *ryō* to repair the village's stone bridge, providing employment and much needed cash income to villagers. In 1837 Nakano loaned rice and millet to over 100 impoverished farmers in nine villages in the area.

Nakano had to provide such funds because the bannerman Tsubouchi proved incapable of offering substantive relief. Tsubouchi granted five bags of rice to impoverished Nakagami villagers in both 1833 and 1836; in 1833 he allowed the payment of ten bags of tax rice to be deferred; and he gave 10 *ryō* of relief to Nakagami in 1837. It was impossible for Tsubouchi to provide more, because declining tax income during the crop failures aggravated his own financial plight. During the height of the crop failures, in fact, he was forced to call upon residents for additional funds. In 1836, for example, he asked Nakano for 100 *ryō* in *goyōkin*; he also demanded that Nakagami village as a whole provide 80 *ryō* in advance tax payment.[97]

Despite the scale of Nakano's various business activities, in 1874 creditors and relatives conferred to discuss ways to restructure the family's operations. With debts totaling over 40,000 *ryō*, Kyūjirō XI had to divest himself of most of his property, suspend his activities in the silk trade, and release all his employees.[98] Let us examine the various factors that led to the family's demise.

Instability in headship was a contributing factor, though hardly decisive, in the family's decline. In 1865–66 Kyūjirō VIII and his successor Kyūjirō IX died within six months of one another. Kyūjirō IX's successor Kyūjirō X had died in 1862, so the headship passed to the latter's younger brother, now the eleventh head of the Nakano household.[99] Kyūjirō XI was twenty-seven years old in 1866, so undoubtedly he had been well trained in the family business.

Nevertheless, the death of his father and grandfather made for instability in the family's activities. The economic success of rural elites depended on countless relationships of mutual trust built up over a number of years. The importance of such relationships can be deduced from an 1875 record listing the former sales destinations for the family's fabrics. Included were twenty-four merchants from Ōmi, thirteen from Osaka, eleven from Kyoto, and nine from Nagoya.[100] An heir could not expect to simply follow in his father's footsteps. He had to constantly strive to maintain those relationships his father had so assiduously created and nurtured. The tasks that lay before Kyūjirō XI were no doubt enormous.

To compound his misfortunes, participants in a major uprising that swept the Musashi area in 1866 destroyed his home and much of his property. The causes of the uprising were similar to those behind the Shindatsu uprising the same year: farmers' indignation at the institution of a raw silk inspection system and the precipitous rise in rice prices. That participants demanded the return of pawned goods without compensation and the cancellation of loans reflects the extent to which they resented the activities of the rural elite.[101] The relief funds provided in the past no doubt meant very little to area farmers, because Nakano continued to accumulate their fields as they defaulted on their loans. In 1865, in fact, 70 percent of Nakagami residents rented land from the family.[102]

After the rebellion was suppressed, Kyūjirō XI began to return some of the lands his family had accumulated. In 1867 alone he sold back over 1.9 *chō* to their original owners. Kyūjirō XI did this not so much to acquire income, because he returned the lands at well below cost. The uprising had perhaps given him cause to reflect on his family's activities and the effects such activities had on others, especially in the area of land accumulation and moneylending. Around the same time, other rural elites in the area adopted similar measures to appease poorer farmers. A few village officials even petitioned their samurai overlords to release members of their communities who had been arrested for participating in the uprising. Concern about further uprisings was another reason to adopt such measures. Even in 1868, rumors spread about a possible uprising against local silk cloth merchants, and farmers continued to demand the return of pawned articles, either without compensation or at reduced rates.[103]

The social disorder gripping most of the Kantō region in the years immediately before and after the Restoration aggravated the family's financial woes. Bands of samurai dissidents (some of them imperial loyalists, others claiming to be), masterless samurai, and gangs of youth roamed the countryside, demanding and extorting money from people of wealth. Nakano had to provide money to such groups on a number of occasions. In 1868 a band of Tokugawa loyalists, the Jingitai, demanded 90 *ryō* for "military expenditures"; another samurai group of indeterminate origin demanded 75 *ryō*.[104] Thieves robbed Kyūjirō XI's brother of 332 *ryō* on a return trip from Edo the same year. In 1869 a former bakufu retainer forced Nakano to give him 20 *ryō* so that he and other retainers could provide for their families and travel to Nikkō to commit ritual suicide. Nakano did not believe him but, fearing further destruction to his property, had no choice but to comply.[105]

Massive debts and unrecoverable loans also drained Nakano's operations of capital. In 1874 the family's debts totaled over 40,000 *ryō*. A small portion derived from its cloth purchases, on which the family had made no payments, but it owed the bulk to merchants and wholesalers in Tokyo, Kyoto, Osaka, Ōmi, and Owari who had advanced it money for purchases. It owed 4,500 *ryō* to Mitsukoshi (formerly Echigoya), for example, and 7,500 *ryō* to Tanaka Jirōzaemon, both major Tokyo wholesalers.[106]

Loans owed the family totaled over 28,900 *ryō*, much of it stemming from credit sales to other merchants, for which the family could expect repayment. Loans with scant likelihood of repayment, though, came to over 11,000 *ryō*: "old loans accumulating since 1819" (over 2,060 *ryō*), most of which went probably to poorer farmers; loans to someone by the name of Sōshirō (6,566 *ryō*, 3,500 *ryō* of which was principle); and loans to the bannerman Tsubouchi (about 2,430 *ryō*). We have no information on Sōshirō, but the size of the debt suggests that he was in a business relationship with Nakano.[107]

Loans to Tsubouchi stemmed from the family's position as *kattemakanai*, to which Kyūjirō VIII had been appointed in 1843.[108] The position required that Nakano collect the tax from Tsubouchi's lands and provide him money for monthly expenditures. Tsubouchi's annual income from lands, however, came to only 436 *ryō*, while his expenditures averaged from 780 to 830 *ryō*. Nakano had somehow to make up the difference, either by borrowing from others or from his own pockets.[109]

Nakano had gained much from this relationship with Tsubouchi. He could invest some of the tax income from Tsubouchi's villages, for example, in his business ventures, whether to purchase additional silk or to loan to other parties. In 1836 Tsubouchi granted Kyūjirō VII a stipend, which was to be deducted from the annual tax, as well as a ceremonial robe and permission to wear a sword and use a surname. In 1846 Tsubouchi also bestowed on Kyūjirō VIII a ceremonial garment and permission to wear a sword and use a surname, in recognition of his raising funds for him.[110] These were positive benefits that derived from the family's political ties. But by the end of the Tokugawa, the costs of their close relationship with Tsubouchi proved a drain on their operations.

Another reason for the family's problems can be found in the nature of the silk trade: production in the Hachiōji region, especially from the 1830's, was slowly being incorporated in a putting-out system, while Nakano continued as a mere buyer of finished cloth in the market. Some of those operating putting-out systems sold their finished cloth in the Hachiōji market, but others sold it directly to Edo, thus reducing the quantity available for purchase. Many such people had far less wealth than Nakano, but by gaining tighter control over production they enjoyed an important competitive edge.[111] Control over the production process was especially important to local merchants from the 1830's, given the deteriorating quality of Hachiōji cloth.

Perhaps the most important factor in the family's demise was the opening of Japan to foreign trade. Raw silk became the country's leading export item, depriving the domestic silk cloth industry of its raw material. In the Hachiōji area, merchants who used to sell raw silk in the market now began to ship to Yokohama, reducing quantities available for the local cloth industry. Countless weavers and silk merchants had to suspend their operations. Nakano and three other representatives of fifty Hachiōji-area silk merchants petitioned the bakufu in 1860 for an end to the Yokohama trade. When the petition failed, Nakano himself launched into the raw silk trade, but he handled small quantities and the move did little to improve his operations. He and seventeen other cloth merchants petitioned Edo wholesalers in 1865 for an increase in the commission they received for their cloth, but the wholesalers refused their request.[112]

In 1867 Nakano Kyūjirō XI composed a record in which he replaced the official era and year name, the third year of Keiō, with one of his own invention, the first year of "Chōtoku," "chō" being the character for long and "toku" the character for moral values. The term implied a repudiation of the current age and a longing for a complete change in the social order. Kyūjirō XI left no other records of his views toward the disastrous events of the 1860's, but we can infer that he yearned for some new order, one in which people of virtue would rule eternal.[113] But the problems he encountered—the death of his father and grandfather, the damage to his silk trade, massive debts, unrecoverable loans, and destruction of his property—were far too great to overcome. By 1875 he had sold his store in Tokyo and had put into pawn 11.5 *chō* of his land and his Nakagami store, never to be recovered.

## Conclusion

Ōhashi Gizaemon and Nakano Kyūjirō were among their regions' most powerful merchants. They were involved in other activities, such as moneylending and landlord operations, but their rise to positions of economic prominence derived largely from accumulated profits earned from trade. Like rural elites in western Mikawa, those in the silk regions were a product of the burgeoning protoindustrial economy. As a result of bakufu restrictions on imports and the transmission of Nishijin technology, new raw silk and silk cloth production regions emerged across the country. Ōhashi and Nakano rode the crest of these salutary changes in the rural economy.

Ōhashi and Nakano remained in business for a considerable time, until several factors converged from the 1830's to throw their businesses into tumult. The death of household heads and successors was one such contributory factor. Many *gōnō* operated on a large scale, but they were still family operations. Their continued success was dependent on the perseverance, will, and aptitude displayed by the head of the household. Their successors had to continually strive to nurture and expand the business ties their fathers had established. Both families faced difficulties as a result of the loss of their household heads.

Crop failures were another serious problem. Although heavily engaged in side industry, most farmers were still in fact farmers, and the bulk of their incomes derived from their crops. Damage to their crops set in motion a vicious cycle that affected all classes. Poorer farmers, unable to pay their taxes, had to sell their lands or borrow from the village rich. Rural elites accumulated more land in the process, but they suffered when too many farmers defaulted on their loans or tax payments. Also, the loss of a mulberry crop or cocoon harvest meant smaller quantities of raw silk and cloth went to market, and the rural elites' commercial operations suffered as a result. Finally, crop failures resulted in declining revenues for political authorities, forcing them to seek additional sources of income, especially from the rural elite.

The control wholesalers in the "three cities" exercised over prices in the production regions was yet another source of instability. Ōhashi and Nakano owed their rise to the ties they had established with city wholesalers, which in turn enabled them to establish business relationships with merchants in other parts of the country. But both families were also subject to the dictates of city wholesalers. Kyoto merchants sometimes set unreasonable prices for the raw silk they purchased, forcing rural merchants to absorb losses or to accept minimal profits. The only way to survive was to operate on a very large scale and over a broad region, but even these actions were no guarantee of success. Nakano Kyūjirō, too, found it necessary to expand the destinations of his sales.

The silk elites' conspicuous wealth engendered resentment among smallholders. In the final years of the Tokugawa, hundreds saw their houses and property destroyed in the massive uprisings that swept much of the countryside. Although the immediate cause of the revolts in Musashi and Shindatsu was the rise in the cost of rice following the opening of the ports, in each incident participants demanded the cancellation of loans and the return of pawned items. Many of the activities in which rural elites engaged were clearly exploitative, and common farmers perceived them as such.

Exactions imposed by political authority put additional strains on the activities of silk elites. Most lords in silk regions controlled relatively small territories and were constantly in search of additional funds. As in the cotton regions, in return for contributions and loans silk elites won tacit approval of their new activities in the economy; they also received advances in status. Political authorities in silk regions, however, imposed much heavier exactions on the rural elite. With the Nakano and Ōhashi families, these exactions were so onerous that they became major impediments to the successful functioning of their operations.

The opening of Japan to foreign commerce in 1859 was one of the most important factors behind the demise of *gōnō* families in the silk trade. Weavers and silk merchants were especially hard hit. With much of the country's raw silk destined for export, domestic weavers were deprived of their raw material. Nakano Kyūjirō went bankrupt in the 1860's in large measure because of the damage inflicted by the commencement of foreign commerce. Even those previously active in the raw silk trade, like Ōhashi, experienced difficulties, because they faced ever-growing competition from new merchants.

The fate of the Ōhashi and Nakano families was not unusual. Most of Shindatsu's largest raw silk merchants, like Ōhashi, were forced out of the trade entirely, leaving only a few merchant houses in the towns to act as intermediaries in the Yokohama trade. Countless small and middling merchants now sold the raw silk they purchased to the town merchants.

Even newcomers found the raw silk trade a far too speculative and risky venture. Both Ōhashi Jinbei and Ikeda Tomokichi, for example, had all but abandoned the trade in the early 1870's.[114]

The failure of Shindatsu's most powerful rural elites to capitalize on the export trade was an important factor in the region's sluggish adoption of either mechanization or the Gunma pattern of producers' cooperatives. It was difficult to motivate Shindatsu's numerous and mostly small-scale merchants to cooperate. By the early Meiji many wealthy Shindatsu farmers did not reel silk or deal in raw silk but were engaged in egg card production, so they did not see the need to encourage changes in the reeling industry.[115]

In the 1890's Shindatsu's wealthiest residents remained active in the silk industry, especially in egg card and mulberry leaf sales, but most of their income now derived from land rents and interest on loans. Of Date district's top twenty-four income earners in 1895, all but four were among the district's largest landlords. Ikeda Tomokichi, with the third highest income, received 36 percent of his income from land rents, 38 percent from interest on loans, and only 4.3 percent from the silk industry. He had first started to acquire land on a significant scale in the 1870's and 1880's.[116]

Not all rural Hachiōji-area merchants met the same fate as Nakano Kyūjirō with the opening of the ports, but most were forced to refocus their businesses away from the silk cloth trade. Matsui Kōjirō of Shimo-Ongata village, who had handled silk textiles well before the opening of the ports, fared somewhat better than Nakano. He withdrew from the trade but softened the blow to his finances by shifting his attention to moneylending and land accumulation. Many rural elites sought their fortunes in sales of raw silk destined for overseas markets. Sashida Shichirō-emon of Kamikawahara village, for example, shipped raw silk to Yokohama export merchants and purchased large quantities from Kai province. Yarimizu village sustained at least nine raw silk merchants, three of whom made purchases of over 10,000 ryō in the Hachiōji market from 10/1871 to 9/1872.[117]

The gōnō stood at the pinnacle of rural society but at the same time led a very precarious existence. The instability of the silk trade forced them to diversify their operations, into such areas as moneylending, land accumulation, and the retail trade, but this often came at the expense of poorer members of their communities. The silk elites became easy targets for the social unrest that gripped their regions in the final years of Tokugawa rule.

# 6

## Tea and Sake Elites

There are no households where people do not drink tea daily.
Ōkura Nagatsune, *Kōeki kokusankō* (1842)

Not content with inhaling the freshness of the opening flowers, the men
drink deep of *saki*. . . . In the vice of intemperance the Japanese have
nothing to learn from foreigners. . . .They are as much given to
drunkenness as any of the northern races of Europe.
Sir Rutherford Alcock, *The Capital of the Tycoon* (1863)

PROTOINDUSTRIAL GROWTH was initially predicated on demand
in Japan's major towns and cities, but by the nineteenth century a
growing consumer market could be found in scores of villages across the
country. Not only did village merchants and village stores supply such necessities as pots and pans and fertilizers, but they increasingly handled
items that had once been commonplace only in urban centers and rural
markets. They sold confections, fish, clothes, sake, miso, soy sauce, and
tea, and even various cooked foods. The tea and sake industries best reflect changing consumption patterns in rural areas. Growing numbers of
farmers not only began to cultivate tea but became major consumers of
tea. With sake, too, farmers had brewed inferior sakes in their homes in
the past, but increasingly they began to purchase superior brands from local establishments.

Both tea and sake became important products from the mid-Tokugawa. Superior tea cultivation and tea-processing techniques from the Uji
area of the Kinai began to appear in other regions around the country
from the nineteenth century, and the growth of the tea industry was especially rapid after the opening of the ports in 1859. Within a few years tea
had become Japan's second leading export item, surpassed only by raw
silk, and countless thousands of farmers began to cultivate tea for the first
time. Growth in the sake industry was equally impressive. By the late
eighteenth century, rural brewers in the Nadame area of the western Kinai

had become the country's leading producers, and numerous smaller-scale brewers appeared in villages across the country. By the early Meiji, sake was by far the country's most important manufactured item, even surpassing textiles.

This chapter examines two rural elites, Nakayama Motonari in the tea trade and Ishikawa Yahachirō in sake brewing. Both could be counted among the most successful elites in their regions. Nakayama was one of the first to launch into the export trade and became a leading figure in the Ibaraki tea industry. Ishikawa became one of the most successful brewers in the western Kantō. But each faced tremendous obstacles in their rise to prominence. The major problem for those in the tea industry was competition, both from domestic producers and from other Asian tea production centers. Like other influential tea producers, Nakayama made prodigious efforts to improve the quality of local tea, but in the end he was unable to persist in the trade. Ishikawa faced a different hurdle. In an effort to increase its revenue, the Meiji government imposed oppressive taxes on brewers, forcing thousands out of business. He was one of the fortunate few whose business survived through the turbulent years of the Meiji era.

## Nakayama Motonari and the Sashima Tea Trade

Few people today would think of Ibaraki prefecture as an important tea cultivation site, but in the Tokugawa and Meiji periods it could be counted among the country's leading tea regions. In 1881, in fact, it ranked fourth nationwide in tea cultivation. Farmers in Sashima district in southwestern Ibaraki, in particular, cultivated and processed massive amounts of tea, much of which went to Yokohama for export after the opening of the ports in 1859. Nakayama Motonari of Heta village was Sashima's leading producer and in large measure was responsible for Sashima's important position in the tea industry. In the 1830's he introduced Uji teaprocessing methods to his region, and in the Meiji he traveled around the prefecture instructing farmers on proper cultivation and processing techniques. In the 1870's and 1880's he operated a large tea farm and trained a number of workers in his tea-processing facility. In the end, however, his efforts proved fruitless. Ibaraki lost out in the growing competition in domestic and international markets, and by the turn of the century tea had become a declining sector of the area economy.

The Sashima area had much in common with the Mooka bleached cotton cloth region described in Chapter 4. The productivity of Sashima's soil was quite low: the rice yield per *tan* in 1877 was only 0.46 *koku* in Sashima, one-half that of the Mooka area, one of the least productive regions in the northern Kantō.[1] Even at the end of the Meiji period in 1911, Sashima's average rice yields were 1.173 *koku/tan*, about 18 percent below those of Ibaraki as a whole.[2] Sashima villages also witnessed serious population decline. The population of Shimo-Deshima dropped 20 percent from 1706 to 1769, from 109 people to 87. Yahagi village suffered a 22 percent decline over the same period.[3] Also like villagers to their north, Sashima farmers were in many ways self-sufficient, their major crops being rice, barley, and millet. They grew cotton, hemp, and tobacco, some of which might have been for sale in the market, but they were not major products of the area.[4]

Sashima's one important marketable product was tea. Sashima tea cultivation dates from the early seventeenth century. Because of the low productivity of the soil, political authorities in the region recognized tea's important role, not only in providing much-needed revenue to domain coffers but in enabling farmers to earn a livelihood from the soil. Sekiyado domain, which controlled much of the Sashima area, actually encouraged tea cultivation in the 1640's. From time to time it ordered farmers to cultivate more, so that it could increase its tax income.[5] Judging from the manner in which domains taxed tea, it was clearly a profitable item. The political overlord in control of Tanaka village, near the town of Shimodate and to the north of Sashima, assessed the best tea fields at 3 *koku* per *tan*, as compared with 1.2 *koku* for the highest grade paddy fields.[6]

Village records contain scant mention of the extent of tea cultivation. If tea taxes serve as any indication of scale, however, it was without a doubt one of farmers' most important cash crops. Tea taxes in Modo village in 1673 came to 12 *kanmon*, compared with 75 *kanmon* on other dry fields.[7] In many other villages, they averaged about 15 to 20 percent of dry-field crop taxes.[8] Sashima's proximity to Edo, the country's foremost consumer market, elevated tea's economic importance to area farmers. The Tone River, a major transportation artery nearby, facilitated the shipment of tea to the Edo market.

The Nakayama family of Heta village attained prominence in the tea industry from the 1830's, but before this time tea production was only one of several of its pursuits. Little is known of the early history of the family, but it clearly had a distinguished lineage. In the 1620's it owned over 15 *chō* of land, and even after awarding some to a branch household, it remained the most powerful household in the village. Successive heads also served continually in the position of village headman.

Like other rural elites, the Nakayama family engaged in extensive production for the market from the mid-Tokugawa. In 1756 it launched into the brewing industry. In 1825 its licenses stipulated a rice usage of 500 koku, so it obviously operated on a large scale. The family also became active in the forestry industry. It shipped lumber and firewood, some of which it purchased from domain forests, to the Edo market. It also accumulated sizable forest tracts by providing Sekiyado domain large loans and contributions, which the domain repaid in the form of forest land. By 1785 the family had acquired over 160 *chō* of the domain's forests. In the 1810's it started a pawn business. Through profits earned from these various activities, the family acquired sizable lands, some of which it rented out to area farmers. In 1825 it owned about 75 *koku* of land in Heta, about 17 percent of the village's assessed productivity and over nine times greater than the village average. It also had land in several other area villages.[9]

In the 1830's the Nakayama head, Motonari (1818–92), aggressively entered the tea industry on a major scale. In part, this was an attempt to revitalize the fortunes of area farmers. Like other Sashima villages, Heta witnessed a steep drop in its population over the course of the eighteenth century, from 439 in 1706 to 328 in 1770.[10] Equally important, the reputation of Sashima tea had fallen in the Edo market and in markets in the northeast, causing its price and sales to plummet. Its reputation had fallen owing to growing expectations for tea in consumer markets. As improving farmers introduced superior Uji processing techniques to their communities, those regions producing teas using traditional techniques, especially the sun-drying of tea leaves, lost their market share. This was the case with tea produced in the Sashima area.[11] Unable to profit from its sale, many farmers began to abandon or uproot their plants, and there was no viable cash product to take tea's place.[12]

Perhaps, too, Motonari was seeking ways to reingratiate his family into the good graces of his community. Two incidents in the early nineteenth century pitted the family against the village. Farmers in twenty-three Sashima villages, suffering from serious crop failures and damage to their tea plants, petitioned Sekiyado domain in 1810 for a tax reduction. When officials agreed only to a postponement in tax payment, farmers initiated an uprising, demanding a substantial reduction in the annual tax and food relief. Denjirō, then head of the Nakayama household, took the side of the domain and got the farmers to disperse. This was not the way rural elites were expected to act. In the first half of the Tokugawa, village headmen stood firm with their communities in disputes with the outside. When farmers rebelled against the excessive taxation of their ruler, headmen often served as their leaders.

A second incident in 1830 served as a poignant reminder of the tensions that often existed between the village rich and the village poor. Heta villagers filed suit with the domain against the village headman, Nakayama, over ownership of 5 chō of land. Villagers claimed that this was commons and that they needed the wood there to sell in the market, so that they could survive as farmers. The headman, they said, had cut the wood and sold it for his own profit. Nakayama, on the other hand, argued that this was his right, since Sekiyado domain had given the land to his family in reward for contributing funds. The domain ruled in Nakayama's favor.[13] As we saw in Chapter 4, rural elites were in a symbiotic relationship with their communities. Much of their success depended on the existence of a thriving community of farmers enmeshed in market relationships whom they could sell to and purchase from. A serious rupture with their village could threaten the very basis of their survival as rural elites.

Yet another form of self-interest was at work in Motonari's resolve to seek to revitalize the local tea industry. Despite outward signs of prosperity, in the 1820's the family business was in poor health, forcing the sale of its brewing licenses in 1825. Details concerning the family's activities before the 1830's are sketchy, but the area's population decline undoubtedly contributed to the family's problems. With people leaving the village and having fewer children, there were far fewer customers, especially those with the necessary resources, for the family's goods. Katsuta Rinzō, discussed in Chapter 4, faced the same predicament.

To overcome problems in the family business and to elevate farmers' fortunes, Motonari began his self-appointed task of improving the Sashima tea industry. In 1834 he met an Uji tea specialist, Tada Bunpei, in Edo and invited him to his village. The following year Motonari built several hearths for firing tea and began instructing area farmers in Uji processing and tea-picking methods. To process tea in quantity and to ensure a high standard of production, he purchased large amounts of tea leaves from area farmers. From 1834 to 1842 the amount of leaves used in his processing operations increased almost fivefold. He hired several workers in his tea-processing facilities, deploying 400 man-days of labor in 1839 alone. He also began to clear some of his mountain forest land to expand his cultivation of tea.[14]

Despite his growing emphasis on tea cultivation and processing, Motonari continued to engage in diverse economic activities. He perpetuated the family trade in lumber and firewood, for example. With mountain forests amounting to over 210 chō in the 1830's, he could readily obtain whatever the market could bear. Using family members and hired laborers, Motonari cultivated about 0.7 *chō* of his paddy lands and 2 *chō* of his dry fields to meet the food consumption needs of his family and employees. He also received income from the rental of lands; he rented out about 3.6 *chō* of paddy lands alone in 1851.

Motonari had to remain diversified, because his tea operations were not a profit-making venture. In 1849, for example, he had income of 148 *ryō*, most of which came from three sources: 23 *ryō* from tenants' rents, 29 *ryō* from tea sales, and 85 *ryō* from income from his forests. His expenditures that year, however, totaled over 157 *ryō*, and he had about 580 *ryō* in debts. To acquire income and to recover some of his losses, Motonari had to put into pawn some of his forest lands. In 1842 alone he pawned over 38 *chō* of his mountain forests.[15]

Despite a dismal showing, Motonari remained optimistic about the possibilities for expansion of the market for Sashima tea. The prospects of foreign trade were particularly alluring. Motonari's first contact with the West came in 1854, when a bakufu official invited him to Shimoda to observe negotiations with Commodore Matthew C. Perry. In the expectation that Japan would soon be opened to foreign trade, Motonari traveled to Nagasaki in 1855 to learn about the possibilities for trade with and conditions in Europe and the United States. Along the way, he observed those regions renowned for their superior teas. In 1857 he managed to get Townsend Harris's private secretary Henry Heusken to taste Sashima tea. To prepare for the opening of Yokohama, he opened a store in Edo in 1858, and with the commencement of foreign trade the following year, he entered into negotiations with a Western merchant, Francis Hall, using a Chinese as intermediary.[16]

Nakayama was quite successful in the initial stage of the export trade, but he soon encountered several difficulties. The political disturbances of the 1860's were especially crippling to many in the export trade. Radical samurai began to press for the "expulsion of the barbarians," making it difficult for merchants to ship their goods to Yokohama. As Motonari described the situation:

> In 1863 expel-the-barbarian debates and incidents arose, creating a tumultuous climate. As a result . . . tea prices plummeted and merchants suffered losses. I and my companions also failed, leading to the loss of half of my family's assets.[17]

In the fall of 1865 tea sales recovered, and Western merchants briskly competed to buy Japanese tea. Shortly afterward, though, conditions again deteriorated, and Motonari was daily in fear of being killed by "expel-the-barbarian" fanatics. His experience in the export trade proved costly. As a result of massive losses, he was forced to put another 100 *chō* of his mountain forests into pawn between 1863 and 1865. Frustrated by his failure, he closed his Edo store in 1867 and returned home.[18]

The actions of Sekiyado domain undoubtedly contributed to Motonari's plight. As a result of the expansion and improvement of the Sashima tea industry, in 1851 the domain enlisted Motonari's assistance in establishing a tea sales office at its Edo residence. Sashima producers had to take their tea to the domain office, which then sold it to Edo wholesalers. To tighten its hold over Sashima production and to more fully exploit opportunities generated by the opening of the ports, in 1862 officials established monopoly branch offices in the three major towns of the domain and collected a 6 percent commission on all tea sales.[19] For Motonari, the domain monopoly was surely a most unwelcome intrusion into the tea trade. Through the monopoly, the domain sapped many of the profits to be gained through exports.

Upon his return to Heta in 1867, Motonari found himself thrust into the turmoil pitting imperial loyalists against supporters of the bakufu. Sekiyado domain had formed farmers' militia (*nōheitai*) in 1862 to defend both the castle town and the villages against the rampages of masterless samurai and imperial loyalists. As a member of the local militia, Motonari's son Saburō attacked, sometimes killing, marauding samurai. He also aided bakufu forces in suppressing rebellious bands from nearby Mito domain. When imperial loyalists took control of Edo castle in 1868, a number of bakufu supporters fled north, hoping to make their way to Nikkō. Some of these troops camped en route in Heta village, and they took Motonari prisoner, along with a well-known imperial loyalist from the area. Both managed to flee from bakufu troops with the arrival of forces from the new Meiji government.[20] The reasons for Motonari's seizure are not clear—he had close ties with some bakufu officials, and his son, as head of the local militia, had provided food to fleeing bakufu troops—but it does reflect the tremendous disorder gripping the area in the final years of Tokugawa rule.

Despite massive losses in the export trade and his disastrous experiences around the time of the Restoration, the eternally optimistic Motonari did not at all abandon his hopes of developing the local tea industry. In fact, he redoubled his efforts at expanding his tea fields and tea-processing facilities. He increased his groves from about 2 *chō* in the mid-1860's to almost 13 *chō* in 1879. In addition to tea grown on his own

fields, he continued to purchase large quantities of tea leaves and processed tea from area farmers.[21]

After the Restoration, Motonari became an enthusiastic supporter of
the encouragement-of-industry initiatives of the central and prefectural
governments. From 1869 to 1870 he served as an official (goyōgakari) in
the Tokyo Products' Bureau (Bussankyoku), where he worked to encourage the tea industry and to improve the quality of Japanese teas. He did
much the same as an encouragement-of-industry official for the prefectural administrations in control of the Sashima area. As an official for Inba
prefecture in 1872 and for Chiba prefecture in 1873, he traveled to villages within their jurisdictions, instructing farmers on how to clear fields
for tea groves, proper processing techniques, and methods to market their
tea.[22] He also wrote two brief treatises in 1873. In his tract on tea cultivation, he espoused the merits of clearing new fields for tea cultivation.[23]

Motonari's ties with Ibaraki prefecture, which assumed jurisdiction
over the Sashima area in 1875, were especially close. As a prefectural encouragement-of-industry official in 1880–81, he traveled throughout the
region and wrote countless reports. He described such things as the weather conditions each month, the types of activities in which farmers engaged,
and the state of tea production and the tea market.[24]

Motonari benefited greatly from this relationship with Ibaraki. Together with his son Saburō, he petitioned the prefecture in 1880 for an in-
terest-free 4,000 yen loan to hire workers from the two leading production regions, Kyoto (Uji) and Shizuoka, to train area farmers in the proper
processing techniques, as well as to develop a 20 chō experimental farm
through the clearing of some of his mountain forests. The prefecture approved a loan for half the amount requested. Despite the noble intentions,
self-interest was an important motivating factor behind his petition. While
seeking to diffuse superior techniques to his locality, Motonari hoped to per-
sonally profit through expanded tea production.[25] In 1885 Motonari and
Saburō received an additional loan of 700 yen to support their training facility and experimental farm.[26] These were perks that few others received.
As we saw in Chapter 1, prefectures were quite parsimonious in dispens-
ing encouragement-of-industry funds.

The family's close relationship with Ibaraki came despite Saburō's active participation in the Popular Rights Movement. After serving in various assemblies at the local level, Saburō was elected to the Ibaraki prefectural assembly in 1879. He and others clashed repeatedly with prefectural
officials over the budget and other policies. Saburō also headed a local

group of activists known as the Kainaisha, which was dedicated to extending popular rights, safeguarding people's welfare, and promoting local enlightenment (*chihō kaimei*). Members met once a month to discuss issues of concern and invited activists from other parts of the country to speak. The Kainaisha was particularly active in demanding the establishment of a nationally elected assembly.[27] Saburō's activities obviously had little bearing on Ibaraki's decision to finance the family's projects. Officials surely recognized Motonari's indispensable role in the improvement of the Ibaraki tea industry.

Largely through the efforts of improving farmers like Nakayama Motonari, Sashima district strengthened its position as one of the country's leading tea cultivation regions. In 1877 processed tea accounted for 17.9 percent of the value of all products in the district, following rice, barley, and wheat.[28] The extent of tea cultivation had also increased exponentially. Two-thirds of the tea fields in 1883 in Shimōsa province, where Sashima is located, had only been started within the previous decade.[29] The quality of its tea ranked among the country's best. Although Sashima tea brought a lower price in 1884 than tea from Suruga and Sayama, it surpassed that from other important production regions, including Tōtōmi and Ise.[30]

While thoroughly immersed in the tea industry, the family continued to engage in diverse economic activities. In 1877 it owned 18.26 *chō* of paddies and dry fields. With the exception of its tea groves, however, the family cultivated very little land itself; instead, it rented most of it out to others. Its residence alone covered 0.9 *chō*, about twice the size of most villagers' farms.[31] Motonari also continued in the lumber and firewood trade, though he had put into pawn or sold off all but 43.3 *chō* of his mountain forests in the decade bracketing the Meiji Restoration because of problems in his tea business.

Despite his Herculean efforts, Motonari's tea business continued to falter, and from 1882 he gradually distanced himself from the industry. In 1886 his tea grove acreage had declined from a peak of 20 *chō* earlier in the decade to 10 *chō*. It declined further still in later years, falling to 6 *chō* in 1888. The amount of tea the family processed fell from a high of 3,500 *kanme* in 1881 to only 412 *kanme* in 1889.[32] By the late 1890's the family had largely withdrawn from tea cultivation and processing.

There were several reasons for Motonari's abandonment of the tea industry, but the low price of tea was the most serious problem. Although no continuous price data are available for Sashima tea, the price for Shizuoka tea on the Tokyo market plummeted by almost half between 1873 and 1878.[33] Declining prices stemmed from both growing competition, domestic and international, and the production of inferior teas. Japan's tea industry simply could not compete with the massive tea plantations being established in such places as India and Ceylon. At the same time, as growing numbers of Japanese farmers began to cultivate and process tea for the first time, they were forced to compete among themselves for an ever-constricting market overseas.

The production of inferior teas plagued Japan's tea industry from the opening of the ports. Farmers, most of whom were making their first venture into the industry, produced tea with little concern for quality. In response to a prefectural inquiry in 1881 concerning ways to improve the Ibaraki tea industry, respondents uniformly cited the production of inferior teas as a most serious problem. Ibaraki farmers mixed in dirt and green vitriol with their teas, and because of high prices for charcoal and firewood, some had reverted back to old processing methods, especially sun-drying. Nakayama Motonari suggested that unscrupulous merchants, domestic and foreign, compounded the problem. Seeking to profit from the moment, they cared little about the quality of the tea they sold.[34] Poor quality was hardly a problem unique to Ibaraki. The same complaints were lodged against Shizuoka's tea farmers, who sometimes laced their teas with willow and vine leaves and applied various dyes.[35]

Ibaraki's preeminent tea producers suggested three remedial measures: the enactment of tough regulations concerning product quality, the formation of companies, and the establishment of tea cooperatives.[36] Ibaraki prefecture does not appear to have ever enacted measures to control the production of inferior teas, and it is not at all clear that they would have had much effect. Hamamatsu prefecture in the Shizuoka area enacted very tough regulations on its tea producers and tea merchants in 1874, but they had to be abandoned within a few months. Producers and merchants, especially those with links to the Popular Rights Movement, vigorously protested government interference in private industry.[37]

A few large-scale Ibaraki producers formed companies to combat the production of inferior teas, but for the most part these were "inspection companies." Producers submitted their teas to the company for inspection, grading, and collective sales, and the companies also offered guidance to area farmers on proper processing methods.[38] Nakayama's own tea operations were clearly on a "factory" scale, despite the extremely seasonal nature of tea processing. All such "companies," though, could enjoy only limited success in correcting abuses without the participation of a majority of the area's producers. If large numbers of farmers produced inferior teas, the entire region's reputation suffered in domestic and international markets, regardless of the existence of a few superior producers.

The formation of tea producers' cooperatives was a far more efficacious solution to the quality control problem. Ibaraki producers first formed such cooperatives in 1884, and Motonari served as the initial director of the prefectural organization. It proved no easy matter, however, getting producers into such groups. Ibaraki farmers cultivated and processed tea on a very small scale, to supplement their income from other agricultural pursuits. They made little from the sale of their tea, and few were willing to sacrifice a portion of their already small profits to the cooperatives.[39]

Again, the above problems were not unique to the Sashima area. What did set Sashima apart, and compounded its tea producers' difficulties in earning a profit, was the poor quality of the soil. As with its paddy lands, Sashima tea fields were far less productive than those in other parts of the country. The tea yield per *tan* in Sashima, in fact, was only about one-third that of Shizuoka prefecture and one-fifth that of the Kyoto metropolitan area.[40] Because of poor soil quality, Sashima farmers had to apply liberal amounts of cash fertilizers, especially on newly reclaimed lands, thus reducing their profits all the more. This was clearly the case on Motonari's fields, where the labor and fertilizer requirements on his reclaimed lands were far greater than on his older fields.[41] With declining tea prices, it proved difficult even for farmers operating on a large scale to earn a minimal profit.

In place of tea cultivation and processing, the Nakayama household shifted its focus to land accumulation. Though forced to sell some of its lands in the 1880's to recoup losses from the tea industry, in the 1890's it turned its attention back to the land. In 1893 it owned within Heta village itself 2.5 *chō* of paddy lands, 15.5 *chō* of dry fields, and 47 *chō* of mountain forests.[42] Although no information is available on the family's activities in the early twentieth century, we can assume, in the light of its acquisition of forest lands, that it also continued in the lumber trade.

Like Nakayama, most Sashima farmers abandoned tea in the 1890's and early years of the twentieth century. Some switched to another cash crop, tobacco, and others turned to sericulture and raw silk production, but these products never came to dominate the area economy to the same degree as tea once had. By 1912 tea had become relatively insignificant, accounting for less than 5 percent of the value of all agricultural products.[43] And farmers continued to produce an inferior product. As in the past, they mixed other leaves with their tea, and few applied the fertilizers necessary to obtain a superior crop.[44]

The Sashima area became further crippled with the advent of the railroad age. As railroads came to monopolize the transport of goods nationwide, especially by the early twentieth century, those areas without railroads suffered. Sashima elites lost out in their repeated bids to bring a railroad through the area. Proximity to the Tone River, which had served the region so well in the past, signified little in this new age of mass transportation, and the government neglected riparian repairs. Like Ibaraki as a whole, the Sashima area had thoroughly deindustrialized by the end of the Meiji era, with the production of staple grains dominating the local economy.[45]

## Ishikawa Yahachirō and Sake Brewing in the Western Kantō

Sake was one of the leading growth sectors of the protoindustrial economy. By the nineteenth century countless large and small breweries dotted the countryside, meeting growing demand not only in towns and cities but in the rural areas themselves. The same process occurred in the western Kantō, where dozens of brewers appeared in villages throughout the region. The Ishikawa family was one of these new brewing houses. Successive Ishikawa heads, adopting the hereditary name Yahachirō, served as headman of the bakufu-controlled segment of Kumagawa village in Musashi province, currently part of Fussa city in western Tokyo.[46] After a short but successful stint in the cloth trade, the family began producing sake in 1863. By the end of the Meiji, it had become one of the region's premier brewers, having survived not a few crises along the way.

Throughout the latter half of the Tokugawa, textiles, not sake, dominated the local economy. Situated in the greater Hachiōji area, Kumagawa was well situated to take advantage of the opportunities offered by the local textile industry. The earliest record detailing conditions in the village, dating to 1760, notes that women wove Ōme striped cloth, a silk/cotton blend, while men cut grasses (magusa) and firewood. Farmers cultivated mulberry trees and engaged in sericulture on a small scale, and there was also one carpenter.[47] These side industries were undoubtedly critical to the village economy. There were hardly any rice paddies in the village, and the quality of its soil was poor.

By the nineteenth century growing immersion in the market had spawned important changes to the village economy. Sericulture and the weaving of Ōme cloth continued as vital side industries, but a number of new occupations appeared that had little to do with farming. In addition to three carpenters, one sawyer, and one cooper, two Kumagawa merchants sold sake and *soba*, two specialized in grains in the Itsukaichi market, two handled salt and fish, and two dealt in used clothes.[48] In an 1829 document the transformation of village life becomes all the more apparent. Of 144 households in the village as a whole, 52 engaged in occupations in addition to agriculture. There were six establishments serving sake and one selling it retail. The oldest had started business forty-five years earlier and another forty years earlier, but the remaining were newcomers, having commenced within the previous eleven years.[49]

Since there were as yet no brewers in the village, the Kumagawa establishments had to purchase their sake from brewers in other villages. Two families with close ties to the Ishikawa household, the Morita family of Ogawa village, across the Tama River from Kumagawa, and the Tamura family in neighboring Fussa village, were both important brewers in the area. The Morita family had been engaged in brewing from an early date, perhaps from the 1660's, and operated on a fairly large scale, using 432 *koku* of rice in its brewing operations in 1787. The Tamura family only started in brewing in 1822 but by the end of the Tokugawa had become one of the Kantō's largest brewers.

Greater immersion in the market economy created a growing chasm between the village rich and the village poor. The size of the gulf was abundantly apparent in a survey the Ishikawa head undertook in 1869 at the behest of Shinagawa prefecture, which had just assumed jurisdiction over the area. As part of a food relief system instituted that year, Shinagawa ordered farmers to submit a portion of their harvest every year, which the prefecture would use to provide relief during times of need. It requested headmen to classify villagers into four ranks, based on their resources: the top rank included those with over 5 *koku* of land, and there were three categories of poorer farmers with less than 5 *koku*. The methods Ishikawa used to classify farmers are not known, but size of landholdings was only one of the determinants used. This is clear from the fact that a few farmers appeared in higher-ranking categories who owned smaller holdings than those in lower categories. Appendix Table 15 shows the results of Ishikawa's survey.

There was a clear disparity in the fortunes of Kumagawa households. The thirty-one families in the top rank comprised 21 percent of the households but owned almost 56 percent of the land. The bottom three ranks, comprising half of the households, owned only 16.5 percent of the land. Judging from their landholdings, they had become thoroughly semiproletarianized. Owning insufficient fields, they tenanted the lands of others and hired themselves out as laborers. This is clear from an 1870 report on village conditions. The primary side industry for men in the slack season was not cutting grasses and firewood, as in the past, but packhorse work and daily wage labor.[50]

Despite the existence of a large segment of poorer farmers, the gap between rich and poor was far smaller than in many other villages around the time of the Meiji Restoration. Ishikawa, with 18.2 *koku*, owned the most land in Kumagawa, and seven other families owned over 10 *koku*, but they were hardly on the scale of many rural elites, including others in our case studies. Consider, for example, Nakano Kyūjirō of nearby Nakagami village, discussed in the previous chapter. Nakano owned about 23 *chō* in 1850, or 30 percent of village lands. This probably explains why Kumagawa experienced few of the tensions, indeed the tremendous class conflict, of the 1860's. As a consequence, he was spared the destruction the Nakano family suffered in the uprising that swept the western Kantō in 1866.

Despite the tremendous changes in the area's economy, the Ishikawa household was slow to take advantage of the opportunities the market offered. Although hailing from distinguished lineage and having successive heads serving in the position of headman, the family was at best modestly involved in market production until 1839, when Wakichi assumed the headship. Its landholdings in 1869 were not much different from those 100 or even 200 years before.

Like the Nakayama family, the Ishikawas engaged in diverse economic activities. Agriculture was its primary pursuit. The family cultivated its own lands, using a combination of family and hired labor. From the notations in a diary maintained by Kamesaburō (b. 1778), who served as family head from 1800 to 1839, the family planted a few cash crops, such as cotton, tea, and mulberry trees, but the crops were primarily for use by the household itself, not for sale in the market.[51] Kamesaburō oversaw all aspects of the family business, but other family members and employees carried out much of the actual work in the fields and around the house. One employee, Senzō, was a jack-of-all-trades. He worked in the fields, undertook repairs around the house, helped in the spring cleaning, and made rope and reed mats.[52]

Kamesaburō engaged in charcoal sales, but this was largely through the happenstance of marriage. His wife's family was one of the area's largest charcoal manufacturers.[53] He also loaned money, but he could hardly be considered a typical moneylender. Most of the loan notations in his 1832 diary were for amounts of less than 1 *ryō*, and they went primarily to farmers in his community.[54] Though the family was prominent in local politics, it could hardly be counted among the western Kantō's elite business families.

The most important side industries for the family were sericulture and weaving. A copy of the introduction to Tsukada Yoemon's 1757 sericultural treatise remains among the family papers, suggesting that it consciously worked to introduce superior techniques.[55] In the 1820's Kamesaburō sold about half of his cocoons and used the remainder to reel silk, from which the family wove silks and silk/cotton blends. Judging from notations in his diary concerning their sale, neither cocoon production nor weaving was carried out on a large scale. His cocoon sales in the 1820's and 1830's ranged from only 5 to 14 *ryō*. He also sold about 10 *tan* of cloth every year, far more than most farm families produced, but hardly sufficient to generate wealth.[56]

With cocoon production, in particular, the family relied heavily on assistance provided by neighbors. According to Kamesaburō's diary entry for 6/1/1832, over thirty neighbors came to the family's aid when its silkworms were spinning their cocoons.[57] When the neighbors needed similar assistance, Kamesaburō sent family members to help out.[58] Neighbors also provided labor when Kamesaburō's rice was ready to be transplanted.[59] Here, too, we find strong ties between the Ishikawa family and others in the community.

It was only upon Wakichi's assumption of the headship in 1839 that the Ishikawa family embarked into rural commerce. Family connections played an essential role in this transformation of the family business. Being childless, Kamesaburō in 1835 adopted as his heir Wakichi from the Sashida family of Kamikawahara village. Sashida was one of the area's leading families and was very active in commerce, especially in the cocoon and raw silk trade. Even after being adopted into the Ishikawa household, Wakichi maintained close ties with his house of birth, and in the initial years after his adoption he returned home from time to time to assist his older brother in the family trade. Wakichi's brother Sashida Jūhei in 1838 became the adopted heir of the Tamura family of Fussa village, another powerful local household, active in the sake industry since 1822.[60] The ties between the Ishikawa and Tamura households were further solidified in 1865, when Wakichi, lacking a male heir, took in as adopted son-in-law Chiyozō (b. 1849), the third son of his brother, Tamura Jūhei.[61] Having close ties with two of the leading families in the region, Sashida and Tamura, signaled an auspicious start to Wakichi's management of the Ishikawa household.

With extensive experience in the Sashida business, Wakichi immediately took the Ishikawa family into the cloth trade. In 1841 he sold over 1,000 *tan* of cloth annually, which he purchased from farm families and sold to merchants operating out of the local markets.[62] Although on a far smaller scale than merchants like Nakano Kyūjirō, Wakichi's trade was of far greater magnitude than most cloth merchants in the area.

Wakichi also started a pawn business in 1849.[63] Pawn shops were an indispensable part of village life in the late Tokugawa, and almost every village in the western Kantō had one. Whenever farmers needed cash, they would put into pawn one or more of their possessions, often an item not currently in use, such as a formal garment or a mosquito net out of season. They usually reclaimed their items within a year, but farmers steeped in debt often had to let them go unredeemed.[64] Considering that Ishikawa and other pawn brokers charged 20 percent interest on the pawn items they took in, this is hardly surprising.[65] In general, however, Ishikawa faced few of the tensions with his community that other rural elites encountered. Family heads maintained close ties with their neighbors and provided them relief in time of need.

The greatest departure in the family business came in 1863, when Ishikawa Wakichi rented a brewery from the Morita family of Ogawa. From the beginning, Wakichi's brewing facility was closely tied to the brewing operations of his brother Tamura Jūhei, and he used the Tamura logo on his sake. Several other breweries shared a similar relationship with Tamura. Between 1839 and 1889, in fact, the Tamura "group" (*tanauchi*) consisted of thirty-five facilities in villages throughout the western Kantō. Included within the Tamura group were those related by blood and those who rented facilities from the family. Tamura Gin'emon, for example, branched from the main family in the 1830's and received funds to rent and eventually purchase a brewing facility. Iwajirō, on the other hand, was completely unrelated to the Tamura family. He served as one of its brewmasters and eventually rented a brewing facility from the family.

The skillful deployment of relatives and close associates was an important means by which Tokugawa-period brewers oftentimes expanded their operations. Rather than increasing the size of their facilities to benefit from economies of scale, they added new facilities through the purchase or rental of brewing licenses and breweries. As shown in Mark Fruin's study of Kikkoman, the Mogi family of Noda employed a similar strategy in the soy sauce industry. Rather than establishing branch houses in diverse industries so as to minimize competition, Mogi used household branching as a device to expand his total capacity in the same industry.[66]

The most important role of the Tamura group head was in extending financing to the individual brewers. According to Ishikawa's brewing ledgers, annual interest on loans, presumably from the Tamura household, ranged from about 61 *ryō* to 600 *ryō* over the period 1865 to 1889.[67] Also, those running the breweries, like Ishikawa Wakichi, met once a year with Tamura to go over their accounts. They also convened meetings when serious problems arose. When it was discovered, for example, that the manager of Ishikawa's Ogawa brewery had misappropriated 300 *ryō* to engage in moneylending, the brewery heads within the Tamura group launched an investigation and sent the manager to another facility.[68] In other ways, the breweries appear to have been relatively independent in the day-to-day operation of their facilities. When Ishikawa sold his sake, for example, he shipped only a small portion, often less than 10 percent of the total brewed, to Tamura.[69] He sold the remaining sake to whomever he pleased.

The Ishikawa family ran the Ogawa sake facility for ten years, until 1873, when it moved its operations to a new plant in Kumagawa itself. Sales of the family sake increased steadily over the course of the Meiji, growing from 934 *ryō* in 1865 to 7,224 in 1889, and the family operated in the black for all but five of the twenty-five years. But in the 1880's the outlook for its operations appeared rather bleak. As a result of a marked growth in sales through the late 1870's, the family decided to build a new, larger, facility in Kumagawa itself, but this timing proved most inopportune. The Matsukata deflation hit the brewing industry hard, and Ishikawa faced successive years of operating in the red. Recovery only came from 1886, but even thereafter profits were sluggish for several years.

In addition to the Matsukata deflation, one of the primary reasons for Ishikawa's difficulties was the onerous taxes the Meiji government levied on the industry. As we saw in Chapter 1, the leadership increased the sake tax with almost every passing year. Between 1871 and 1880 the yearly operating fee increased from five to thirty yen. The tax on sake sales leaped from 5 percent in 1871 to 10 percent in 1875. The government replaced the tax on sake sales in 1878 with a tax of one yen per *koku* of sake brewed. In 1883 it increased the tax to 4 yen per *koku* and to 20 yen in 1908. All these taxes were levied on the brewer, not on the consumer.

The new taxes placed a tremendous burden on brewers. In the early 1870's rice was by far the most costly item among Ishikawa's brewing outlays, accounting for 50–60 percent of the total, while sake taxes comprised only 2.5 percent. In 1885 rice accounted for about 44 percent and sake taxes for 31.5 percent.[70] This was another reason why Ishikawa decided to build the new brewing facility. Under growing pressure from taxation, he sought to take advantage of economies of scale and lower overall operating costs.

All brewers faced tremendous instability, as a result of both bakufu curtailment orders and burdensome taxation in the Meiji. Of the thirty-five breweries in the Tamura group over the period 1839–89, twelve remained in business for ten years or less. Nine abandoned brewing in the turbulent decade preceding the Meiji Restoration, and another thirteen went under in the 1880's. There were only twelve breweries remaining in the group in 1889.[71] Beset by insurmountable difficulties, the Tamura head decided to dissolve the group in 1903.[72] The individual brewers remained in business, though now on an independent footing.

Tremendous instability was one reason why so many brewers engaged in other activities at the same time. Even into the 1890's, for example, the Ishikawa family continued to engage in cocoon production. In 1893 the family and its employees produced cocoons that brought a net profit of about 13 yen.[73] Sericulture and cocoon production had become all the more important to Kumagawa's economy since the opening of the ports, and several filatures were started there beginning in the 1870's.[74] The family also continued to cultivate some of its lands, using a combination of household and hired labor.[75] Profits from these activities paled in comparison to those obtained from its sake operations, but rural elites such as Ishikawa continued to see the need for multifarious business activities. If one of their activities proved a failure, at least they would have some other activity to fall back on.

The volatility of the sake industry also explains why Ishikawa Chiyozō embarked into the beer industry in 1887. An American of Norwegian extraction, W. Copeland, started Japan's beer industry around 1869–70, and by the early Meiji dozens of Japanese brewers could be found throughout the greater Tokyo-Yokohama area. Beer had obvious allure. It served as a potent symbol of *bunmei kaika*, or "civilization and enlightenment," one of the slogans of early to mid-Meiji modernizers who wanted to propel their country into the front ranks of the world's leading powers. Ishikawa Chiyozō no doubt felt some of this passion. Together with his older brother, he got a Western-style haircut in the foreign concessions area of Yokohama in 1872.[76] The fact that beer did not become an object of taxation until 1901 contributed to its appeal.[77] Sake brewers saddled with onerous taxes found the production of beer enticing, despite high startup costs. Ishikawa Chiyozō's initial plant, equipment, and raw material costs came to over 5,000 yen, and his beermaster received an annual salary of 200 yen, about three times the salary of his sake brewmaster.[78]

Ishikawa made his foray into beer brewing through the assistance of yet another powerful household in the area, the Yamaguchi Chūjirō family of Toyota village (Hino city). Chūjirō brewed sake for the Tamura group and had started in the beer industry only a few months earlier. Before Chiyozō became the Ishikawa heir, Wakichi in 1858 had brought Chūjirō into his household as his adopted son-in-law, but Chūjirō soon had to return with Wakichi's daughter to take over the headship of the Yamaguchi house. Despite the disorder this caused in the Ishikawa succession, the two families remained on close terms thereafter, and Chūjirō provided the Ishikawa family valuable assistance when it launched into beer production. The two families, in fact, sometimes advertised their beers together.

Under the trademark Japan Beer, Ishikawa sold his product primarily to establishments in Tokyo and Yokohama, because beer was not yet a popular beverage in rural areas. The entire venture proved a costly failure. In a six-month period in 1888, he sold only 1,212 large bottles of beer and 414 small bottles. Also, the bottle caps he used sometimes cracked under pressure, and he had enormous problems collecting money on his beer sales. He abandoned beer production after being in the business for less than two years.[79]

Perhaps because of its failure in the beer industry, from the late 1880's the Ishikawa family made a conscious attempt to modernize its sake operations. Ishikawa Taisuke (b. 1871), in particular, brought the family business into the modern age. Taisuke received a modern education in local schools and in 1891 entered the Nishinomiya Brewing School, where he learned both the advanced techniques of Nadame breweries and modern management principles. Taisuke's philosophy was that brewing should not be simply entrusted to brewmasters. Owners had to take an active role in the management of their facilities, and brewing itself had to be based on modern scientific methods.[80]

Largely as a result, the Ishikawa brewery soon recovered from the problems of the 1880's. In 1889 the Kumagawa brewery had higher sales than any other in the Tamura group, including the brewery Tamura himself operated. Ishikawa's operations continued to expand in later years. Between 1889 and 1896 both its income from sales and its total production volume increased over fivefold. It won a prize for its sake at the Fourth National Encouragement of Industry Exhibition in 1894, and it began to make increasing inroads into the Tokyo market.[81] In 1907 it brewed over 3,000 koku of sake.[82] The family's brewery operated on a much smaller scale than those in the Nadame area, where thirteen brewers produced over 5,000 *koku* in 1895, but for the Tokyo area Ishikawa Brewery was among the largest.[83]

Income from land rents was another important component of rural elites' activities. The Tamura family, for example, became one of the area's most powerful landlords, with over 257 *chō* of land in 1890. It also owned stocks in banks and railroads valued at 34,770 yen.[84] The Ishikawa family, too, engaged in land accumulation, though not on such a grand scale. In 1871 it owned only about 2.1 *chō*, primarily dry fields in Kumagawa itself.[85] Judging from its land certificates, it owned over 16.6 *chō* of paddies and dry fields around 1900. About half of these fields were obtained through land clearings along the Tama River, which Wakichi and others undertook from 1867 to 1882. In addition, the family owned about 17.8 *chō* of mountain lands and 8.5 *chō* of uncultivated grasslands (*shibachi*), and it held certificates for 1.9 *chō* of lands once belonging to the Yamaguchi and Tsuchiya families.[86]

Ishikawa's land accumulation brought him into conflict with poorer members of the community, just as it had with other rural elites a half a century before. In 1907, for example, he faced the wrath of angry tenants suffering from crop failure whom he had removed from his lands for failure to pay their rents. All tenants in the village decided to boycott the cultivation of his fields for one year. Faced with the loss of significant income from tenancy rents, Ishikawa caved in and apologized to his tenants for his action.[87]

## Conclusion

Diversification was a hallmark of all rural elites' business operations, and it was nowhere so evident as in the activities of the Nakayama and Ishikawa families. Despite Nakayama's total immersion in the cause of Sashima tea and the expansion of his tea fields and processing facilities, he continued to engage in other activities, especially the lumber industry and landlord operations. The same was true of the Ishikawa household. Even after building a large brewing facility, the family persisted in activities in which it had engaged well over one hundred years before, such as sericulture. In the Meiji period it added landlord operations and the brewing of beer to its other activities, rather than specializing in sake alone. Both families also continued to cultivate their own lands well into the Meiji period.

Rural elites in the sake and tea industries had little choice but to remain diversified, because the economic climate was far too volatile. Tea producers faced growing competition in domestic and international markets, causing prices to plummet. They also faced the problem of inferior production. Japan's system of small family farms made it difficult to produce goods of uniform standard and quality. Producers in the raw silk industry solved this problem either by establishing modern filatures, as in Nagano, Yamanashi, and Aichi, or by instituting producers' cooperatives, as was the case in Gunma. Some tea regions, such as Shizuoka, eventually established modern tea-processing factories with mechanized machinery, as well as powerful producers' cooperatives. Ibaraki producers, however, were unable to make the transformation and lost out in the increasing competition.

Sake brewers faced a different set of problems. Many went out of business during periods of political and economic uncertainty, as in the years preceding the Restoration and the early 1880's. Equally disastrous for brewers were the policies of the new Meiji government. A growing portion of brewers' annual expenditures went to the central government in the form of taxes. Only brewers who were able to modernize and take advantage of economies of scale survived.

Our examination of the Ishikawa family illustrates the importance of family connections in some rural elites' business operations. The ties Ishikawa Kamesaburō forged with the Tamura family, in particular, were critical in his family's later entry into the sake industry. The loans he received from Tamura, too, undoubtedly tided the family over in years of uncertainty. Its connection with the Yamaguchi family facilitated its launch into beer brewing. These ties were enduring. A century later, in 1988, the wife of the president of Ishikawa Brewing, Ishikawa Yahachirō, hailed from the Morita household, his mother from the Tamura household, and a grandmother from the Yamaguchi household.[88]

All rural elites maintained close ties with other rural elites, especially through the institution of marriage. Not all were so closely wedded in business as the Ishikawa and Tamura households, but such connections were critical in the successful functioning of their business endeavors. The extension of loans was especially important, as we saw in our case study of the Nakano family in the previous chapter. Equally important, these ties, whether in the form of interrelated businesses or financing, served to set the rural elite apart from others in their villages. The Ishikawa family closely nurtured ties with poorer Kumagawa residents, at least until the early years of the twentieth century, but this was not the case with most rural elites. The *gōnō* were of their communities but not always a part of them.

# Conclusion

Item. If the master of the household conducts himself poorly, if he has a fondness for ostentation and extravagance, or if he indulges in entertainments, and he completely neglects the family business, then his brothers [*ichizoku*] and related households [*fudai no mono*] should carefully deliberate and force him into retirement. . . .

Item. All things, from the fields, mountain thickets, the house and its contents, money, rice, and wheat and barley, are not our personal possessions. For generations they have been entrusted from our ancestors down to our parents. Now I have been bestowed the honor of taking care of them, and I will entrust them to my children. . . .

Item. Frugality means to be moderate in appearance, to ensure that one's wife and children are warned to practice economy, to grant such luxuries as clothing, playthings, food and drink, and amusements, but to prohibit splendor in residence, worldly goods, tidings [*otozure*], and gifts.

Ono Family House Codes, Fukuda Village (1795)

TO HEAD A GŌNŌ HOUSEHOLD was a most serious undertaking, requiring unflagging dedication to all aspects of the family business and household management. Few were successful in maintaining their household's prosperity in the long run. Political authorities' onerous exactions, their region's loss of market share, market volatility, and instability in headship propelled many wealthy families into steep decline and others into drastic changes in the nature of their businesses. The Ono family knew full well just how volatile Japan's protoindustrial economy could be. Despite owning over 500 *koku* of land, the head found it necessary to compile precepts to be followed by current and future family members. If everyone maintained constant vigilance, he perhaps thought, they would be more fortunate than others. He was wrong. In the 1830's the family faced insurmountable problems deriving from declining profits from cotton cultivation, high wages for agricultural laborers, and a shortage of tenants to cultivate its fields.[1]

The *gōnō* initiated many of the changes ushering in the volatile protoindustrial economy. They introduced new forms of side industry to their communities and improved upon existing techniques. They traveled oftentimes long distances to learn superior techniques or to purchase better seeds and seedlings. Some composed agricultural treatises and kept detailed agricultural diaries for the purpose of improving techniques and yields. Virtually every region of Japan had these improving farmers. Largely as a result of their efforts, the Kinai lost its dominance in some of the country's most important areas of production, including the weaving of luxury silks, cotton cultivation and weaving, the brewing of refined sake, and the production of superior teas. By the nineteenth century, farmers in most areas of the country produced goods for sale in distant markets. The opening of the ports stimulated some sectors of the economy all the more, affording growing numbers of farmers the opportunity to benefit from the sale of their goods in international markets.

The gōnō were also the beneficiaries of the changes in regional production patterns. Advances in agricultural productivity and the introduction of new forms of production generated higher levels of surplus, enabling them to increase their economic fortunes. As the conduits linking the production regions with centers of consumption, the gōnō performed an invaluable function in rural society. The ties they established with powerful merchants in the cities spurred the growth of production, providing farmers with an important source of outside income.

By the end of the nineteenth century, the protoindustrial era had come to a close, especially with the advent of mechanized factories in many of the important production regions. So, too, did the era of the gōnō. Several institutional innovations obviated the need for improving farmers. Government and private institutes conducted research on improved techniques in modern laboratories, and agricultural specialists with scientific training assumed the leadership of local agricultural societies. By selling directly to consumer markets and export ports, producers' cooperatives and modern factories undercut a once vital rural elite activity, interregional commerce. Many gōnō found investments in areas outside agriculture, such as modern industry, banks, and railroads, far more profitable and largely abandoned the cultivation of their own lands. Others amassed sizable landholdings and lived off the rents of their tenants.

As with any economic system, there was no decisive closure to the protoindustrial era. Well into the twentieth century, many Japanese engaged, and continue to engage even today, in protoindustrial-like activities, whether in weaving, the making of briefcases, or the manufacture of automotive parts. Similar conditions obtained in many European countries. In France, for example, the advent of modern industry did not displace protoindustry but often perpetuated it and encouraged new forms, and many industries did not witness mechanization at all until the twentieth century.[2] But at the same time, the Japanese economy was a much different entity, both in qualitative and quantitative terms, in the twentieth century than before. Especially when viewed through the lens of the rural elite, the world was now a much different place.

Volatility was a hallmark of Japan's protoindustrial economy, and few *gōnō* survived intact into the industrial era. My case studies of the Fukami, Nakano, and Ōhashi families illustrate how critical headship was to the success of their businesses. The household steward had to be continually attuned to market supply and demand and to cultivate close ties with other merchants, both locally and in distant parts of the country. There was some flexibility in the headship system. If there were no sons, or if a son was unsuited to assume the headship, for example, the head would adopt an heir. But there were no real safeguards against the head's or the heir's own premature demise. Nor were there guarantees that future heads would maintain a steadfast devotion to the preservation and expansion of the family businesses.

Crop failures were another element of instability. The *gōnō* obviously suffered because they were farmers themselves, although the relative weight of this activity declined as they became involved in other activities. More important, such disasters devastated the primary pillar sustaining the *gōnō* in positions of economic consequence, smallholders. When crop failures struck, smallholders were unable to pay their taxes, forcing them to borrow from farmers of means. If crop failures occurred in successive years, it was not at all unusual for smallholders to default on their loans. Bankrupt smallholders also lacked the resources to purchase goods sold by the wealthy. Finally, when there was damage to the cotton or mulberry crop, the *gōnō* had far less to sell in distant markets.

The policies of political authorities, too, greatly influenced the activities of village elites, as we saw in Chapter 1. From the mid-eighteenth century, domains called upon their wealthier residents for contributions and loans, and their requests came with growing frequency. As we saw with the Nakano and Ōhashi families (Chapter 5), political authorities' demands became a tremendous drain on *gōnō* resources. Through monopolies, domains sought to appropriate much of the surplus generated from increasing market production within their territories. Although a number of rural merchants increased their economic fortunes as a result of being appointed as officials overseeing these monopolies, those outside the official purchasing networks often went bankrupt. It was only with the overthrow of the Tokugawa regime in 1868 that these policies and exactions were abolished, but sake brewers found no relief whatsoever with the establishment of the Meiji state.

The introduction of new or improved forms of production also generated stiff competition among production regions and their rural elites for market share. The decline of a production region could easily signal the demise of its rural elite, who had their foundations in the market economy. In an attempt to save themselves and their regions, many called upon political authorities for protection against competition. They also formed guilds to restrict newcomers to the trade and to improve the quality of goods bound for outside markets. This market competition intensified over the course of the protoindustrial era and became especially pronounced in key sectors of the economy with the opening of the ports. By the end of the Meiji era, only those regions with a strong competitive advantage—whether in the form of mechanization, superior product, market niche, or, in the case of tea, relatively high levels of land productivity—survived.

The machinations of city wholesalers were yet another source of instability. From the early to mid-eighteenth century, merchants in the "three cities" extended their reach into the production regions by establishing oftentimes elaborate purchasing networks and by positioning rural merchants to oversee the flow of goods. Although the networks had considerably weakened by the early nineteenth century, city wholesalers continued to exercise appreciable influence over rural merchants. On occasion they increased the number of their agents in the production regions to foster competition, and they played off production regions against one another to bring down prices.

How typical was this volatility among Japan's protoindustrial elites? The literature on European protoindustrialization in the last decade and a half has suggested tremendous diversity both among and within countries, so sweeping comparisons are hazardous. In some areas of France, market conditions appear to have been fairly stable. A significant number of those starting factories in the cotton industry, in fact, had their start as protoindustrial merchants.[3] Conditions in eighteenth-century England were far more unpredictable. About 33,000 businesses filed for bankruptcy under the legal statutes, and many more simply failed. The leading sectors of bankruptcy were textiles and clothing (about one-quarter of the total) and the wholesale and retail trades (another one-quarter of the total). Both were the most vibrant sectors of the British economy at the time, full of growth and opportunity but also fraught with risk and intense competition.[4]

Japan's rural elites faced a similarly unpredictable economic climate. Many rural elites did not survive in their particular trades for long, and even those who persisted encountered countless obstacles. At the end of the Meiji era, some protoindustrial merchants had successfully made the transition to industrial modes of production, but they came primarily from among the intermediate stratum of merchants, not from among the rural merchant elite.

The high failure rate among Japan's rural elites, however, did not at all stem the tide of new entrants to commerce and industry. It is not difficult to understand why newcomers might have been enticed by examples of the successful, the Ōhashi Gizaemons and Nakano Kyūjirōs, those who had made fabulous sums in their trades. Many new entrants were risk-takers, but they had little sense of the degree of the risk they were taking. This was nowhere more evident than in the Yokohama trade, where merchants quickly made enormous sums and just as quickly lost them. As the historian Julian Hoppit explained the situation for England, "eighteenth-century businessmen appear to have had a good sense of the availability of opportunities, but were rather less successful in their attempts to judge the degree of risk involved."[5] Like that of Western Europe, the Japanese experience reminds us that capitalism results not simply from the initiatives of a handful of prescient entrepreneurs. It was a far more dynamic, dialectical process than commonly assumed, with as many losers as winners and no guarantee of continued success.

It is also safe to say that the gōnō cannot be understood as an incipient bourgeoisie, conducting their trades in an unfettered manner. In the initial stage of protoindustrialization, the gōnō, indeed, had to fight the entrenched interests of urban merchants, especially those enjoying monopolistic privileges in the castle towns. But in other areas this view appears overly simplistic. Rural protoindustry and rural elites did not displace but oftentimes coexisted with wholesalers and their guilds in the major cities. By establishing purchasing networks in the countryside, in fact, city wholesalers spurred the process of protoindustrialization itself. Although many rural merchants sought to break free from their dependence on city wholesalers by trading with other parts of the country, the tremendous demand that urban consumers generated ensured that vast quantities of goods flowed to the major cities. This accorded city merchants broad powers over rural production and prices, even in the Meiji period—far less power than they exercised in the mid-eighteenth century, it is true, but important nonetheless.

Moreover, it is far from obvious that in the nineteenth century there existed clear lines demarcating town and village merchants, or that village merchants were opposed to the more traditional, feudal patterns of organization. As in the Hachiōji area (Chapter 5), both groups coexisted in the local textile merchants' association. The same was true in the Kiryū weavers' guild, where the majority of members were from surrounding villages, not from the town of Kiryū itself. The greatest problem for both town and village merchants was the arrival of newcomers to their trade, and they did whatever was necessary to erect barriers to their entry. Many early gōnō rose to positions of economic prominence employing the logic of free trade, especially in their battles against castle town merchants, but once achieving success they settled comfortably back into more traditional modes of organizational activity, especially guild groupings. When rural elites established themselves as powerful regional merchants, their interests became similar to those of merchants operating out of the towns and cities. In sum, Japanese protoindustrialization entailed a clear shift in the major sites of production but there was no radical departure in modes of business activity.

Despite remarkable similarities to Western Europe's pattern of protoindustrialization, the Japanese pattern contained a distinctive element, namely, as Saitō Osamu has indicated, its transformative effects on the rural economy. Unlike the Western European pattern, Japanese protoindustrialization did not lead to an exodus from the countryside to urban areas, nor did it engender a division of labor between those regions specializing in commercial agriculture and those specializing in rural industry. Farmers continued to engage in both cash crop production and rural industry, with few abandoning one to specialize in the other. Also, Japan experienced no transformation to capital-intensive large-scale agricultural methods.[6]

Saitō reminds us that, even as factory output began to outdistance traditional industry at the close of the Meiji era, Japan remained heavily wedded to traditional modes of production. Well into the twentieth century, farmers in areas with high levels of agricultural productivity supplemented their incomes through various forms of side industry, and those in regions with high levels of rural industry continued to cultivate the land. The differences with Europe are especially striking when one compares occupational distribution. About 72 percent of Japan's population

worked in agriculture and forestry in 1872, not much below the percentage for the Tokugawa period as a whole. In 1905 the figure had fallen only
slightly, to about 64 percent.[7] In most advanced countries of Western
Europe, in contrast, well under half the population were employed in the
agricultural sector: 41 percent in Holland in the late eighteenth century,
36 percent in England in 1801, and 39 percent in France in 1881. Ger-
many, with 62 percent of the population employed in agriculture in 1800,
comes closest to Japan, but it witnessed a much steeper decline in later
decades, reaching 43 percent in 1882.[8]

The reasons for this dissimilarity are undoubtedly complex and varied,
but a significant part of the explanation surely lies in the more prominent
role of rural elites in Japan's protoindustrialization process. By introducing new seed varieties and production techniques, rural elites provided Japan's smallholders the ability to survive as farmers, thus impeding the
process of proletarianization common in Western European countries.
Even the industries that sprouted in the closing years of the protoindustrial era scarcely influenced the basic structure of rural society. Most such
industries could be found in rural areas and provided employment to surplus members of farming families, especially women.

The influential role of Japan's rural elites can be seen in several areas. It
is most obvious when considering the relative weakness of regional specialization. As the statistical data included in Chapter 2 clearly demonstrate, an important characteristic of Japanese protoindustrialization is
not the emergence of regions with clear dominance in particular protoindustrial sectors. Indeed, what is most striking is the spread of protoindustrial activity to almost every corner of the country. The gōnō, as improving farmers and diffusionist elites, were largely responsible for this development, and they were quite conscious of their role as promoters of industry. They recorded their accomplishments in order to provide a model for
later generations to emulate, as well as to impart to them the gravity of
their duties as household heads.

The role of Japan's rural elites can also be seen in the ties they maintained with city-merchant capital. As this study shows, wholesalers exercised numerous controls over rural merchants, but they hardly orches-
trated protoindustrial activity. This was quite unlike the pattern found in
parts of Western Europe. Wholesale merchants in Nimes, France, for example, financed the cultivation of mulberry trees, sericulture, and the
throwing of silk thread and were largely responsible for the growth in the
rural linen industry. Town merchants in Rouen initiated and directed the
diffusion of spinning and cloth manufacture in rural Normandy. In Hol-

land, textile manufacturers in Leiden shifted some of their weaving to rural households, and merchants in Haarlem had poorer farmers spin linen yarn.[9] Japan's rural elites, in contrast, acted as buffers between city wholesalers and the rural economy. Merchant capital provided funds, but rural elites themselves dominated rural commerce and industry.

Our case studies suggest that the *gōnō* existed in an oftentimes tenuous relationship with their communities. The activities in which they engaged depended on the labor and purchasing power of others. Landlords and those involved in putting out or in manufacture required the labor of other farmers, and merchants needed the goods smallholders produced. The *gōnō*'s introduction of new forms of production and improvement efforts provided poorer farmers additional sources of income, enabling them to survive as farmers and to remain on the land. At the same time, the *gōnō* profited when smallholders engaged in market-related production.

A tension between the two groups was inherent in their relationship from the beginning. As we saw in our discussion of the Mooka region (Chapter 4), rural elites' activities often led to the impoverishment of people in their villages. Less pronounced versions of this precarious balance between the two groups probably existed to one degree or another in every village in Japan. The *gōnō* and their communities were in a symbiotic relationship, with each dependent on the other for continued survival.

Many of the *gōnō*'s activities were clearly exploitative. Their money-lending activities, in particular, led them to appropriate land from those who defaulted on their loans. The extent of polarization of landholdings often varied significantly by region, but it was an unmistakable phenomenon in all parts of Japan from the mid-Tokugawa. By the close of the Tokugawa, many elites owned sizable portions of their village arable. As we saw with the Nakayama and Ishikawa families, the accumulation of lands intensified all the more in the Meiji period.

How did the Japanese pattern of protoindustrialization influence social inequality? A wide gulf between rich and poor had existed in all Japanese farming villages well before the advent of protoindustry. But in general, most poorer farmers in the early Tokugawa were closely tied to village patriarchs, with whom they lived or from whom they rented fields. In return for ritual obeisance and labor services, the patriarchs provided them protection in times of difficulties. By the mid-eighteenth century, most farmers had acquired independence from village patriarchs. Although some rural elites still commanded various forms of labor services, in most areas immersed in a vibrant protoindustrial economy such relationships existed in only attenuated form and labor had become commodified.

For many poorer farmers, protoindustry afforded the opportunity to escape the clutches of their patriarchs. As in the northern Kantō (Chapter 4), some farmers found it necessary to leave their villages in order to acquire complete independence. This desire for independence, which has not been a central concern of this study, might also explain why, when farmers went out to work, on a daily, seasonal, or yearly basis, they often found employment outside their villages, and why rural elites hired people from other villages to tend to their fields or to assist in the family business. A rigorous examination must be conducted to test this claim, but it provides interesting fodder for speculation concerning intravillage interpersonal relationships.

The effect of protoindustry on standards of living is far more difficult to gauge. Several recent studies of Europe have found that protoindustrialization, far from impoverishing farmers, as had been assumed in the earlier literature, often created prosperity for many.[10] For Japan, the response must be more tempered. Many rural elites made fabulous sums through interregional commerce, manufacture, and tenancy rents. For poorer farmers, by-employments provided additional income to increase their landholdings, as was the case in Ōishi village (Chapter 5). There are also examples of poorer farmers' increasing their fortunes and rising to the top ranks of their region's elites. Most Japanese farmers, too, saw qualitative improvements in their lives in the nineteenth century. They became consumers of goods, purchasing tea, sake, clothing, and confections and other foods from local markets and village stores.

At the same time, in many areas the already wide disparity between rich and poor widened all the more in the final decades of Tokugawa rule. Large numbers of farmers had become semiproletarianized and forced to earn much of their income from activities outside agriculture, by way of side industry, by selling their labor, and by tenanting land. Many rural elites, on the other hand, had amassed considerable fortunes and sizable landholdings, often one-third or more of their village fields.

The extreme volatility of the protoindustrial economy, probably more than protoindustry itself, produced these growing class cleavages. Crop failures and economic downturns, in particular, devastated large numbers of farmers. In the nineteenth century alone, there were at least three periods of severe distress (and many more periods of shorter economic downturns): the 1830's, a time of successive crop failures and depressed demand for goods in consumer markets; from the mid-1850's to the early 1870's, a period of tremendous political uncertainty, crop failures, and an inflationary spiral unleashed by the opening of the ports; and the early

1880's, when Matsukata's deflationary policies drastically curtailed the demand for goods from the traditional sector of the economy. Gōnō suffered as well when economic conditions were unfavorable, but most could use their vast accumulated assets to tide themselves over until recovery set in. Some rural elites, such as Nakano Kyūjirō (Chapter 5), even accumulated significant landholdings during the 1830's, when many poor farmers defaulted on their debts. There were, of course, good times for farmers, especially the first three decades of the nineteenth century and the inflationary years of the late 1870's, when many undoubtedly improved their fortunes. The succession of downturns, however, injected a powerful note of instability and impermanence.

What effect did the Japanese pattern of inequality have on economic growth? In a recent comparative study of New World economies, Stanley Engerman and Kenneth Sokoloff argue that the distribution of wealth might well have determined the evolution of political, legal, and economic institutions that influenced later patterns of growth. High material living standards and relative equality among elites and commoners alike in the northern United States and Canada encouraged the evolution of extensive networks of markets and commercialization, as well as the establishment of egalitarian political institutions that facilitated further market growth and market participation. In many Latin American countries, on the other hand, high levels of inequality—characterized by significant numbers of unfree labor, state-privileged elites, and restrictive immigration policies—limited participation in the market and impeded economic and political growth in the long term.[11]

Japan can be situated between the two extremes in Engerman and Sokoloff's model. The gōnō stood at the pinnacle of rural society and commanded immense influence over others in their communities, but they shared few other similarities with Latin American elites. Japan's rural elites fostered, and their activities were grounded upon, large numbers of *independent* farmers actively participating in market-related activities. This was quite unlike the Latin American pattern, where only a select few maintained strong market ties. Moreover, Japan's rural elites were privileged only in a very narrow sense. As we saw in Chapter 1, despite a host of perks Tokugawa and Meiji political authorities deigned to grace them with, very few had access to corridors of power in any significant manner, at least not until the convening of the Diet in 1890.

Nor was the Japanese wealth distribution pattern comparable to that of the northern states and Canada. Large segments of Japan's rural populace engaged in production for the market by the nineteenth century, but there were stark differences in the degree to which individual farmers benefited. A large segment of the rural farming class had become semi-proletarianized, which made them extremely susceptible to the ravages of market fluctuations.

Furthermore, it is far from clear that the relative equality of Japanese farmers vis-à-vis their counterparts in Latin America contributed to the later formation of egalitarian political institutions. The political institutions created by the Meiji leadership after 1868 were far from democratic, and the enactment of a Constitution in 1889 was as much the product of international pressures and the desire among some in the leadership to emulate Western industrial democracies as the result of any perceived need to extend guaranteed rights to the people of Japan. But at the same time, government leaders clearly recognized the benefits of active participation in the market by all members of society, as is evident in their speedy abolition of feudal restrictions and class privileges. They subsequently neglected the traditional sector of the economy, as the *gōnō* rightly perceived, but their inattention stemmed more from a different vision of how the country was to modernize than from a complete disregard for the traditional sector itself.

The *gōnō* contributed to economic progress, technological development, and organizational change in their communities, and in myriad ways they prepared Japan for the industrialization that was to take place in the twentieth century. But their role in the transition to the industrial era was complex. Few survived the gruelingly competitive and volatile economic climate of the protoindustrial era, and their activities sometimes fostered social and economic divisions within their communities.

# Reference Matter

# Tables

TABLE 1

*Nationwide Goods by Sector, 1874*

| Sector | Value (*yen*) | Percent of total |
|---|---|---|
| Agricultural goods | 227,286,701 | 61.0 |
| Manufactured goods | 111,891,559 | 30.0 |
| Primary goods* | 33,128,714 | 9.0 |
| TOTAL | 372,306,974 | 100.0 |

SOURCE: Yamaguchi Kazuo, *Meiji zenki keizai*, 5.
*Forestry, fishing, mining, and livestock products.

TABLE 2

*Leading Agricultural Products, 1874*

| Item | Value (1,000 *yen*) | | Percent of agricultural total | |
|---|---|---|---|---|
| Rice | 142,799.0 | | 62.8 | |
| Special-use agricultural goods | 27,915.2 | | 12.3 | |
| Cotton (seed and ginned) | | 7,434.5 | | 3.3 |
| Rapeseed | | 6,036.8 | | 2.7 |
| Cocoons | | 4,917.3 | | 2.2 |
| Indigo | | 3,422.1 | | 1.5 |
| Tobacco | | 2,939.7 | | 1.3 |
| Other agricultural goods | 56,572.5 | | 24.9 | |
| TOTAL | 227,286.7 | | 100.0 | |

SOURCE: Yamaguchi Kazuo, *Meiji zenki keizai*, 6–9.

TABLE 3

*Leading Manufactured Goods, 1874*

| Item | Value (1,000 yen) | Percent of manufacturing total |
|---|---|---|
| Sake | 18,605.5 | 16.6 |
| Textiles | 17,159.1 | 15.3 |
| Soy sauce | 6,338.5 | 5.7 |
| Raw silk | 6,164.8 | 5.5 |
| Other manufactured goods | 63,623.7 | 56.9 |
| TOTAL | 111,891.6 | 100.0 |

SOURCE: Yamaguchi Kazuo, *Meiji zenki keizai*, 14.

TABLE 4

*Leading Cotton Regions, 1874 and 1901*

(* denotes Kinai)

| 1874 | | | 1901 | | |
|---|---|---|---|---|---|
| Prefecture | Total (1,000 kanme) | Percent of natl. total | Prefecture | Total (1,000 kanme) | Percent of natl. total |
| Aichi | 1,819.6 | 15.4 | Osaka* | 686.7 | 15.4 |
| Kyoto* | 1,348.8 | 11.4 | Hiroshima | 580.3 | 13.0 |
| Osaka* | 1,058.3 | 8.9 | Tottori | 481.0 | 10.8 |
| Sakai* | 810.7 | 6.8 | Ibaraki | 428.1 | 9.6 |
| Myōtō | 541.5 | 4.6 | Aichi | 306.1 | 6.9 |
| NATL. TOTAL | 11,850.0 | 100.0 | NATL. TOTAL | 4,468.6 | 100.0 |

SOURCES: 1874 data, Yamaguchi Kazuo, *Meiji zenki keizai*, 9–10; 1901 data, *Nihon teikoku tōkei nenkan*, 22: 471–73.
NOTE: Figures for 1874 refer to seed, ginned, and other semi-processed cottons; those for 1901 refer to seed cotton alone. Prefectures (and metropolitan areas) and their borders changed considerably between 1874 and 1901. Myōtō refers to present-day Tokushima prefecture.

TABLE 5

*Leading Cocoon Production Regions, 1874 and 1891*

| 1874 | | | 1891 | | |
|---|---|---|---|---|---|
| Prefecture | Total (1,000 yen) | Percent of natl. total | Prefecture | Total (1,000 koku) | Percent of natl. total |
| Kumagaya | 1,245.2 | 25.3 | Nagano | 281.9 | 17.8 |
| Yamanashi | 799.2 | 16.3 | Gunma | 193.7 | 12.3 |
| Nagano | 415.9 | 8.5 | Fukushima | 144.8 | 9.2 |
| Chikuma | 308.3 | 6.3 | Saitama | 93.7 | 5.9 |
| Fukushima | 300.2 | 6.1 | Shiga | 91.4 | 5.8 |
| NATL. TOTAL | 4,917.3 | 100.0 | NATL. TOTAL | 1,580.2 | 100.0 |

SOURCES: 1874 data, Yamaguchi Kazuo, *Meiji zenki keizai*, 9–11; 1891 data, *Nihon teikoku tōkei nenkan*, 12: 393–95.
NOTE: Kumagaya includes present-day Gunma and Saitama prefectures. Chikuma includes Gifu and four districts in northern Nagano prefecture.

TABLE 6

*Leading Raw Silk Production Regions, 1874 and 1902*

| 1874 | | | 1902 | | |
|---|---|---|---|---|---|
| Prefecture | Total (1,000 kanme) | Percent of natl. total | Prefecture | Total (1,000 kanme) | Percent of natl. total |
| Kumagaya | 65.5 | 17.4 | Nagano | 492.9 | 19.3 |
| Toyooka | 29.9 | 7.9 | Gunma | 337.4 | 13.2 |
| Chikuma | 21.9 | 5.8 | Yamanashi | 157.2 | 6.2 |
| Nagano | 18.0 | 4.8 | Fukushima | 149.7 | 5.9 |
| Fukushima | 16.8 | 4.4 | Saitama | 129.4 | 5.1 |
| NATL. TOTAL | 377.0 | 100.0 | NATL. TOTAL | 2,549.4 | 100.0 |

SOURCES: 1874 data, Yamaguchi Kazuo, *Meiji zenki keizai*, 14–16; 1902 data, *Nihon teikoku tōkei nenkan*, 22: 557–59.
NOTE: Toyooka included all of the former Tanba province and three districts in Tango; in 1876 it was incorporated in Hyōgo prefecture and the Kyoto metropolitan area.

*Appendix*

TABLE 7

*Leading Silk Textile Regions, 1874 and 1891*

(* denotes Kinai)

| 1874 | | | 1891 | | |
|---|---|---|---|---|---|
| Prefecture | Total (1,000 yen) | Percent of natl. total | Prefecture | Total (1,000 yen) | Percent of natl. total |
| Kyoto* | 1,503.0 | 32.8 | Gunma | 2,658.6 | 21.2 |
| Tochigi | 649.9 | 14.2 | Kyoto* | 2,648.4 | 21.1 |
| Toyooka | 446.0 | 9.7 | Fukui | 1,586.2 | 12.6 |
| Kumagaya | 347.9 | 7.6 | Yamanashi | 701.9 | 5.6 |
| Yamanashi | 206.7 | 4.5 | Fukushima | 649.9 | 5.2 |
| NATL. TOTAL | 4,581.1 | 100.0 | NATL. TOTAL | 12,543.7 | 100.0 |

SOURCES: 1874 data, Yamaguchi Kazuo, *Meiji zenki keizai*, 15; 1891 data, *Nihon teikoku tōkei nenkan*, 12: 457–59.

TABLE 8

*Leading Cotton Textile Regions, 1874 and 1891*

(* denotes Kinai)

| 1874 | | | 1891 | | |
|---|---|---|---|---|---|
| Prefecture | Total (1,000 yen) | Percent of natl. total | Prefecture | Total (1,000 yen) | Percent of natl. total |
| Aichi | 751.4 | 6.9 | Aichi | 2,433.6 | 14.9 |
| Osaka* | 698.1 | 6.4 | Tochigi | 1,455.2 | 8.9 |
| Nara* | 690.7 | 6.4 | Saitama | 1,295.5 | 7.9 |
| Saitama | 631.8 | 5.8 | Osaka* | 1,150.3 | 7.0 |
| Niikawa | 610.0 | 5.6 | Wakayama | 1,135.9 | 6.9 |
| NATL. TOTAL | 10,856.3 | 100.0 | NATL. TOTAL | 16,344.9 | 100.0 |

SOURCES: 1874 data, Yamaguchi Kazuo, *Meiji zenki keizai*, 15; 1891 data, *Nihon teikoku tōkei nenkan*, 12: 457–59.
NOTE: Niikawa is roughly coterminous with present-day Ishikawa prefecture.

TABLE 9

Leading Silk/Cotton Blend Textile Regions, 1874 and 1891

(* denotes Kinai)

| | 1874 | | | 1891 | |
|---|---|---|---|---|---|
| Prefecture | Total (1,000 yen) | Percent of natl. total | Prefecture | Total (1,000 yen) | Percent of natl. total |
| Tochigi | 1,061.1 | 76.9 | Kyoto* | 1,787.5 | 34.6 |
| Kyoto* | 269.2 | 19.5 | Gifu | 981.5 | 19.0 |
| NATL. TOTAL | 1,379.1 | 100.0 | Tochigi | 589.5 | 11.4 |
| | | | Aichi | 571.0 | 11.0 |
| | | | Saitama | 303.6 | 5.9 |
| | | | NATL. TOTAL | 5,167.8 | 100.0 |

SOURCES: 1874 data, Yamaguchi Kazuo, Meiji zenki keizai, 15; 1891 data, Nihon teikoku tōkei nenkan, 12: 457–59.

NOTE: Tochigi in 1874 included the rural town of Kiryū, which later became part of Gunma prefecture.

TABLE 10

Leading Sake-Brewing Regions, 1874 and 1891

(* denotes Kinai)

| | 1874 | | | 1891 | |
|---|---|---|---|---|---|
| Prefecture | Total (1,000 koku) | Percent of natl. total | Prefecture | Total (1,000 koku) | Percent of natl. total |
| Hyōgo* | 255.5 | 7.4 | Hyōgo* | 436.5 | 12.8 |
| Aichi | 165.9 | 4.8 | Fukuoka | 159.2 | 4.7 |
| Niigata | 148.2 | 4.3 | Nagano | 136.3 | 4.0 |
| Tochigi | 122.2 | 3.6 | Aichi | 135.1 | 4.0 |
| Kyoto* | 119.0 | 3.5 | Osaka* | 128.2 | 3.8 |
| NATL. TOTAL | 3,431.4 | 100.0 | NATL. TOTAL | 3,408.0 | 100.0 |

SOURCES: 1874 data, Yamaguchi Kazuo, Meiji zenki keizai, 17; 1891 data, Nihon teikoku tōkei nenkan, 12: 466–68.

TABLE 11

*Leading Tea Cultivation Regions, 1881 and 1912*

(* denotes Kinai)

| | 1881 | | | 1912 | |
|---|---|---|---|---|---|
| Prefecture | Arable (chō) | Percent of natl. total | Prefecture | Arable (chō) | Percent of natl. total |
| Shizuoka | 9,045.4 | 21.5 | Shizuoka | 12,812.1 | 26.3 |
| Mie | 4,117.6 | 9.8 | Mie | 2,946.0 | 6.1 |
| Gifu | 4,101.1 | 9.8 | Kagoshima | 2,399.0 | 4.9 |
| Ibaraki | 2,690.0 | 6.4 | Ibaraki | 2,344.2 | 4.8 |
| Kyoto* | 2,635.9 | 6.3 | Kyoto* | 2,287.8 | 4.7 |
| NATL. TOTAL | 41,998.0 | 100.0 | NATL. TOTAL | 48,693.8 | 100.0 |

SOURCES: 1881 data, *Nihon teikoku tōkei nenkan*, 2: 65–67; 1912 data, ibid., 32: 98–99.

TABLE 12

*Leading Tea-Processing Regions, 1881 and 1911*

(* denotes Kinai)

| | 1881 | | | 1911 | |
|---|---|---|---|---|---|
| Prefecture | Total (1,000 kanme) | Percent of natl. total | Prefecture | Total (1,000 kanme)) | Percent of natl. total |
| Shizuoka | 695.8 | 12.4 | Shizuoka | 2,676.3 | 30.9 |
| Mie | 516.9 | 9.2 | Mie | 678.8 | 7.8 |
| Kyoto* | 467.5 | 8.3 | Kyoto* | 498.7 | 5.8 |
| Gifu | 320.8 | 5.7 | Kumamoto | 478.1 | 5.5 |
| Shiga | 304.4 | 5.4 | Nara* | 372.9 | 4.3 |
| NATL. TOTAL | 5,601.2 | 100.0 | NATL. TOTAL | 8,660.2 | 100.0 |

SOURCES: 1881 data, *Nihon teikoku tōkei nenkan*, 2: 65–67; 1911 data, ibid., 32: 204.

## TABLE 13
### Ōishi Landholdings, 1820 and 1846

| Size (koku) | 1820, Shimo-Ōishi | | 1846, entire village | |
|---|---|---|---|---|
| | Households | Percent | Households | Percent |
| over 40 | 1 | 0.8 | 0 | 0.0 |
| 30–40 | 4 | 3.1 | 1 | 0.4 |
| 20–30 | 2 | 1.5 | 10 | 4.1 |
| 15–20 | 12 | 9.2 | 11 | 4.5 |
| 10–15 | 16 | 12.3 | 44 | 18.0 |
| 5–10 | 23 | 17.7 | 85 | 34.7 |
| 1–5 | 18 | 13.8 | 76 | 31.0 |
| 0–1 | 54 | 41.5 | 18 | 7.3 |
| TOTAL | 130 | 99.9 | 245 | 100.0 |

SOURCE: Adapted from Hasebe, "Kinsei kōki," 129.

## TABLE 14
### Landholdings in Nakagami Village, 1872

| Land size (koku) | Families | | Total land owned | | No. of people employed outside village |
|---|---|---|---|---|---|
| | No. | Percent | Koku | Percent | |
| 0–0.1 | 6 | 5.7 | 0.4 | 0.1 | 2 |
| 0.1–0.5 | 29 | 27.6 | 7.3 | 1.6 | 15 |
| 0.5–1 | 17 | 16.2 | 11.5 | 2.5 | 1 |
| 1–5 | 35 | 33.3 | 89.8 | 19.7 | 9 |
| 5–10 | 8 | 7.6 | 63.5 | 13.9 | 0 |
| 10–15 | 8 | 7.6 | 94.5 | 20.7 | 1 |
| over 20 | 2 | 1.9 | 189.3 | 41.5 | 0 |
| TOTAL | 105 | 99.9 | 456.3 | 100.0 | 28 |

SOURCE: Adapted from Table 13 in Akishima shishi, 981.

## TABLE 15
### Classes of Kumagawa Villagers, 1869

| Category | No. of families | Avg. landholdings per family (koku) | Percent of village lands owned |
|---|---|---|---|
| Over 5 koku | 31 | 8.58 | 55.9 |
| Under 5 koku—top rank | 12 | 3.61 | 9.1 |
| Under 5 koku—middle rank | 32 | 2.94 | 19.8 |
| Under 5 koku—low rank | 40 | 1.52 | 12.8 |
| "Extremely impoverished" | 17 | 0.55 | 2.0 |
| "Broken Farmers" | 19 | 0.47 | 1.7 |

SOURCE: Calculated from Doc. 222, Tama Jiman, 5: 71–77.

# Glossary

*Bakufu.* Administrative organ of the Tokugawa house.

*Chō.* Land measurement, equivalent to 2.45 acres or 1 hectare.

*Daikan.* Intendant. Used here to refer to overseers of bakufu lands.

*Daimyo.* Feudal lords (*daimyō*), numbering about 250.

*Fudai.* Lords who were direct vassals of the Tokugawa house.

*Gōnō.* Rural elites; literally, "wealthy farmers." Used by Japanese historians to denote a particular socioeconomic class.

*Goyōkin.* Extraordinary funds levied by political authority on villages or wealthy residents.

*Goyōtashi.* The most common term referring to financial purveyors. Early *goyōtashi* were often castle-town merchants providing particular goods or services to the domain. In the second half of the Tokugawa, *goyōtashi* refers primarily to those procuring funds for domains, either directly or indirectly. There were often several *goyōtashi* ranks.

*Hatamoto.* Bannermen of the Tokugawa house; all had fiefs of less than 10,000 *koku.*

*Hōkōnin.* Contract laborers.

*Intendant.* See *Daikan.*

*Izari.* Inclining loom.

*Jinya.* Administrative offices maintained by small domains in a major town in their territory. The *jinya* served the functions of a castle town, but the lord often permanently resided in Edo or another major city.

*Kaitsugi.* Rural agents of city wholesalers.

*Kaiyado.* Rural agents of city wholesalers; often lodged city buyers and facilitated purchases for them.

*Kan.* Silver coinage used in western Japan; one of three primary monetary units in the Tokugawa.

*Kanme.* Unit of weight, equivalent to 8.72 pounds. Often referred to simply as *kan.*

*Kanmon.* Copper coinage; one of three primary monetary units in the Tokugawa. In 1700 the official exchange rate was 4 *kanmon* of copper to 1 *ryō* of gold.

Kantō.  Region surrounding Edo; often used to denote eight provinces around the city.

*Kin.*  Unit of weight, equivalent to 1.32 pounds.

Kinai.  Region in west-central Japan encompassing areas around Osaka and Kyoto; includes the five provinces of Yamato, Kawachi, Izumi, Settsu, and Yamashiro.

*Koku.*  Measurement of land productivity; equivalent to 4.96 bushels of rice or the corresponding value of other crops.

*Kuni don'ya.*  Wholesalers who received goods from particular provinces.

*Nakagai.*  Jobbers, often positioned between producers and wholesalers or between retailers and wholesalers.

*Niuke don'ya.*  Consignment merchants; wholesalers who received goods on consignment rather than through direct purchase.

*Ryō.*  Gold coinage used in eastern Japan; one of three primary monetary units in the Tokugawa.

*Sankin kōtai.*  System by which most domain lords were required to spend alternate years in residence in Edo and to permanently station their families there.

*Seishō.*  Large merchant houses and other Meiji-period firms with close ties to the government, including ties through official contracts, tax breaks, and subsidies.

*Shiire don'ya.*  Wholesalers who purchased directly from production regions using their own capital.

*Shinomaki.*  Ginned cotton that was beaten until soft; the fibers were straightened and bundled in preparation for spinning into yarn.

*Takahata.*  High loom or draw loom, used to produce ornate cloths.

*Tan.*  Measurement used for cloths, equivalent to about 9 yards. Also measurement of land, equal to one-tenth of a *chō*.

Tōhoku.  Region encompassing the northeastern section of the main island of Honshū.

Tōkai.  A region of central Japan, facing the Pacific and including Mikawa province, examined in Chapter 4.

*Yashikisha.*  One of several terms used to refer to hereditary servants. In the northern Kantō, *yashikisha* maintained separate residences but provided labor and other services to their patriarch.

*Zaguri.*  An improved device for reeling raw silk from cocoons. Through the use of cogwheels or belts, it doubled the speed of earlier devices. Several improvements were made to the *zaguri* in the Meiji period.

# Notes

Complete authors' names, titles, and publication data are given in the Works Cited, pp. 237–51.

## Introduction

EPIGRAPH: Hashimoto, *Nōgyō keizai no omoide*, 32.

1. Denda, *Gōnō*, 25–27.
2. Smith, *Agrarian Origins*, chap. 11.
3. Crawcour, "Changes," 189–202; Hauser, *Economic Institutional Change*; and Hanley and Yamamura, *Economic and Demographic Change*.
4. Smith, "Landlords' Sons," 93–107. For a summary of similar studies, see T. Nakamura, *Economic Growth*, 104–11.
5. Yamamura, "Entrepreneurship," 300; and the Introduction by Teruko Craig in Shibusawa, *Autobiography of Shibusawa Eiichi*, ix–x.
6. Yamamura, "Entrepreneurship," 310–13; and Denda, *Gōnō*, 127–34.
7. Smethurst, *Agricultural Development*, esp. 142–52.
8. See Table 50 in Ishii, *Nihon keizaishi*, 202.
9. Compiled from "Zenkoku tagaku nōzeisha meibo (Meiji 44-nen)," reprinted in Shibuya, comp., *Meijiki Nihon zenkoku shisanka*, 223–31.
10. Bix, *Peasant Protest*; Kelly, *Deference and Defiance*; Vlastos, *Peasant Protests*; Walthall, *Social Protest*; and White, *Ikki*.
11. Walthall, "Family Ideology," 463–83; and Walthall, "Life Cycle," 42–70.
12. One possible exception is William Jones Chambliss's study of Chiaraijima village, birthplace of Shibusawa Eiichi, but his primary focus was socioeconomic change in one particular village, rather than the role of rural elites. See Chambliss, *Chiaraijima Village*.
13. See Waswo, *Japanese Landlords*; and Smethurst, *Agricultural Development*.
14. T. Nakamura, *Economic Growth*, 77–83; see especially Table 3.3.
15. Some notable exceptions include recent studies of the Furuhashi family. See Inui, *Gōnō keiei*; and Haga, ed., *Gōnō Furuhashi-ke*.

16. Fujita Gorō was the first to take up the role of the *gōnō* in a substantive manner. Rejecting the view that Japanese capitalism sprouted solely as a result of contact with the West after the Restoration, Fujita contended that agriculture and industry in the Tokugawa displayed limited, but nonetheless important, modern traits. The *gōnō* were largely responsible for this transformation, Fujita asserted, but they were not simply a European-type bourgeoisie. Indeed, they had bourgeois characteristics in that they were entrepreneurial and employed labor, but merged with this were traits that were decidedly less progressive. As "parasitical landlords," they lived off the sweat of their tenants and, as "resurrected serf-master-type landlords" (*saihan nōdoshuteki jinushi*), they kept poorer farmers indebted to them through their moneylending activities. For a summary of Fujita's views, see Kidota, *Ishin reimeiki*, 8–29. Fujita's two most important works are *Nihon kindai sangyō no seisei* and, together with Hattori, *Kinsei hōken shakai*.

Subsequent research revised Fujita's thesis concerning the *gōnō*. In a 1963 article Yamazaki Ryūzō posited two development patterns in the late Tokugawa, one bourgeois and the other not. Bourgeois development was largely confined to the Kinai and the Seto Inland Sea area of the main island of Honshū. With the growth of a market economy from the eighteenth century, middling and upper-class farmers became petty commodity producers, and a few eventually became rich farmers (*funō*) by expanding their operations and by employing wage labor. In less productive regions, on the other hand, the path to wealth was greatly circumscribed, obviating any chance for bourgeois development. The market economy impoverished the majority of farmers, while a few wealthy farmers (*gōnō*) accumulated the land of poorer farmers and used them as their tenants and piece-wage laborers under the putting-out system. See Yamazaki, "Edo kōki," 331–74.

Sasaki Junnosuke criticized Yamazaki's two-pattern typology. All villages by the nineteenth century, he asserted, witnessed a bipolar class differentiation into *gōnō* and semiproletarians. Even Yamazaki's rich farmers turned into landlords, which led to the collapse of so-called "bourgeois development." Sasaki maintained that the two most important functions of wealthy farmers were moneylending and commerce. Through such activities, the *gōnō* subordinated and controlled the activities of poor and middling farmers. Furthermore, the particularities of market relationships in the Tokugawa, by which rural merchants were dependent on city merchant capital, blocked a more independent, bourgeois, form of development. See Sasaki, *Bakumatsu shakairon*, esp. 252–55.

17. For one example, see Nakamura Masanori, *Kindai Nihon jinushiseishi*. Richard Smethurst offers an interpretation of Japanese landlord studies in *Agricultural Development*, 7–32.

18. Ogilvie and Cerman, "Theories of Proto-industrialization," 1.

19. Smith, "Farm Family By-Employments," 71–102.

20. Smith, "Premodern Economic Growth," 15–49.

21. Howell, *Capitalism*.

22. Wigen, *Making of a Japanese Periphery*.

23. Berg, "Markets," 6–9; and Berg, Hudson, and Sonenscher, "Manufacture," 25–28.

24. See Giddens, *Central Problems*, chap. 2 passim; and Lloyd, *Explanation*, chaps. 9 and 14 passim.

25. Unlike the conservative urban merchants who lived in the shadow of political authority and sought its protection at every turn against competitors, Smith's "rural entrepreneurs" were a totally different breed. Lacking the special privileges and trade monopolies enjoyed by castle-town merchants, they amassed wealth primarily through their own hard work and initiative. This assumption comes out most clearly in Smith, "Premodern Economic Growth," 25–39.

26. Hauser, *Economic Institutional Change*.

## Chapter 1

1. A 1722 bakufu edict is included in Ōishi Kyūkei, supplemented by Ōishi Shinkei, *Jikata hanreiroku*, 2: 112–13.

2. For a taxonomy of domains, see Bolitho, "The *Han*," 185–91.

3. Kitajima, ed., *Seishigyō no tenkai*, 19–42. Many domains, such as Ueda, placed controls on products coming in and going out, in effect creating a domain market sphere. To ensure compliance, they established checkpoints (*kuchidome bansho*) along the major arteries leading outside their territories. See Ōishi Shinzaburō, *Nihon kinsei shakai*, 42–65.

4. Bolitho, "The *Han*," 215–17, 224–25.

5. For Matsue and Yonezawa domains, see Takeuchi Makoto, *Taikei Nihon no rekishi*, 10: 181–91. For Akita, see Watanabe Fumio, *Yonezawa-han no tokusangyō*, 149–50.

6. Ono, "Bakuhansei seiji kaikakuron," 318–19; and *Aizu shuzōshi*, 9, 45–48.

7. For Sendai and Kaga, see Kudō and Kawamura, "Kinsei kinu orimonogyō," 144–45. For Ibaraki, see *Ibaraki kenshi, Kinseihen*, 364–65.

8. Murakami, *Edo bakufu no daikan*, 155–56, 225–26.

9. Kodama et al., eds., *Nihon rekishi taikei*, 3: 1071. For examples of early monopolies in Sendai and Aizu, see Yoshinaga, *Kinsei no senbai seido*, 20–22. Nishikawa Junsaku prefers the term monopsony over monopoly to signify that domains had exclusive rights to purchase particular goods produced within their territories but competed in central markets with goods from other parts of the country. See Nishikawa and Amano, "Shohan no sangyō," 176–78.

10. *Nihon sangyōshi taikei*, 6: 166–72; and *Shinshū Ōsaka shishi*, 4: 636–39.

11. For Hiroshima, *Hiroshima kenshi, Kinsei 2 tsūshi IV*, 415–19. Tottori had first instituted a monopoly on cotton cloth in 1818, but it proved unprofitable and had to be abandoned in 1823; see *Tottori kenshi*, 5: 562–78.

12. *Nihon sangyōshi taikei*, 6: 166–72.

13. Konta, *Mogami benibanashi*, 61–83. Some regions of fragmented rule did adopt inspection systems, usually at the urging of rural elites. Wealthy farmers and merchants in Musashi and Kōzuke provinces petitioned the bakufu in 1781

to establish forty-seven stations across the Kantō region to inspect raw silk. Again in the 1860's, two wealthy Shindatsu producers of egg cards petitioned the bakufu for the institution of an inspection system, so as to prevent the production of inferior egg cards. See Vlastos, *Peasant Protests*, 114–20; and Walthall, *Social Protest*, 11–13.

14. For Himeji, see Hozumi, *Himeji-han mengyō keizaishi*, 250–52. For Hikone's monopoly, see Yoshinaga, *Kinsei no senbai seido*, 100–101; and Mishima, *Nagahama chirimen*, 8–23.

15. The following discussion of Nagaoka domain is from *Niigata kenshi tsūshihen*, 4: 108–17 and 5: 98–113, 794–801.

16. *Tatsuno shishi*, 2: 173–77, 316–23.

17. *Hiroshima kenshi, Kinsei 2 tsūshi IV*, 63–100.

18. *Kindai Ashikaga shishi*, 1: 594–95, 637–44.

19. The bakufu allowed land put into pawn to go unredeemed but never repealed its ban on the sale of land; see Yamaguchi and Sasaki, *Taikei Nihon rekishi*, 4: 164–67.

20. Kitajima, ed., *Seishigyō no tenkai*, 19–42. The Meiji government in 1872 finally removed all restrictions on farmers engaging in commerce; see *Gunma kenshi tsūshihen*, 8: 271.

21. Shimoseki village, in fact, was bakufu territory; Yonezawa only had custodial jurisdiction over the village from 1753 to 1789. See Omura, *Hokuetsu no gōnō*, 15–17.

22. For Maeki, see *Hobara chōshi*, 1: 361. For Shimosato, see Shinoda, "Chita shuzōgyō," 36–37.

23. *Nishio shishi*, 3: 946–47.

24. Ooms, *Tokugawa Village Practice*, 2–6, chaps. 2–3 passim. In her study of house codes and diaries maintained by rural elites, Anne Walthall makes a similar argument; see "Family Ideology," 463–83.

25. Quoted in Deyon, "Proto-industrialization," 44.

26. For a summary of his views, see Kidota, *Ishin reimeiki*, chap. 1.

27. For an interesting example of rural elites marrying into high-ranking samurai families, see *Kindai Ashikaga shishi*, 1: 843.

28. For Chōshū, see Craig, *Chōshū in the Meiji Restoration*, 268–301. For Mito, see Kidota, *Ishin reimeiki*, chap. 3 passim; *Ibaraki kenshi, Kinseihen*, 809–34; and Koschmann, *Mito Ideology*, 131–39.

29. I share Koschmann's view that "rather than an alliance between equal and autonomous parties, this relationship is better viewed as part of the process of ideological hegemony that sometimes allowed non-samurai to become involved in certain aspects of reformist politics"; see *Mito Ideology*, 139.

30. For Nakajima, see *Ibaraki kenshi, Kinseihen*, 459–60. For Watanabe, see Omura, *Hokuetsu no gōnō*, 34–47.

31. Dohi, "Kinsei ni okeru bukka kisei," 58–59; Nakai, *Tenkanki bakuhansei*, 237–42; Tsuda, *Nihon no rekishi*, 22: 118–37, 297–303; Hayashi Reiko, *Edo ton'ya nakama*, 262.

32. For bakufu edicts concerning sake brewing, see Yunoki, *Sakazukuri*, chap. 3 passim.

33. Ibid., 112–15, 128–33.

34. See Tables 19, 23, and 64, ibid., 125, 133, 300–301.

35. The Satō family of Katakai village in Echigo, for example, started in sake brewing in 1701; in 1831 it operated on a fairly large scale, using 1,742 *koku* of rice for brewing. As a result of bakufu restrictions on sake brewing around 1842 and 1843, it was forced to reduce the scale of its operations significantly, instead emphasizing moneylending and landlord operations. See *Niigata kenshi tsūshihen*, 4: 525–26, 5: 352–56.

36. Yunoki, *Sakazukuri*, 122.

37. Mishima, *Nagahama chirimen*, 54–57, 77–83. In general, however, producers in the region needed Hikone domain for the sale of their product, so there was less resistance there to the monopoly than in other areas; see Arai, "Kinu orimonogyō," 70–72.

38. For Himeji, see Yoshinaga, *Kinsei no senbai seido*, 109–11; and Hozumi, *Himeji-han mengyō keizaishi*, 132–215, 245–86. For Tottori, see *Tottori kenshi*, 3: 523–25. For Hiroshima, see *Hiroshima kenshi, Kinsei 2 tsūshi IV*, 415–19.

39. Kodama, *Kinsei nōmin seikatsushi*, 90–91.

40. Ogilvie, "Social Institutions," 28–29. For concrete examples, see Myška, "Proto-industrialization," 200–203.

41. I have found little evidence of significant contributions and loans from rural elites to prefectural administrations. In 1882 donations to Gunma came to 3,200 yen, or about 0.76 percent of prefectural income that year. We can safely assume that such contributions and loans were more important in the early 1870's, but available records do not afford an accurate assessment. See *Gunma kenshi tsūshihen*, 7: 86, 118.

42. *Shinshū Ōsaka shishi*, 5: 321.

43. Unno, "Shokusan kōgyō," 180–82; *Kawamata chōshi*, 1: 517–18.

44. *Yamashiro chagyōshi*, 13.

45. For Osaka, see *Shinshū Ōsaka shishi*, 5: 295. For Ibaraki, see *Ibaraki-ken shiryō, Kindai sangyōhen I*, 31. For examples from Okayama and Tottori prefectures, see *Okayama kenshi*, 10: 266–68; and *Tottori kenshi kindai*, 3: 12–13, 18–21.

46. For Tottori, see *Tottori kenshi kindai*, 3: 160–66. For Aichi, see *Shinpen Okazaki shishi*, 4: 622. For Mie, see Doc. 93, *Mie kenshi shiryōhen*, 285–87. For Okayama, see *Okayama kenshi*, 10: 267–68. For Fukui prefecture, see *Fukui kenshi tsūshihen*, 5: 542. For Gunma, see *Gunma kengikaishi*, 1: 292–93.

47. For Okayama prefecture, see *Okayama kenshi*, 10: 248. For Mie prefecture, see Docs. 10, 13, and 14, *Mie kenshi shiryōhen*, 102–9, 114–20, 120–23.

48. For Shindatsu, see *Kawamata chōshi*, 1: 520–30. For examples from the Ibaraki tea industry, see *Ibaraki-ken shiryō, Kindai sangyōhen I*, 25; and Doc. 495, *Ibaraki-ken shiryō, Kindai sangyōhen II*, 311–13. For examples from the Ibaraki silk-reeling industry, see Doc. 456, ibid., 244–45.

49. For Nakayama, see *Ibaraki-ken shiryō, Kindai sangyōhen I*, 37. For Tajima, see Unno, "Shokusan kōgyō," 182. Tajima received a salary of 10 yen a month in this position; see Doc. 41, *Gunma kenshi shiryōhen*, 17: 858–59.

50. For Itohara, see Oka et al., eds., *Nihon keizaishi*, 212–13. For Mutō, see *Gunma kenshi tsūshihen*, 8: 90–91.

51. For Furuhashi, see Inui, *Gōnō keiei*, 237–46, 263–64. For Iwamoto, see *Tottori kenshi kindai*, 3: 113–14.

52. Oka et al., eds., *Nihon keizaishi*, 217. This does not mean that the government totally halted subsidies to industries deemed important to Japan's balance of trade. In 1902 the Ministry of Agriculture and Commerce purchased 100,000 yen of textile machinery from abroad, which it loaned out to important export production regions. Those establishing joint stock companies to produce silk cloth and capitalized at 30,000–40,000 yen would receive textile machinery from the government valued at 20,000 yen, as well as an annual subsidy of 10,000 yen for five years. See *Kindai Ashikaga shishi*, 1: 1184–88.

53. Oka et al., eds., *Nihon keizaishi*, 218.

54. For Ibaraki, see *Ibaraki-ken shiryō, Kindai sangyōhen I*, 30–35. Some *rōnō* had acquired a nationwide reputation, and prefectures in succession invited them to lecture. Between 1884 and 1891, for example, eighteen prefectures invited Hayashi Onri to teach the farming methods he was championing. See *Fukushima-ken nōgyōshi*, 2: 130–31.

55. *Fukushima-ken nōgyōshi*, 2: 123–24, 146–47.

56. Ibid., 2: 146–47.

57. Ibid., 2: 123.

58. *Okayama kenshi*, 10: 250.

59. The best discussion of this is still Smith, *Political Change*, chap. 8 passim.

60. For Ibaraki, see *Daichi ni midori*, 38, 47. The Ibaraki assembly voted to reduce this insignificant amount by 81 percent, down to 2,100 yen. For Gunma, see *Gunma kenshi tsūshihen*, 7: 118.

61. Soda, *Chihō sangyō*, 26–29.

62. For early assemblies in Niigata, see *Niigata kenshi tsūshihen*, 6: 175–76. For the Fukuyama area, see Arimoto et al., eds., *Meijiki chihō keimō shisōka*, 53–68. For a general discussion, see Arimoto, "Chiso kaisei," 190–94. For government leaders' views, see Umegaki, *After the Restoration*, 148–56.

63. *Gunma kenshi tsūshihen*, 7: 116, 122–23.

64. Figures are from Table 1 in Ikegami, "Meijiki no shuzei," 70. See also Yunoki, *Sakazukuri*, 331–332; and Ishii, *Nihon keizaishi*, 135.

65. Yunoki, *Sakazukuri*, 321–24; and *Akita-ken shuzōshi, honpen*, 91–95.

66. In spite of their efforts, the brewers lacked unity of purpose and the movement quickly fizzled. There were simply too many types of brewers. In addition to the large-scale brewers, such as those in Nadame who concentrated on sake production alone, numerous rural elites engaged in sake production as only one of several other activities. In addition, there were countless households that brewed sake for family consumption only. See Yunoki, *Sakazukuri*, 335–37.

67. Emura, *Jiyū minken kakumei*, 35–38. Neil L. Waters gives an interesting

example of this close relationship between business and politics in his study of the Kawasaki region; see *Japan's Local Pragmatists*, 98–99.

68. Waters, *Japan's Local Pragmatists*, 86–87; and Emoto, *Daichi ni midori*, 33–34.

69. For Fukuoka, see Oka et al., eds., *Nihon keizaishi*, 218. For Fukushima, see *Fukushima-ken nōgyōshi*, 2: 124. For Okayama, see *Okayama kenshi*, 10: 268. For Ibaraki, see Emoto, *Daichi ni midori*, 47–50.

70. *Gunma kengikaishi*, 1: 416–29, 1443–56.

71. For Hagiwara, see Sasaki, ed., *Mura ni ikiru hitobito*, 214–16. For Fukushima, see *Fukushima-ken nōgyōshi*, 2: 123–27.

72. Arimoto, "Chiso kaisei," 197.

73. *Fussa shishi, jōkan*, 700, 710–11. Compounding the brewers' problems, in 1890 the government initiated a system to ensure that brewers in weak financial shape did not default on their taxes: brewers designated by the government had to put up personal property—such as stocks, bonds, buildings, or land—as collateral for one-fourth of their estimated sake tax. In 1896 the government expanded the system to include all brewers and increased the collateral to one-half of their estimated tax. Sakurai Hirotoshi argues that this system encouraged brewers to accumulate far more land than they had in the past, for two reasons: the government allowed land to be placed as security, and brewers could earn income from tenants renting their land. It is important to keep in mind, however, that many brewers had been landlords well before this new regulation. See Sakurai, *Seishugyō no rekishi*, 30–32, 487–88.

74. *Fussa shishi, jōkan*, 711.

75. For Niigata, see *Niigata kenshi tsūshihen*, 6: 769–70. For Okayama, see *Okayama kenshi*, 10: 526. For Chita, see Shinoda, "Chita shuzōgyō," 51. In the long run, government tax policies worked to the benefit of larger-scale brewers. Through economies of scale, larger brewers were able to produce more high-quality sake at less cost. A number of other government policies, too, advantaged larger brewers. In 1882 the government ordered that brewers of refined sake had to be at a scale of over 100 *koku* of rice, while unrefined brewers had to produce more than ten *koku*; a new regulation in 1898 increased the minimum for unrefined sake to fifty *koku*. The government also placed restrictions on sake for home consumption. In 1880 it limited home-brewed sake production to one *koku* per household, in 1886 it prohibited home brewing of refined sake, and in 1899 it prohibited home brewing entirely. See Ikegami, "Meijiki no shuzei," 73–77.

76. *Fukushima-ken nōgyōshi*, 2: 147, 154.

77. Soda, *Chihō sangyō*, 63–78. E. S. Crawcour provides an introduction to Maeda Masana and his thinking in *Kōgyō Iken*. Carol Gluck situates Maeda within Japan's late Meiji agrarianist tradition; see *Japan's Modern Myths*, 179–80.

78. Soda, *Chihō sangyō*, 135–39, 152.

79. *Fukushima-ken nōgyōshi*, 2: 150.

80. Soda, *Chihō sangyō*, 186–87, 234–50. Thomas R. H. Havens provides a discussion of Ishikawa in *Farm and Nation*, 58–60.

81. Soda, *Chihō sangyō*, 133–52.

82. Ogura, *Can Japanese Agriculture Survive?*, 302–5.

83. *Fukushima-ken nōgyōshi*, 2: 136.

84. Havens, *Farm and Nation*, 64–72.

85. *Fukushima-ken nōgyōshi*, 2: 136–41. By the end of the 1890's a number of prefectural agricultural schools had been established. They played a critical role in diffusing agricultural technology. See *Gunma kenshi tsūshihen*, 8: 88.

86. *Fukushima-ken nōgyōshi*, 2: 152–53. Some prefectures had been moving in this direction well before the agricultural association law of 1899. Okayama prefecture established regulations for agricultural societies in 1895. The regulations stipulated that such societies were to be formed at three levels: town and village; district and city; and prefecture. There was a clear hierarchy, with selected town and village members in the district society, and selected district and city society members in the prefectural organization. The prefectural association employed agricultural agents who traveled around the prefecture and assisted in the establishment of agricultural schools and agricultural experiment stations. See *Okayama kenshi*, 10: 427–30.

87. The government made membership in agricultural societies compulsory in 1905 and enacted mandatory dues in 1922. The National Agricultural Association (Zenkoku Nōjikai), renamed the Imperial Agricultural Association (Teikoku Nōkai) in 1907, won recognition in 1910 as the national organization for agricultural societies at the local level. The government allowed producers' cooperatives to engage in more than one activity in 1906 and allowed federations of cooperatives in 1909.

88. For Gunma, see *Gunma kenshi tsūshihen*, 8: 134. For Fukui, see *Fukui kenshi tsūshihen*, 5: 507–8.

89. *Gunma kenshi tsūshihen*, 8: 84–85; and Oka et al., eds., *Nihon keizaishi*, 225.

90. The following discussion of Meiji landlords is based on Waswo, *Japanese Landlords*, chaps. 1–4.

91. Richard J. Smethurst argues that much of the increase in tenancy was the result, not of rural impoverishment and foreclosure, but of the addition of new lands under cultivatioi. see *Agricultural Development*.

92. For the reasons for the shift, see Banno, *Establishment of the Japanese Constitutional System*, 170–99; and Fraser, "Land Tax Increase."

93. For Oda and Yokoi, see Oka et al., eds., *Nihon keizaishi*, 225. For Yanagita, see Denda, *Gōnō*, 218–20; and Gluck, *Japan's Modern Myths*, 160. For Ishikawa, see Soda, *Chihō sangyō*, 176–78.

## Chapter 2

1. A good discussion of the early history of Osaka can be found in Hauser, *Economic Institutional Change*, 8–23.

2. *Kyōto no rekishi*, 5: 125–27.

3. Hayashi Reiko, *Shōnin no katsudō*, 14–18. In 1697 alone, Kinai brewers

shipped 640,000 barrels of sake to Edo. In 1821 over 1.2 million barrels entered the port of Edo. See Yunoki, *Sakazukuri*, 78, 133.

4. Hauser, *Economic Institutional Change*, esp. chap. 6. For the origins of cotton cultivation in the Osaka region, see Takebe, *Kawachi momenshi*, 2–10; and Nagahara, "Mensaku no tenkai," 70–88.

5. The best English-language account is still Smith, *Agrarian Origins*. See also Yamazaki, "Edo kōki," 337–41; and Kodama et al., eds., *Nihon rekishi taikei*, 3: 688–99. Total arable increased from an estimated 1.64 million *chō* in the early seventeenth century, to 2.97 million by the mid-eighteenth, and to 3.05 million in the early Meiji. The majority of land clearings thus took place around the first century of Tokugawa rule. The irrigation projects carried out around the same time allowed rice to be cultivated in areas where it had been impossible before, and they contributed to productivity advances on a host of crops.

Political authorities (the bakufu and individual domains), villages, and individuals undertook land reclamation in the Tokugawa. The most common form in the seventeenth century consisted of massive projects initiated by the domains and bakufu. Upon their enfeoffment by the Tokugawa house, daimyo immediately used these projects to solidify and to expand the fiscal basis of their economies. Such land reclamations and irrigation projects could be found in many parts of the country. Hiroshima domain, for example, undertook large-scale projects in the first half of the seventeenth century, especially in the coastal areas. It also carried out repairs on major rivers, as well as a number of flood control and irrigation projects. For examples from Hiroshima domain, see *Hiroshima kenshi, Kinsei 1 tsūshi III*, 394–97. Farmers themselves carried out some additional projects in the eighteenth century, albeit on a much smaller scale; see *Hiroshima kenshi, Kinsei 2 tsūshi IV*, 756–57. For examples from Tottori and Bizen, see *Tottori kenshi*, 4: 143; and *Okayama kenshi*, 7: 192–94.

For the importance and extent of use of cash fertilizers in Hiroshima, see *Hiroshima kenshi, Kinsei 2 tsūshi IV*, 774–77.

6. Smith, *Agrarian Origins*, chaps. 7–9; Kodama et al., *Nihon rekishi taikei*, 3: 406–8; and Araki, "Kinsei shoki," 14–43. With regard to case studies of the breakdown of patriarchal farming units, several scholars have examined the family of Sase Yojiemon, author of the agricultural treatise *Aizu nōsho*. See especially Fujita and Hatori, *Kinsei hōken shakai*, 71–94. Also see *Fukushima-ken nōgyōshi*, 1: 421–26, 451–61; and Shōji, "Kaidai," 229–36.

7. For cotton cultivation in Mikawa, see *Shinpen Okazaki shishi shiryō*, 7: 530–31; *Nihon sangyōshi taikei*, 5: 54–55; *Hyakushō denki*, 227; Iwasaki, "Nishi Mikawa chiiki," 350; and Kitajima, ed., *Edo shōgyō to Ise-dana*, 233. For cotton cultivation in Aizu, see Hayashi Reiko, "Kinsei shakai no mensaku," 180–81; and Shōji, "Kaidai," 257. For the Kinai comparison, I have averaged the yields in Table 14 in Hauser, *Economic Institutional Change*, 124.

8. *Nihon sangyōshi taikei*, 1: 223–24. For examples of early silk cloth production, see *Tango kigyōshi*, 3–14; *Hachiōji orimonoshi, jōkan*, 28–36; *Nihon sangyōshi taikei*, 4: 287–88; *Kiryū orimonoshi, jōkan*, 42–62; and Kudō and Kawa-

mura, "Kinsei kinu orimonogyō," 143. For Ashikaga, see Doc. 1, *Kindai Ashikaga shishi*, 3: 444, 450. For Shindatsu, see *Nihon sangyōshi taikei*, 3: 73–75.

9. Katō, *Nihon no sake 5000-nen*, 200.

10. *Ibaraki kenshi, Kinseihen*, 239.

11. *Ōsaka fushi*, 5: 671; and Yunoki, *Sakazukuri*, 32, 76–79.

12. Ōishi Sadao, *Nihon chagyō hattatsushi*, 224–44.

13. For tea-processing methods, see *Shizuoka-ken chagyōshi*, 1: 142; Rein, *Industries*, 117–19; Gribble, "Preparation of Japan Tea," 8–10; *Kikugawa-chō chagyōshi*, 100–101; and *Yamashiro chagyōshi*, 214–17.

14. For examples of some key technological advances, see Morris-Suzuki, *Technological Transformation*, part I passim.

15. Smith, *Agrarian Origins*, chap. 7 passim; and Smith, "Ōkura Nagatsune." Domains, too, took an avid interest in Miyazaki's work. In 1702 a farmer notified Kaga domain of his experimentation with making wax and cotton cultivation. The domain responded, "Is this something written about in *Nōgyō zensho*?" See Hayama, "Shōnō nōhō," 80.

16. For interesting comparisons, see Mingay, ed., *Arthur Young*.

17. Arizono, *Kinsei nōsho*, 16–23. Agricultural treatises, with the exception of *Nōgyō zensho* and Ōkura Nagatsune's treatises of the early nineteenth century, were rare in advanced regions like the Kinai and points west along the Seto Inland Sea. Arizono argues that the agricultural patterns developed there were diffused to less advanced areas and were modified to conform to local conditions.

18. For a discussion of Meiji agricultural techniques (known as the *Meiji nōhō*) and efforts at diffusion, see Francks, *Technology*, 55–63.

19. In a 1796 inventory of the trousseau for the daughter of a landlord in Matsukamiko village in what is today Ehime prefecture, twenty-nine of the fifty-eight articles of clothing listed were made of silk and purchased in Kyoto and Osaka. See Oka, "Nōson no henbō," 57–58.

Frequent bakufu and domain edicts against commoners wearing silks suggest that the populace largely ignored the prohibitions. In 1643 the bakufu issued an edict restricting farmers' clothing to hemp and cotton; village headmen and townspeople were allowed to wear pongee and unpatterned silks, as long as they were not dyed purple or plum. See Hayashi Reiko, *Shōnin no katsudō*, 12–13. See also *Nihon sangyōshi taikei*, 1: 223–24; Yoshimura, "Bakuhansei shakai to hatasaku gijutsu," 111–15; and Inoue, "Kaidai 1," 458.

20. Vlastos, *Peasant Protests*, 92–96; *Nihon sangyōshi taikei*, 3: 75; *Fukushima kenshi*, 2: 488–89. There may have been as many as 200 breeds of silkworm by the end of the Tokugawa; see Morris-Suzuki, *Technological Transformation*, 39–40. For the oftentimes slow pace of diffusion, see Kudō et al., "Kinsei no yōsan," 112–15.

21. Some treatises noted differences between the colder northeastern Japan and the more moderate climes, such as Shinano and Ōmi. Satō Tomonobu of Kakeda village in Ōshū criticized Tsukada Yoemon's treatise *Shinsen yōsan miroku* because it failed to take significant account of climatic differences between Shinano, where Tsukada lived, and Ōshū. Soon after, Tsukada issued a revised

version of his treatise which corrected this important omission. See Shōji, *Kinsei yōsangyō hattatsushi*, 73–74.

22. Inoue, "Kaidai 1," 465–69.

23. Uegaki, *Yōsan hiroku*, 151–69.

24. Inoue, "Kaidai 2," 484. Uegaki's work made its way to Europe, where a Dutch scholar translated it into French. It was published in Paris and Turin (Italy) in 1848. See Inoue, "Kaidai 1," 443.

25. *Yūki shishi*, 6: 186–94. Shima village was Gunma's most important egg card production region in the early Meiji, and the Tajima household was the village's preeminent producer. See *Gunma kenshi tsūshihen*, 8: 141–42.

26. Inoue, "Kaidai 2," 476; and Kudō et al., "Kinsei no yōsan," 116.

27. Umemiya, "Kaisetsu," 886–88.

28. Sugiyama refers to these as "sedentary reeling machines"; see Sugiyama, *Japan's Industrialization*, 80. For more on the technological aspects of the *zaguri*, see *Nihon sangyōshi taikei*, 1: 236–39; Ishii, "Meijiki no Gunma," 111; Duran, *Raw Silk*, 97–98; and Negishi, "Bakumatsu kaikōki," 10–19.

29. Ueda domain in Shinano banned the use of the *zaguri* on three occasions from the 1830's, because officials believed that it damaged the reputation of the local industry in national markets. Yonezawa took similar measures for the same reason. See Negishi, "Bakumatsu kaikōki," 13–14, 19–22. Even producers in Ōshū and Shinano, where the devices were first invented, rarely used them before the opening of the ports; see Kudō et al., "Kinsei no yōsan," 130–32; Morris-Suzuki, *Technological Transformation*, 37–39; and Takamura, "Suijō no shiruku rōdo," 332.

30. Ishii, "Meijiki no Gunma," 111–13; and Sugiyama, *Japan's Industrialization*, 81–82.

31. For Yonezawa, see Watanabe Fumio, *Yonezawa-han no tokusangyō*, 153. For Okaya, see *Okaya shishi, chūkan*, 450–51. For other areas, see Table 2 in Negishi, "Bakumatsu kaikōki," 8. Some forms of *zaguri*-reeled silk, however, did not have a high reputation in European markets, because the quantity of thread in each hank varied, the thread would break and was not uniform, and there were too many imperfections in the thread, such as lumps and knots. See Takeuchi Sōichi, "Kindai seishigyō e no ikō," 211–14.

32. *Tango kigyōshi*, 27–38.

33. *Kiryū orimonoshi, jōkan*, 112–24, 132; and Kudō and Kawamura, "Kinsei kinu orimonogyō," 149. The *takahata* was used to weave figured fabrics and was similar in design to European looms of the seventeenth and eighteenth centuries; the major difference was the positioning of the draw boy. See Nakaoka et al., "Textile History," 120. Smaller variations of the *takahata* allowed less ornate cloths to be produced more efficiently. See *Hachiōji orimonoshi, jōkan*, 441–43. Another such loom monopolized by Nishijin was the *sorahikibata*, also used to produce high-quality silks with complicated designs. A device from this loom was eventually added to the *takahata*, enabling it to do the same. See *Nihon sangyōshi taikei*, 1: 260–61.

34. Kudō and Kawamura, "Kinsei kinu orimonogyō," 148; and Mishima, *Nagahama chirimen*, 7.

214     NOTES TO CHAPTER 2

35. For Ashikaga, see *Yūki shishi*, 5: 438. For Echigo, see *Niigata kenshi tsū-shihen*, 5: 322. For Iyo, see Tsunoyama, "Nihon no shokki," 292.

36. We know little about the extent of small-scale sake production in the To-kugawa. Figures for the mid-Meiji, however, suggest that it was extensive. See Saitō and Tanimoto, "Zairai sangyō," 268–70. Most brewers in the Gunma area were very small, producing only about 2–10 *koku* of sake, suggesting that it was for household use. See *Gunma kenshi tsūshihen*, 8: 283.

37. Yunoki, *Sakazukuri*, 32–46, 104–5. In 1715 the eastern part of Mikage village used only about 41 *koku* in making sake, probably just enough for village consumption. In 1777 Kanō Jihei, who became one of the region's largest brewers, produced 320 *koku*. See *Nihon sangyōshi taikei*, 6: 182–83.

38. *Ibaraki kenshi, Kinseihen*, 384.

39. For the Nakamura example, see ibid., 242. For Satō, see *Niigata kenshi tsūshihen*, 5: 354. For Watanabe, see Omura, *Hokuetsu no gōnō*, 7, 14–15.

40. For Echigo brewmasters in the Kantō, see *Niigata kenshi tsūshihen*, 6: 771; *Nihon sangyōshi taikei*, 4: 118; and *Itsukaichi chōshi*, 600–602. For Tanba, see *Nada no sakazukuri*, 199; and Yunoki, *Sakazukuri*, 197–202.

41. *Hiroshima kenshi, Kindai 1 tsūshi V*, 847–49.

42. *Ibaraki kenshi, Kinseihen*, 360–64.

43. For Nakayama, see *Ibaraki-ken shiryō, Kindai sangyōhen I*, 23–24. For Nomura, see Doc. 498, *Ibaraki-ken shiryō, Kindai sangyōhen II*, 317; and *Ibaraki kenshi, Kinseihen*, 364. For Sakurai, see *Ibaraki kenshi, Shichōsonhen II*, 205–7.

44. Ōishi Sadao, *Nihon chagyō hattatsushi*, 246; and *Shizuoka-ken chagyō-shi*, 1: 1315–16.

45. *Nihon sangyōshi taikei*, 5: 132. The primary market for green tea until the end of the nineteenth century, when consumers shifted to black tea, was North America. See Sugiyama, *Japan's Industrialization*, 146–52. Japanese made a number of efforts in the early and mid-Meiji to produce the kind of black tea desired by Europeans but met with unsatisfactory results. According to J. J. Rein, "The black tea prepared in Japan, lacking the characteristic good taste and aroma and the strength, does not furnish an agreeable beverage. For reasons not fully learned, the Japanese tea-leaf cannot stand the process of fermentation so important in the production of the black sorts of Chinese tea." See Rein, *Industries*, 122–23.

46. For Shizuoka, see Unno and Katō, eds., *Shokusan kōgyō to hōtoku undō*, 37. For Niigata, see *Niigata kenshi tsūshihen*, 6: 773–74. According to Rein, "In Tokio itself . . . many a piece of ground has been transformed, even from the former parks of Daimyo residences, into tea-gardens. The Japanese government had reckoned that in this way altogether 4,600 chō of land have in recent times been withdrawn from cultivation for other crops and devoted to raising tea." See Rein, *Industries*, 127.

47. *Nihon sangyōshi taikei*, 5: 132; and *Yokohama shishi*, 2: 666–68. For these and other examples of the diffusion of Uji tea methods to Shizuoka, see *Shi-*

*zuoka-ken chagyōshi,* 1: 1290–1357; and *Shizuoka-ken Fuji-gun chagyōshi,* 664–77.

48. Because of significant underreporting at the local level, there are clear problems with statistical sources from the early Meiji. For a discussion of such problems, see Nakamura Satoru, *Meiji Ishin no kiso kōzō,* 113–21; and J. Nakamura, *Agricultural Production,* chap. 1. Since underreporting was probably common to all regions and for all products, the 1874 data still afford an idea of the extent of the diffusion of commodity production, at both the regional and the national level.

49. Yamaguchi Kazuo, *Meiji zenki keizai,* 5. Ishii Kanji, building on data presented in the 1874 *Bussanhyō,* has estimated that 58.2 percent of the value of all products came from the agricultural sector, 33.7 percent from the industrial sector, and 8.1 percent from livestock, forestry, marine products, and mining. Ishii, "Kokunai shijō," 10–11.

50. Yamaguchi Kazuo, *Meiji zenki keizai,* 38–43. Regional variations, of course, were great; some regions, such as Niigata and Akita along the Japan Sea, produced massive surpluses of rice, while others were net importers. One wealthy farmer in Eguchi village in Settsu province, part of the Kinai, sold 55.2 percent of his rice in the 1790's, the remainder going toward taxes and household consumption. By the nineteenth century the Kinai had large numbers of rural rice merchants and retail rice establishments. See *Shinshū Ōsaka shishi,* 4: 266–68.

51. Calculated from Ishii, "Kokunai shijō," 10–11.

52. The per capita production of manufactured goods in 1874 was 6.79 yen in the Kinki, 3.84 yen in the Kantō, 3.83 yen in the Tōkai, 2.89 yen in the Tōhoku, and 1.97 yen in Kyūshū. Calculated from data presented ibid., 10–11.

53. Wigen, *Making of a Japanese Periphery,* chap. 4 passim.

54. Fukuyama domain to the west continued as a major cotton cultivation region until around the mid-nineteenth century. Some villagers in neighboring Hiroshima domain devoted about fifty percent of their dry fields to cotton by the time of the Meiji Restoration; see *Hiroshima kenshi, Kinsei 2 tsūshi IV,* 252–73. Villages in southern Bitchū along the Oda and Takahashi rivers found cotton cultivation more profitable than other crops and turned over more and more of their paddies to its cultivation; see *Okayama kenshi,* 7: 331–33. The Kantō region had cultivated rather small amounts of cotton in the first half of the Tokugawa but accounted for 9.1 percent of national production in 1877. See Oka, "Nōson no henbō," 49–50.

55. Oka et al., eds., *Nihon keizaishi,* 55–56. For Tottori, see *Tottori kenshi,* 5: 542–46.

56. For the Kinai, see *Shinshū Ōsaka shishi,* 5: 305–6; *Ōsaka fushi,* 6: 696–700; and Oka, "Nōson no henbō," 47–49. For cotton cultivation rates and the importance of cash fertilizers, see Hauser, *Economic Institutional Change,* 126–36. For Fukuyama, see Hamada, "Bakumatsuki nōgyō seisanryoku," 341–45, 366–71. For Okayama, see Oka, "Nōson no henbō," 54. The price of dried sardines consumed one-half of the income from cotton; see Oka et al., eds., *Nihon keizaishi,* 55.

57. Takebe, *Kawachi momenshi*, 185, 218–35. Prices for seed cotton fell 16 percent over the period 1874–85; see Inoue et al., eds., *Nihon rekishi taikei*, 4: 464–65.

58. For Hiroshima, see *Hiroshima-ken no rekishi*, 192, 195. In neighboring Okayama prefecture, cotton harvests declined by over 90 percent between 1888 and 1900; calculated from tables in *Okayama kenshi*, 10: 274, 437. For Tottori, see *Tottori-ken no rekishi*, 170–71; and *Tottori kenshi kindai*, 3: 145–49. For Ibaraki, see *Ibaraki kenshi, Kingendaihen*, 268–69.

59. Abe Takeshi, "Kinsei Nihon," 75.

60. *Tottori kenshi*, 5: 555–57.

61. Abe Takeshi, "Kinsei Nihon," 75.

62. For Shimotsuke and Hitachi, see *Ibaraki kenshi, Kinseihen*, 376–82. For Chita, see Hayashi Hideo, *Zaikata momen ton'ya*, 50.

63. Unno, "Shokusan kōgyō," 188–89; Ishii, *Nihon keizaishi*, 110. Saitō and Tanimoto cite a figure of 34 percent; see "Zairai sangyō," 240–41.

64. Saitō and Tanimoto, "Zairai sangyō," 247–53.

65. Ibid., 241–44. The British, in fact, were disappointed with their showing. Confined to the treaty ports, Western merchants had to work through Japanese intermediaries and had scant knowledge of ever-changing domestic demands and fashions. See Sugiyama, *Japan's Industrialization*, 65–71.

66. Uchida, "Narrow Cotton Stripes," 165.

67. Nakamura Satoru, *Nihon shoki shihonshugi shiron*, 18.

68. Saitō and Tanimoto, "Zairai sangyō," 247–53. This is not to assert, however, that Sennan was without its problems. Competition with other production centers, not to mention competition among Sennan producers themselves, was intense. Of twenty-one prominent Sennan weaving establishments active in the early Meiji, only three survived into the early twentieth century. See Amano and Abe, "Zairai sangyō ni okeru shihon," 313–36.

69. Abe Takeshi, "Menkōgyō," 186–91.

70. By the 1770's, in fact, Shindatsu villages accounted for over seventy percent of total production in the Ōshū, Kōzuke, and Yūki regions. See *Fukushima kenshi*, 2: 377–78.

71. *Fukushima-ken nōgyōshi*, 1: 516.

72. Hasegawa Akira, "Bakumatsuki no Tatsuno shōyugyō," 54–59.

73. *Fukushima kenshi*, 2: 379, 489.

74. Kudō et al., "Kinsei no yōsan," 116–20.

75. Narita, *Kogai kinu burui taisei*, 413. The treatise was written around 1813–14.

76. Inoue et al., *Nihon rekishi taikei*, 4: 134–35; and Unno, "Shokusan kōgyō," 181.

77. For Ibaraki, see Hayasaka, "Meiji shoki ni okeru seishikatachi," 55–56. For Aichi, see *Anjō shishi*, 886–87. For Gunma, see *Gunma kenshi tsūshihen*, 8: 192.

78. Takamura, "Suijō no shiruku rōdo," 334.

79. See Table 5-1A in Saitō and Tanimoto, "Zairai sangyō," 237.

80. Ishii, *Nihon keizaishi*, 161–63; and Ishii, "Meijiki no Gunma," 79–83. "Improved *zaguri*" refers to the process of re-reeling; see *Gunma kenshi tsūshihen*, 8: 224.

81. The number of power looms in the United States increased from 5,321 in 1880 to 20,822 in 1890 and to 44,257 in 1900. See Matsui, *History*, 34.

82. Ishii, *Nihon keizaishi*, 161; and Ishii, "Meijiki no Gunma," 148. Both areas, in fact, were eventually consigned to primarily domestic sales because of the inferior grades of silk they produced; see Sugiyama, *Japan's Industrialization*, 115, 118.

83. Ishii, *Nihon keizaishi*, 112.

84. *Hachiōji orimonoshi, jōkan*, 403, 456–57.

85. *Nihon sangyōshi taikei*, 4: 293–95.

86. Negishi, "Bakumatsu kaikōki," 23–24.

87. *Kindai Ashikaga shishi*, 1: 832.

88. Ishii, *Nihon keizaishi*, 42; and Nakaoka et al., "Textile History," 133.

89. Even the most entrepreneurial weaving establishments, however, faced difficult times during the deflationary years of the early 1880's. The number of weavers in Kiryū, in fact, declined by two-thirds. See *Gunma kenshi tsūshihen*, 8: 255–56; and *Kindai Ashikaga shishi*, 1: 834–35.

90. For Yūki, see *Yūki shishi*, 6: 235–43. For Onozato, see *Kiryū orimonoshi, chūkan*, 234; and *Gunma kenshi tsūshihen*, 8: 257–60.

91. The greater humidity in Fukui was also more conducive to habutae production; dry air produced static electricity, giving rise to nap or fuzz, complicating the weaving process. It was only after the Russo-Japanese War, with the increased use of electric power and the diffusion of cheaper domestic power looms, that mechanized weaving factories took hold in the Kiryū area. Fukui prefecture, however, became the leading production region for silk textiles in 1903. See *Gunma kenshi tsūshihen*, 8: 258, 260–62, 265–67, 561–64; *Fukui kenshi tsūshihen*, 5: 540–47.

92. *Kawamata chōshi*, 1: 579, 627–29. Whereas habutae production in Fukui and Ishikawa prefectures was centered in cities, production in the Kawamata area was rural-centered. See Nakamura Tsunejirō, ed., *Kawamata kigyō*, 3.

93. Yunoki, *Sakazukuri*, 112–14.

94. Shinoda, "Chita shuzōgyō," 32–33.

95. Yunoki, *Sakazukuri*, 299–301.

96. Ibid., 325–41. In the Meiji era, the area known as Nadame included the city of Nishinomiya. In the Tokugawa, however, Nishinomiya was not considered part of this area.

97. There were twenty tea wholesalers in Edo in the 1810's; see *Nihon sangyōshi taikei*, 5: 125. We also know that merchants in Sunpu in Suruga province handled over 10,651 ryō of tea in 1856, most of which was sold outside the area. See *Shizuoka-ken chagyōshi*, 1: 303–4; and *Yokohama shishi*, 2: 646.

98. For Niigata, see *Niigata kenshi tsūshihen*, 6: 772, 777. For Ise, see *Yokohama shishi*, 2: 674.

99. Yokohama kaikō shiryōkan, ed., *Yokohama shōnin*, 177.

218                    NOTES TO CHAPTER 2

100.  Yūki shishi, 6: 194–95.
101.  For Tokugawa guild functions, see Miyamoto Mataji, Kabunakama no kenkyū, 151–57.
102.  Nihon sangyōshi taikei, 4: 295; Kudō and Kawamura, "Kinsei kinu orimonogyō," 148.
103.  For Kiryū and Isezaki, see Gunma kenshi tsūshihen, 8: 256–57. For Ashikaga, see Kindai Ashikaga shishi, 1: 1194–1205.
104.  Fukuyama, Kinsei nōson kin'yū, chap. 3.
105.  Havens, Farm and Nation, 41–49, 70–71.
106.  Gunma kenshi tsūshihen, 8: 148–58.
107.  For raw silk cooperatives organized by Hoshino and Hagiwara, see Soda, Chihō sangyō, 238–47. For the Kawamata cooperative, see Kawamata chōshi, 1: 614–17. For an example of a tea cooperative, see Shizuoka-ken Fuji-gun chagyōshi, 81–86.
108.  Doc. 488, Ibaraki-ken shiryō, Kindai sangyōhen II, 300–306.
109.  Ibaraki kenshi, Shichōsonhen II, 218–20; and Ibaraki-ken shiryō, Kindai sangyōhen II, 29–30.
110.  Vlastos, Peasant Protests, 114–20; and Yamaguchi and Sasaki, Taikei Nihon rekishi, 4: 205–6. For much the same reason, wealthy farmers and merchants in the provinces of Musashi and Kōzuke petitioned the bakufu in 1781 for permission to establish forty-seven raw silk inspection stations across the Kantō. See Walthall, Social Protest, 11–13; and Yamaguchi and Sasaki, Taikei Nihon rekishi, 4: 205–6.
111.  Local governments in the major cities, too, had encouraged or ordered their formation from the early 1870's, invariably with the active support of their merchants and tradesmen. With the abolition of guilds in the early Meiji, trade had become disrupted, and local governments wanted to restore order to the commercial system. The Kyoto metropolitan government, for example, was especially active in the formation of trade and industry associations well before the central government stepped in. See Yamashiro chagyōshi, 13; and Kikugawa-chō chagyōshi, 103–5.
112.  For weavers in Kiryū and Ashikaga, see Gunma kenshi tsūshihen, 8: 256; and Kindai Ashikaga shishi, 1: 1194. For tea, see Kikugawa-chō chagyōshi, 131–32; and Yokohama shishi, vol. 3 (jō), 822–32.
113.  For trade and industry associations, see Fujita Teiichirō, Kindai Nihon dōgyō kumiai shiron, 59. For tea producers' associations, see Yokohama shishi, vol. 3 (jō), 835–38.
114.  Francks, Technology, 150–52.
115.  For examples from Kiryū and Isezaki, see Gunma kenshi tsūshihen, 8: 257.
116.  Morris-Suzuki, Technological Transformation, 101–3; Katō, "Nihon no sake zukuri," 264–68; and Akita-ken shuzōshi, 104. Sericultural schools established at the prefectural and central government levels, too, made many private schools unnecessary. In 1881, for example, leading sericulturists in Kakeda in the

Shindatsu region established a sericultural training center. It attracted 70–80 students a year from almost every part of the country. It closed in 1894 because it duplicated functions performed by government schools; the central government had opened a national sericultural training school in 1886, and individual prefectures had established their own sericultural schools. See *Ryōzen chōshi*, 1: 679–80.

## Chapter 3

1. For the rise of Osaka as a powerful commercial and manufacturing center, see Hauser, *Economic Institutional Change*, 7–23; and Wakita, "Kinsei Ōsaka chiiki."

2. By the 1720's there were 1,727 *kuni don'ya* in Osaka. See *Shinshū Ōsaka shishi*, 3: 488–90; and Hauser, *Economic Institutional Change*, 24–25.

3. *Shinshū Ōsaka shishi*, 3: 358–62.

4. In the early years of the Tokugawa, there were a number of very powerful merchants in Kyoto who were active in both finance and foreign and domestic trade. Many of the country's most powerful financiers in the early seventeenth century lived in Kyoto. Tottori domain, for example, obtained loans from Kyoto merchants until the 1670's, not from merchants in Osaka. See *Tottori kenshi*, 4: 608–9. With the growing importance of Osaka, however, many Kyoto financiers moved or set up branch stores there. See *Shinshū Ōsaka shishi*, 3: 363–68, 370–75. A number of others went bankrupt as a result of some domains' inability to repay their loans. See *Kyōto no rekishi*, 5: 112–19, 136–39.

5. *Kyōto no rekishi*, 5: 125–27.

6. There were forty-eight such merchants in 1685; see ibid., 5: 135–36.

7. Kitajima, ed., *Edo shōgyō to Ise-dana*, 74–75.

8. Watanabe Morimichi, *Ōmi shōnin*, 75–78, 132–46.

9. Hayashi Reiko, *Edo ton'ya nakama*, 15–33; and Hayashi Reiko, *Shōnin no katsudō*, 19–42. There was also vibrant commercial activity in the Shindatsu region in the seventeenth century. We know, for example, that Fukushima castle town merchants sold raw silk to Kyoto as early as the 1650's. See *Fukushima shishi*, 2: 233–34. In 1636 two flood victims in the town of Kawamata were from Ise and Kyoto, suggesting that commerce may have been carried out with these regions. Several periodic markets were also in existence in Shindatsu from an early date, providing merchants from distant regions convenient locations to conduct business. See *Kawamata chōshi*, 1: 347–51.

Merchants in Kiryū, Kōzuke province, also shipped silk to other parts of the country in the early Tokugawa. The first record indicating ties between Kiryū and Edo merchants dates from 1684, and the first showing transactions with Kyoto from 1696. A periodic market visited by merchants from various parts of the country was in existence in Kiryū from much earlier, so we can assume that Kiryū silk found its way to other areas before this time. See *Kiryū shishi, jōkan*, 773–77, 873–75. In 1700 a dispute arose over the dispersal of the assets of a bankrupt Edo silk dealer, Kiryūya, who did business with a number of rural Kantō silk and pongee merchants. The previous year the rural merchants had sent over 7,626 *ryō* worth of goods to Kiryūya but had never received payment. This suggests that Kiryūya was a consignment merchant and had no control over local production. See Kitajima, ed., *Edo shōgyō to Ise-dana*, 122–23.

A 1682 record from Ōmama indicates that a local merchant by the name of Inojū began purchasing substantial quantities of ginned cotton from an Edo merchant twenty years before. Inojū sold the ginned cotton to area residents. See Doc. 293, *Gunma kenshi shiryōhen*, 15: 647. This record also suggests that farmers in the region still combined silk cloth manufacture with other forms of side industry, reflecting the still immature nature of the silk industry.

10. Mitsui, one of Japan's largest merchant houses, operated fifteen stores in the early 1720's; see Tanaka, "Mitsui Echigoya no 'Jōshūdana,'" 27. Many also employed large numbers of workers. Around 1740 the average Edo silk wholesaler employed around eighty people. Mitsui's main Edo store, Hondana, had 225 workers in 1733. Another of its Edo stores, Mukaidana, employed 105 in 1729. See *Mitsui jigyōshi, honpen* 1, 176, 185.

11. Around 1700 the Hasegawa merchant house in Edo, for example, received most of the cotton it sold from the stem family in Matsuzaka in Ise, which obtained the cotton from the surrounding region. The purpose of the Edo store was clearly to sell the cotton the stem family collected. By the mid-eighteenth century, however, the proportion obtained in this manner drastically declined. See Kitajima, ed., *Edo shōgyō to Ise-dana*, 90–91. In the early years many of these new merchant houses maintained their head operations in their native areas, supplying their city stores with capital and supplies, and their operations were rather loosely organized. From the early eighteenth century, however, they began to tighten control over their diverse operations, putting them under greater unified management. Their main operations also moved to the cities. See *Ōsaka fushi*, 6: 89–92.

12. There was also a marked expansion in the number of merchants dealing in products not handled to any considerable extent before, such as processed agricultural products (ramie, indigo balls, lacquer, etc.) and products derived from the mining and manufacturing industries (nails, swords, copper and lead, carpentry tools, etc.). Food products and raw materials from agriculture comprised a large portion of the imports into the port of Osaka in 1714. These were either consumed in the region or processed and shipped to other parts of the country. Large quantities of rapeseed, for example, were imported into Osaka and then shipped out in the form of oil (*mizu abura*). See *Shinshū Ōsaka shishi*, 3: 496–509.

13. Wakita, "Kinsei Ōsaka chiiki," 312–16.

14. Mitsui, for example, shipped 80 percent of its Kyoto main headquarters' purchases in 1711 to its largest store in Edo; see *Mitsui jigyōshi, honpen* 1, 148–54.

15. Evidence of this change in Edo commerce is that in 1694 ten organizations of Edo merchants united to form the Tokumi Wholesalers' Guild, the main purpose of which was to ensure the reliability of ocean transport to Edo from the west, especially from the Kinai. Ocean transport at the time entailed numerous problems, including frequent shipwrecks and pilferage by the ships' crews. Tokumi devised means to better control the shipping establishments handling the goods and to

spread losses from lost or damaged freight. The organization presupposed the existence of Edo merchants who themselves purchased from production regions. Under a commercial system dominated by consignment merchants, such a system would have been unnecessary because such merchants did not own the freight being shipped. See Hayashi Reiko, *Edo ton'ya nakama*, 56–63.

It was also from the second half of the seventeenth century that weights, measures, and currency began to move toward common standards. Although the bakufu set these standards, domains increasingly adopted them as well. The sale of goods in the "three cities" often necessitated a common currency and uniform standards of measurement, so it was in the domains' interests to enforce such policies. See Takeuchi Makoto, "Kinsei zenki no shōgyō," 151–53.

16. Wholesalers also charged *kaiyado* with overseeing the buyers themselves, ensuring that there were no irregularities. Mitsui, for example, imposed a long and detailed set of regulations on the buyers it dispatched to the Echigo region to buy crepe. Individual items ranged from prohibitions against drunkenness, gambling, and consorting with prostitutes to regulations about what food buyers were allowed to eat at every meal. Mitsui required the *kaiyado* to read these regulations aloud to the buyers upon their arrival. See Watanabe Kazumi, *Echigo chijimi*, 343–53.

17. *Mitsui jigyōshi, honpen 1*, 449.

18. The following discussion of market hierarchy in the Tōkai is based on Kitajima, ed., *Edo shōgyō to Ise-dana*, chap. 5.

19. Ibid., 107–16. For an example of a *kaitsugi* from the Chita region of Owari, see Hayashi Hideo, *Zaikata momen ton'ya*, 42–48.

20. Terada Denbei of Hanazono village, for example, launched into the cotton cloth and ginned cotton trade from the late 1760's and became a rural agent for Edo wholesalers. The Terada family was a largeholder, at various times engaged in sake brewing, acted as financial purveyor (*goyōtashi*) to the domain, and served as village headman. Saitō Kanzaemon of Enokimae village is a good example of a small jobber. Saitō purchased very small lots of cotton cloth from farm households, usually in quantities of about two to three *tan*, and sold them to fourteen jobbers in lots averaging from ten to fifteen *tan*. In 1802 he handled a total of 1,019 *tan*, much less than the 28,983 *tan* Terada transacted in 1791. He, too, was a village official.

21. *Shinpen Okazaki shishi*, 4: 535–37.

22. Some wholesalers even engaged in the manufacturing process. Daimaru, for example, operated a dyeing establishment in Kyoto; through the subcontracting system, Echigoya (Mitsui) controlled a large number of establishments there engaged in cloth finishing; see Hayashi Reiko, *Edo ton'ya nakama*, 136–37.

23. Around the 1720's large merchant houses such as Mitsui had agents in a few towns, such as Hachiōji and Fukushima. In the early eighteenth century, Mitsui opened a branch store in Fujioka, which bought silk from the surrounding area and served as a center for payments, shipments, and purchasing for much of eastern Japan. The store also handled a number of products in addition to silk, suggesting that the volume of its silk purchases was not very large. See *Mitsui jigyōshi, honpen 1*, 73–75.

24. As a result, Nishijin's relative position in silk production declined. In the 1750's Mitsui's Kyoto headquarters purchased about two-thirds of the silk for all Mitsui stores, a large portion of which came from Nishijin weavers. By the end of the century, this had declined to about 50 percent. See ibid., 386–87, 435–36.

25. Like cotton wholesalers, silk wholesalers asserted control over shipping establishments. Although cotton shipped to Edo from the Kinai and the Tōkai invariably went by sea, silk went over land routes. Many land freighters started or expanded their businesses through loans from the city wholesalers. See Hayashi Reiko, *Edo ton'ya nakama*, 140–46. By the closing decades of the Tokugawa, however, much silk was transported by sea as well. See Takamura, "Suijō no shiruku rōdo," 335.

26. Kagawa, *Kinsei Mitsui keieishi*, 538–42. Not all rural shippers needed such prepayments in the early years. In the Fukushima area there were a number of wealthy merchants who did not need advance funds for purchases. Sixty percent of the merchants in Kōzuke also did not need such payments, but those in other regions, such as Hida, Mino, Ōmi, and Tango, did; see *Mitsui jigyōshi, honpen 1*, 206. Transportation costs to Kyoto were low: in the early nineteenth century, costs for sending raw silk from Fukushima to Kyoto came to only 3 percent of the price of the silk. See Oka et al., eds., *Nihon keizaishi*, 59.

27. Miyamoto Tsutomu, "Sun'en cha ikken," 382–83.

28. Yunoki, *Sakazukuri*, 241–95.

29. Just as city wholesalers monopolized purchases from production regions, so too they began to assert control over sales to local areas. Whereas in the seventeenth century rural merchants such as Nakamura Sakuemon would purchase ginned cotton and cotton cloth locally and from the Kinai and sell it to cities in the northeast, from the eighteenth century Edo wholesalers usurped this trade. While Mitsui sold primarily within Edo, other houses sold large quantities to towns in the Kantō and northeastern Japan. Seventy percent of Kashiwaya's credit sales in 1764, in fact, were outside Edo. Shirokiya also sold silk and sundries to merchants in various parts of the Kantō. One year around the 1830's, an employee visited ninety-four establishments in Kōzuke alone to collect payment for goods Shirokiya had sold on credit. As a result of these activities, merchants such as Nakamura had to largely abandon their trade in ginned cotton and cotton cloth. See Hayashi Reiko, *Edo ton'ya nakama*, 150–58.

30. Hauser, *Economic Institutional Change*, 40–58.

31. Ebisuya and Kameya's employees increased from 173 and 139, respectively, in 1747 to 277 and 199 in the 1760's. Mitsui's Edo Hondana store, in contrast, increased from 272 to 328 over the same period. See *Mitsui jigyōshi, honpen 1*, 273–82.

32. Hayashi Reiko, *Shōnin no katsudō*, 302–5; Oka et al., eds., *Nihon keizaishi*, 172–73; and Yamaguchi, ed., *Nihon sangyō kin'yūshi kenkyū: orimono kin'yūhen*, 63–65.

33. *Mitsui jigyōshi, honpen 1*, 425–28.

34. In 1814, Edo silk wholesalers were forced to order twenty-five rural agents in the Gunnai area not to sell outside the guild. See ibid., 367, 440–41.

35. Ibid., 367–68.

36. Ibid., 442, 452.

37. Hayashi Reiko, *Shōnin no katsudō*, 292–306.

38. *Shinpen Okazaki shishi*, 4: 539–53.

39. Nakai, *Tenkanki bakuhansei*, 261–64, 268–70, 286–89.

40. Tanimoto, "Bakumatsu Meijiki menpu," 54–56. Some goods found a growing market within their own production regions. In Chōshū domain in the 1840's, for example, 64 percent of the paper was exported, 27 percent of the cotton cloth, 87 percent of the salt, and 5 percent of the sake. In Kaga domain in 1840, the export rates were 75 percent for silk and pongee, 86 percent for hemp and flax, 24 percent for cotton cloth, and 100 percent for sedge hats (*sugegasa*). See Shinbo and Saitō, "Gaisetsu," 14.

41. Sashinami, "Kinsei kindai ikōki," 164–65.

42. *Kiryū orimonoshi, jōkan*, 231–33.

43. Miyamoto Tsutomu, "Sun'en cha ikken," 385–409.

44. *Shizuoka-ken chagyōshi*, 397–98.

45. *Shizuoka kenshi tsūshihen*, 5: 376.

46. Yamaguchi Kazuo, ed., *Nihon sangyō kin'yūshi kenkyū: orimono kin'yūhen*, 43–57.

47. *Mitsui jigyōshi, honpen 1*, 417–20.

48. Ibid., 411–18.

49. Ibid., 441–42.

50. Kitajima, ed., *Edo shōgyō to Ise-dana*, 482–86.

51. *Nishio shishi*, 3: 956–60.

52. *Hobara chōshi*, 1: 359–75.

53. Yamaguchi Kazuo, ed., *Nihon sangyō kin'yūshi kenkyū: orimono kin'yūhen*, 384–87.

54. *Kawamata chōshi*, 1: 643–45.

55. See Table V-2 in *Shinpen Okazaki shishi*, 4: 540–41.

56. Yokohama kaikō shiryōkan, ed., *Yokohama shōnin*, 181.

57. *Yokohama shishi*, 2: 659–66.

58. Yokohama kaikō shiryōkan, ed., *Yokohama shōnin*, 168–78, 181–83.

59. *Mitsui jigyōshi, honpen 2*, 28.

60. Zaidan shōjin Ōmi shōnin kyōdōkan Chōgin-shi kenkyūkai, ed., *Henkakuki no shōnin shihon*, 279–330.

61. *Hachiōji shishi, gekan*, 945–1000.

62. Mori, "Kaikō," 122–33.

63. Ibid., 135–39, 163; and Nishikawa Takeomi, "Meiji shonen," 71.

64. Mori, "Kaikō," 163.

65. See Table 3, ibid., 134.

66. Nishikawa Takeomi, "Meiji shonen," 72–75.

67. Ishii, *Nihon sanshigyōshi bunseki*, 100.

68. Nishikawa Takeomi, "Meiji shonen," 71–72, 75–76, 80–81.

69. Yamaguchi Kazuo, ed., *Nihon sangyō kin'yūshi kenkyū: seishi kin'yūhen*, 10, 26–27.

70. Ishii, *Nihon sanshigyōshi bunseki*, 100–104; and Ishii, "Meijiki no Gunma," 84–87.

71. For Ashikaga, see *Kindai Ashikaga shishi*, 1: 832; for Kiryū, see *Kiryū orimonoshi, chūkan*, 90–93.

72. *Kiryū orimonoshi, chūkan*, 93–113.

73. The order was never rescinded, but changes in the rules concerning its implementation made it completely ineffective. See Inoue et al., eds., *Nihon rekishi taikei*, 4: 133–34; and Takamura, "Suijō no shiruku rōdo," 342–44.

74. *Kindai Ashikaga shishi*, 1: 842–55.

75. Kawamura, "Kinsei Kiryū orimonogyō," 75–77. Area weavers, unable to obtain the raw silk to pursue their craft, were hardly pleased. In a communication to the Kiryū headman, they complained about Fujiu and two other local merchants, who "forgot the place of time-honored customs" and pursued wanton self-profit at the expense of others. See *Kiryū orimonoshi, chūkan*, 98–99.

76. *Gunma kenshi tsūshihen*, 8: 223–40; and Ishii, "Meijiki no Gunma," 137–38.

77. Ishii, "Meijiki no Gunma," 144–45.

78. See Table 60 in *Gunma kenshi tsūshihen*, 8: 240.

79. *Kikugawa-chō chagyōshi*, 163–66.

80. Docs. 50–51, *Shizuoka kenshi shiryōhen*, 17: 399–401.

81. *Shizuoka kenshi tsūshihen*, 5: 588–90.

82. See the examples in *Shizuoka-ken no sangyō kumiai*, 231–34.

83. *Kawamata chōshi*, 1: 632–35, 720.

84. *Shinpen Okazaki shishi*, 4: 575–91.

85. *Nishio shishi*, 4: 779.

86. Yamaguchi Kazuo, ed., *Nihon sangyō kin'yūshi kenkyū: orimono kin'yūhen*, 27–35.

87. Pollard, "Regional Markets," 44.

88. Yamaguchi Kazuo, ed., *Nihon sangyō kin'yūshi kenkyū: orimono kin'yūhen*, 11–13, 357.

89. *Kawamata chōshi*, 1: 610–11, 645, 720.

90. Yamaguchi Kazuo, ed., *Nihon sangyō kin'yūshi kenkyū: seishi kin'yūhen*, 15–17.

91. For Gunma, see Ishii, "Meijiki no Gunma," 92–106. Gunma, of course, had several early filatures, including one at Tomioka initially operated by the government, but most had gone out of business by the 1890's.

92. Ibid., 148–53.

93. Abe Takeshi, "Menkōgyō," 195–97.

94. See Hudson, "Proto-industrialization in England," 60.

## Chapter 4

EPIGRAPH: Miyanaga, *Shika nōgyōdan*, 141. Ōkura Nagatsune makes a similar statement about the widespread weaving of cotton; see Ōkura, *Kōeki kokusankō*, 246.

1. This term is used by Hayashi Reiko in *Shōnin no katsudō*, 9.

2. Several of these names are mentioned in Ōkura, *Kōeki kokusankō*, 326–27.

3. See Table 2-1 in Hasegawa Shinzō, *Kinsei nōson*, 43.

4. *Mooka shishi*, 7: 98–99.

5. Doc. 3, *Makabe-machi shiryō, Kinseihen I*, 66.

6. Docs. 9 and 38, ibid., 98, 255. Similar rates of cotton cultivation can be found in Kameguma and Hajima villages; see Docs. 14 and 16, ibid., 128, 152–53.

7. See "Kaisetsu" to *Makabe-machi shiryō, Kinseihen II*, 26–31.

8. For examples from four villages, see Docs. 9, 14, 16, and 38, *Makabe-machi shiryō, Kinseihen I*, 98, 128, 152–53, 255.

9. *Mooka shishi*, 7: 415–17.

10. *Ibaraki kenshi, Kinseihen*, 377–79.

11. The northern Kantō had produced bleached cotton since the seventeenth century but only in insignificant quantities. In 1789 Kantō bleached cotton accounted for about 77 percent of the Edo Shiroko guild's cotton cloth purchases in the Kantō. See *Mooka shishi*, 7: 406, 413; and *Makabe-machi shiryō, Kinseihen II*, 20.

12. *Mooka shishi*, 7: 414.

13. Ibid., 7: 422–25.

14. Doc. 48, *Ibaraki-ken shiryō, Kinsei shakai keizaihen I*, 241–42.

15. *Mooka shishi*, 7: 433–34.

16. *Ibaraki kenshi, Kinseihen*, 377–78.

17. Doc. 109, *Makabe-machi shiryō, Kinseihen II*, 336–39.

18. Doc. 44, *Ibaraki-ken shiryō, Kinsei shakai keizaihen I*, 198–209.

19. *Ibaraki kenshi, Kinseihen*, 380–82; and *Mooka shishi*, 7: 434–36.

20. Hayashi Hideo, *Zaikata momen ton'ya*, 39–42, 65–67.

21. *Mooka shishi*, 7: 442–47, 463–64.

22. Docs. 9–11 and 38–41, *Makabe-machi shiryō, Kinseihen I*, 94–110, 253–68.

23. For a summary and critique of this argument, see Cornell, "Infanticide," 22–46.

24. For a summary of recent studies, see Ogilvie and Cerman, "Proto-industrialization," 228–29.

25. Jannetta, *Epidemics*, 188–207.

26. For Shimo-Obata, see Doc. 41, *Makabe-machi shiryō, Kinseihen I*, 266; for Kameyama, see Doc. 22, *Mooka shishi*, 3: 245.

27. Docs. 9, 11, 38, 40, *Makabe-machi shiryō, Kinseihen I*, 102, 107, 260, 265.

28. Doc. 22, *Mooka shishi*, 3: 245.

29. Nagatsuka, *The Soil*.

30. Abe Takeshi, *Kinsei sonraku*, 60–62. The figures for the Seto Inland Sea area come from Table 39 in Arimoto, "Jinushisei keiseiki," 460.

31. Hasegawa Shinzō, *Kinsei nōson*, 17–18; and Inui, *Gōnō keiei*, 26–35.

32. Doc. 6, *Mooka shishi*, 3: 204–5.

33. Doc. 3, ibid., 3: 198–203.

226 NOTES TO CHAPTER 4

34. Hasegawa Shinzō, *Kinsei nōson*, 143–50.
35. Ibid., 150–55.
36. Ibid., 175, 196–98.
37. Ibid., 194–200; *Ibaraki kenshi, Kinseihen*, 436.
38. *Ibaraki kenshi, Kinseihen*, 420–23.
39. *Mooka shishi*, 7: 505–14.
40. Hasegawa Shinzō, *Kinsei nōson*, 43, 176–77, 191–93, 200–202.
41. The composition of Makabe's "town merchants," in fact, reflects the degree to which conditions had changed by the closing years of the Tokugawa. Included among the sixty-three signatories to the 1857 pact were seven merchants from neighboring villages and two village merchants with branch stores in Makabe. They signed the pact because they, too, wanted to limit competition from upstart merchants in the countryside. Ibid., 208–9.
42. *Ibaraki kenshi, Kingendaihen*, 353.
43. *Shimodate shishi, gekan*, 375; and Yamaguchi Kazuo, ed., *Nihon sangyō kin'yūshi kenkyū: orimono kin'yūhen*, 755.
44. Doc. 9, *Mooka shishi*, 4: 443.
45. *Mooka shishi*, 8: 57, 172.
46. *Ibaraki kenshi, Kingendaihen*, 353.
47. Yamaguchi Kazuo, ed., *Nihon sangyō kin'yūshi kenkyū: orimono kin'yūhen*, 769–70, 776–78.
48. *Makabe-machi shiryō, Kingendaihen II: seishigyō*, 16–17, 24–26. Sericulture and reeling had not been side industries in Sakurai village before the opening of the ports, and like other northern Kantō villages, Sakurai had suffered from serious population decline until at least the 1840's. See Docs. 32–35, *Makabe-machi shiryō, Kinseihen I*, 223–35.
49. *Ibaraki kenshi, Kingendaihen*, 105, 139–40.
50. See Table 4-2, ibid., 262.
51. *Mooka shishi*, 8: 223–26.
52. *Ibaraki kenshi, Kingendaihen*, 280–89.
53. *Hyakushō denki*, 227–28; and Oka, "Kaidai," 372–74.
54. Uchida Jin'emon of Higashi-achiwa village, for example, obtained yields that were at best 60 percent of those of Yamato province in the Kinai. See Iwasaki, "Nishi Mikawa chiiki," 363.
55. Ibid., 358–64.
56. Ibid., 354, 363.
57. Yoshinaga, "Mikawa momen," 47–49; and *Shinpen Okazaki shishi*, 3: 1222–23.
58. *Anjō shishi*, 482–85; and *Shinpen Okazaki shishi*, 3: 306–20.
59. *Anjō shishi*, 565–67.
60. A number of village documents indicate that farm women engaged in weaving as a side industry. Unfortunately, these documents, known as *sashidashichō (meisaichō)*, in the Mikawa region are very brief compared with other areas and give little information on the extent of side industry. Documents 83 (1705), 89 (1770), 90 (1770), 97 (1784), 99 (1802), and 100 (1802) in the Oka-

zaki city history note that women wove cotton cloth in the slack season. See *Shinpen Okazaki shishi*, 7: 597–600, 610–16, 629–33, 638–48.

61. *Nishio shishi*, 3: 905.

62. Yoshinaga, "Mikawa momen," 50–51.

63. Ibid., 51–53; and *Shinpen Okazaki shishi*, 3: 1232–38.

64. *Shinpen Okazaki shishi*, 3: 815–17, 822–25.

65. *Nishio shishi*, 3: 694–95.

66. Yoshinaga, "Mikawa momen," 52.

67. *Nishio shishi*, 3: 1067.

68. *Shinpen Okazaki shishi*, 3: 1340–43.

69. Ibid., 3: 1187–96, 1257–62.

70. Although crop rotation patterns may account for some of these fluctuations, differences in total arable dedicated to cotton every year were not so great. See Iwasaki, "Nishi Mikawa chiiki," 359–61.

71. *Shinpen Okazaki shishi*, 3: 1188–89. See especially Graph 8-3.

72. Ibid., 3: 1196–97.

73. *Nishio shishi*, 3: 702–4.

74. Doc. 190, *Shinpen Okazaki shishi*, 7: 917–25.

75. Doc. 186, ibid., 7: 903–4.

76. Doc. 187, ibid., 7: 904–7. That they established distinct businesses is not at all surprising. Clans, or *dōzokudan*, consisted of a stem family and a group of branch families. While maintaining individual residences, branch families initially owned little land and depended on the stem family for favors in time of need; in return, they provided labor and other services to the stem at critical times in the agricultural season. With the growth of the market economy, most *dōzokudan* persisted only in attenuated form. See Fukutake, *Japanese Rural Society*, 61–67.

77. Doc. 188, *Shinpen Okazaki shishi*, 7: 908–11.

78. Doc. 189, ibid., 7: 912–17.

79. Doc. 190, ibid., 7: 917–25.

80. *Shinpen Okazaki shishi*, 3: 1119–20, 1159–60.

81. Doc. 190, *Shinpen Okazaki shishi*, 7: 917–25.

82. *Nishio shishi*, 2: 1240–48.

83. Doc. 44, *Shinpen Okazaki shishi*, 8: 191–204.

84. *Shinpen Okazaki shishi*, 4: 534–57.

85. Yoshinaga, "Mikawa momen," 56, 61–63; and *Shinpen Okazaki shishi*, 3: 1245, 1251–54.

86. Toby, "Both a Borrower and a Lender Be," 483–512.

87. Yoshinaga, "Mikawa momen," 63–64; *Shinpen Okazaki shishi*, 3: 1254–55.

88. *Nishio shishi*, 3: 697–702, 716–31.

89. *Shinpen Okazaki shishi*, 3: 1256.

90. *Nishio shishi*, 3: 922–29.

91. Ibid., 3: 929–30; and *Shinpen Okazaki shishi*, 3: 1238–39.

92. Yoshinaga, "Mikawa momen," 52–53; and *Shinpen Okazaki shishi*, 3: 1232–38.

93. Yoshinaga, "Mikawa momen," 56–60; and *Shinpen Okazaki shishi*, 3: 1248–49.
94. *Shinpen Okazaki shishi*, 4: 582–83.
95. Ibid., 4: 573–74.
96. Ibid., 4: 604.
97. Ibid., 4: 581–89.
98. Ibid., 4: 562–68. Ginned cotton merchants faced the same problem. One of Fukami Tarōemon's major responsibilities as a rural agent for ginned cotton was to ensure product quality. In 1846 and again in 1851 Tarōemon told merchants under him that the quality of Mikawa thread had declined, resulting in fewer orders from Edo wholesalers and lower prices. He asked them to inform producers of the problem. See Doc. 183, *Shinpen Okazaki shishi*, 7: 899–901.
99. *Shinpen Okazaki shishi*, 4: 583–84.
100. Ibid., 4: 621–26.
101. Ibid., 4: 540–41.
102. Yoshinaga, "Mikawa momen," 64; *Shinpen Okazaki shishi*, 3: 1255.
103. *Shinpen Okazaki shishi*, 4: 608.
104. *Nishio shishi*, 4: 443. Sugiura continued in the cotton cloth trade and in 1887 acquired the rural agent's license that Fukami Sahei had originally owned. There were violent swings, however, both in the amount of cloth he handled and in the trade's profitability. See ibid., 4: 744, 758–71.

## Chapter 5

EPIGRAPHS: Ihara, *Japanese Family Storehouse*, 26; Ejima Kiseki in Hibbett, *Floating World*, 102.
1. Shively, "Sumptuary Regulation," 123–58.
2. Shindatsu farmers engaged in sericulture from at least the early seventeenth century, and merchants in the town of Fukushima shipped raw silk to other parts of the country, including Kyoto and Gifu; see *Nihon sangyōshi taikei*, 3: 73–75; and *Fukushima shishi*, 2: 233–35. Around the same time, farmers in the Hachiōji area wove pongee, which they took to their local markets for sale; see *Hachiōji orimonoshi, jōkan*, 28–30.
3. Docs. 3-3-5 and 3-6-4, *Ryōzen chōshi*, 2: 290, 433. Kimura Motoi has estimated that the average village contained about 400 people and had an assessed productivity of around 400–500 *koku*; see *Kinsei no mura*, 27.
4. Doc. 3-6-5, *Ryōzen chōshi*, 2: 437–38.
5. See Table 1 in Hasebe, *Shijō keizai*, 139.
6. For an example of Ōishi's tribute assessments, see Doc. 3-4-17, *Ryōzen chōshi*, 2: 342–44. The real productivity of Ōishi's lands and the acreage under cultivation were undoubtedly higher than official records suggest. In 1888, in fact, farmers cultivated 18.5 percent more land than in 1849. For 1888 figures, see Doc. 4-3-9, *Ryōzen chōshi*, 3: 469; for 1849 figures, see Doc. 3-6-1, *Ryōzen chōshi*, 2: 409. The extant records do not tell us when the additional land was cleared, but we can assume that at least a part was already under cultivation in the Tokugawa. Most political authorities undertook no new land surveys after the

late seventeenth century, providing farmers the opportunity to benefit from productivity gains on their fields. The same was true in Ōishi, where political authorities conducted no new land surveys between 1674 and the Meiji land tax reform of the 1870's. See Hasebe, *Shijō keizai*, 140–41.

7. See Table 11 in Hasebe, "Kinsei kōki," 129.

8. *Ryōzen chōshi*, 1: 242–47.

9. Doc. 3-4-2, *Ryōzen chōshi*, 2: 323–26.

10. Doc. 3-6-4, ibid., 2: 425–37.

11. *Ryōzen chōshi*, 1: 418–19; and *Date chōshi*, 4: 873–76.

12. Doc. 3-6-5, *Ryōzen chōshi*, 2: 437–41. Taxes continued to be assessed on these items, however.

13. See, for example, Doc. 3-6-6, ibid., 2: 441–49.

14. The growing parity in sex ratios is clear from Docs. 3-5-10, 3-5-11, 3-5-12, 3-5-13, 3-5-14, 3-5-15, 3-6-1, and 3-6-4, ibid., 2: 380–88, 405–11, 425–37. For similar trends in nearby villages, see Tables 2–4 in Hasebe, *Shijō keizai*, 115–16, 118.

15. See Doc. 3-5-14, *Ryōzen chōshi*, 2: 387–88.

16. There are numerous documents in the Ryōzen town history listing these deductions. For an example from 1864, see Doc. 3-4-23, ibid., 2: 351–54.

17. Doc. 3-18-1, ibid., 2: 748–49.

18. Doc. 3-1-28, ibid., 2: 247–48.

19. See Docs. 3-1-26 and 3-1-29, ibid., 2: 244–55. Assertions of impoverishment were not simply schemes to get political authorities to lower taxes; the miserable conditions have been substantiated in diaries and other private records. For this and numerous other examples of the effects of climate on Ryōzen villagers, see Hasebe, *Shijō keizai*, 159–71.

20. In the late sixteenth century, there were two powerful lineage groups in the village, the Ōhashi and the Kanno. In the late Tokugawa there were seven powerful households claiming distinguished lineage, four of whom had surnames of Ōhashi. See *Ryōzen chōshi*, 1: 242–47; and Hasebe, *Shijō keizai*, 247, 359.

21. Since no information is available on earlier Gizaemon household heads, I have used such appellations as II and III to distinguish known generations of the family.

22. Compiled from Doc. 36, *Fukushima kenshi*, 9: 959–63. In the second half of 1833, Ōhashi sold over 60 percent of his raw silk to rural merchants, to those in Ōmi in particular. See Hasebe, "Kinsei kōki," 120; and Hasebe, *Shijō keizai*, 260–61. One such rural merchant was Fujiu Zenzō of Kirihara village in Kōzuke. In addition to employing weavers to produce silk cloth, Fujiu was a rural agent for Edo silk wholesalers. For a case study, see Pratt, "Village Elites," 248–60.

23. See Doc. 37, *Fukushima kenshi*, 9: 964–78.

24. A number of Shindatsu merchants, especially in the towns, operated putting-out systems in the nineteenth century. The Takahashi family of the town of Kawamata, for example, engaged in a fairly large putting-out operation; see *Kawamata chōshi*, 1: 328–32. The major Shindatsu raw silk markets were in Fu-

kushima, Hobara, Yanagawa, Koori, Fujita, Kawamata, and Kakeda; see *Hobara chōshi*, 1: 351.

25. Hasebe, "Kinsei kōki," 126–27; *Fukushima-ken nōgyōshi*, 1: 520–21; *Ryōzen chōshi*, 1: 481–83. Maeki Kyūhei also purchased extensively from other parts of northeastern Japan; see Yoshida, *Sanshigyō to nōmin ikki*, 105–6.

26. This was certainly the case with the Satō Tomonobu family of Kakeda village; see *Ryōzen chōshi*, 1: 420–22. Ōhashi kept records of raw silk and silk cloth prices in various regions; see Sasaki, *Bakumatsu shakai no tenkai*, 165.

27. Hasebe, *Shijō keizai*, 249.

28. Ibid., 250–51, 274–75.

29. Docs. 3-10-5 and 3-10-9, *Ryōzen chōshi*, 2: 588–89, 593–97. In 1835 the family employed six live-in servants, as well, some of whom undoubtedly assisted in such tasks; see Doc. 3-5-17, ibid., 2: 389–90.

30. Gihei, a branch household, owned over thirteen *koku* of land. The largest landholder in the village was Ōhashi Jinbei, who owned 35.1 *koku*. See Doc. 3-3-5, *Ryōzen chōshi*, 2: 308–12.

31. The majority of Docs. 387–545, Ōhashi Kensuke Family Archives, record loans to people unable to pay their taxes.

32. Hasebe, *Shijō keizai*, 264–73.

33. Doc. 3-15-12, *Ryōzen chōshi*, 2: 665.

34. Ibid., 2: 676.

35. Anne Walthall has argued that Japan's rural elites composed family histories and diaries in a conscious effort to impose specific values and standards of behavior on family members, for the purpose of ensuring the family's reputation and status in succeeding generations. Gizaemon II, while leaving no family histories or long-term diaries, clearly had this in mind when he composed this document. See Walthall, "Family Ideology," 463–79.

36. Doc. 3-16-7, *Ryōzen chōshi*, 2: 725.

37. Hasebe, *Shijō keizai*, 251.

38. Doc. 3-5-18, *Ryōzen chōshi*, 2: 390.

39. Doc. 3-16-3, ibid., 2: 716.

40. Doc. 3-2-16, ibid., 2: 278–79.

41. Doc. 3-16-3, ibid., 2: 709–17. For an example of a request from 1837, see Doc. 3-2-9, ibid., 2: 273–74.

42. Hasebe, *Shijō keizai*, 267. The bulk of Ōhashi's loans went to merchants who purchased raw silk for the family.

43. A large number of documents recording this are in the Ōhashi Kensuke Family Archives. Doc. 567 notes the grant of samurai status; Doc. 568 grants Gizaemon the right to wear a sword because of his relief efforts on behalf of farmers in distress; Doc. 579 records a grant of a 100 *koku* stipend, to be deducted from the village's annual tax. Unfortunately, few of these documents contain dates.

44. Ōhashi kept detailed inventories of gifts received from political authority; for an example, see Doc. 587, Ōhashi Kensuke Family Archives.

45. Doc. 3-15-12, *Ryōzen chōshi*, 2: 663–65.

46. Doc. 3-16-7, ibid., 2: 720–25. Recovering funds from merchant interme-

diaries could be a problem even in better times. Some merchants absconded with the funds Ōhashi provided to purchase raw silk or used the money for other purposes. For an example, see Doc. 914, Ōhashi Kensuke Family Archives.

47. *Hobara chōshi,* 1: 362–63.

48. Docs. 3-11-8, 3-11-9, and 3-11-11, *Ryōzen chōshi,* 2: 617–21, 623–24.

49. Doc. 3-15-3, ibid., 2: 654.

50. Doc. 3-16-3, ibid., 2: 709–17.

51. Ibid.

52. Vlastos, *Peasant Protests,* chap. 6; and Hasebe, *Shijō keizai,* 292–93.

53. Doc. 3-15-1, *Ryōzen chōshi,* 2: 653.

54. See Doc. 901, Ōhashi Kensuke Family Archives.

55. Hasebe, *Shijō keizai,* 361, 378–79.

56. See Table 1, ibid., 309–10.

57. Ibid., 288–89.

58. Doc. 4-1-84, *Ryōzen chōshi,* 3: 134.

59. Hasebe, *Shijō keizai,* 349–51; and Hasebe, "Kinsei kōki," 131–32. Perhaps not coincidentally, Ōishi villagers followed Gizaemon and other powerful households in abandoning raw silk and into the production of egg cards. In 1878 Ōishi villagers produced 584 *kin* of raw silk, 8,960 *kin* of paper mulberry, 1,099 silkworm egg cards, and over 4,000 *kin* of cocoons; see Doc. 4-1-120, *Ryōzen chōshi,* 3: 201. Ōishi had never been a significant production center for egg cards and was not included among the designated "Honba" production centers.

60. Docs. 4-1-3 and 4-3-15, *Ryōzen chōshi,* 3: 36, 475–76.

61. Doc. 4-4-109, ibid., 3: 712.

62. *Akishima shishi,* 680–85.

63. Ibid., 708–10.

64. Ibid., 680, 711, 816–17.

65. Docs. 27–28, *Akishima shishi, fuhen,* 274–81; and *Akishima shishi,* 827–28.

66. *Hachiōji orimonoshi, jōkan,* 553–56; and *Akishima shishi,* 865–69.

67. *Hachiōji orimonoshi, jōkan,* 568–69.

68. Ibid., 608–10.

69. *Akishima shishi,* 943–45.

70. Ibid., 945–53.

71. *Hachiōji orimonoshi, jōkan,* 574–82.

72. Doc. 13, *Nakagami-mura Nakano-ke,* 23.

73. *Akishima shishi,* 953–54.

74. Doc. 1, *Nakagami-mura Nakano-ke,* 13.

75. *Akishima shishi,* 940–41. For a genealogy of the family, see the introduction to *Nakagami-mura Nakano-ke,* 12.

76. Docs. 2, 3, and 8, *Nakagami-mura Nakano-ke,* 13–14, 19–20.

77. Nakano Kyūjirō served as assistant headman (*kumigashira*) in the 1810's and as headman from 1829; see Shirakawa, "Gōshō Nakano Kyūjirō," 23.

78. See Docs. 4–5, *Nakagami-mura Nakano-ke,* 15–17.

79. *Akishima shishi,* 942–43.

80. Ibid., 967–69.
81. Ibid., 962.
82. Shirakawa, "Gōshō Nakano Kyūjirō," 25–29.
83. Doc. 14, *Nakagami-mura Nakano-ke*, 23–24.
84. In 1814, for example, Usui Hachirōbei of Haijima village sold Kyūjirō VII his *kaitsugi* licenses, allowing him to conduct business with seven major Edo wholesalers. See Docs. 17–23, ibid., 26–31.
85. *Akishima shishi*, 969.
86. Ibid., 961.
87. *Hachiōji orimonoshi, jōkan*, 639–41.
88. Ibid., 671–75.
89. *Akishima shishi*, 962–64.
90. Ibid., 964–73.
91. Ibid., 972–74. See also Docs. 84–85, *Akishima shishi, fuhen*, 360–62; and *Hachiōji orimonoshi, jōkan*, 628–32.
92. *Akishima shishi*, 956–57, 974.
93. Ibid., 976.
94. Ibid., 853.
95. Ibid., 983–89.
96. Docs. 9–10, *Nakagami-mura Nakano-ke*, 20–21.
97. *Akishima shishi*, 920–30, 1040–42.
98. Ibid., 989–92.
99. See the genealogical chart in *Nakagami-mura Nakano-ke*, 12.
100. Doc. 61, ibid., 112–14.
101. *Akishima shishi*, 1361–65. A document composed after the uprising contains a list of 166 people who had provided "sympathy gifts" (*mimai junōchō*) to the family. Many appear to have been common farmers in the area, but about half had family names or owned business establishments (with a "ya" designation, such as Hinoya), suggesting that they were families of means. Many such families lived in the greater Hachiōji area, but there were also people and businesses in Edo, Kyoto, Gunnai, Yokohama, and Kawasaki. See Doc. 57, *Nakagami-mura Nakano-ke*, 103–8.
102. *Akishima shishi*, 984.
103. Ibid., 1370–78.
104. Docs. 58–59, *Nakagami-mura Nakano-ke*, 109.
105. *Akishima shishi*, 992, 1336–38.
106. Ibid., 990–92.
107. Ibid., 992–93.
108. Doc. 45, *Nakagami-mura Nakano-ke*, 92–93.
109. *Akishima shishi*, 992–94, 1031–34.
110. Docs. 37, 38, and 46, *Nakagami-mura Nakano-ke*, 67, 93–94.
111. *Akishima shishi*, 994–96. For a good example of someone engaged in putting out, see *Hachiōji shishi, jōkan*, 1013–24, 1041.
112. *Akishima shishi*, 997–99.
113. Ibid., 1361–88. "Chōtoku" has the alternate meaning of the "*Toku-*

gawa" house ruling for a "long" time, but considering previous events it seems unlikely that Nakano wished to see current conditions perpetuated.

114. Hasebe, *Shijō keizai*, 314, 379–82.

115. Ibid., 340–46.

116. Ibid., 315–27.

117. For Sashida, see *Akishima shishi*, 1018–24, 1326; for Matsui, see *Hachiōji shishi, gekan*, 1066–75; and for Yarimizu village, see Sasaki, *Bakumatsu shakairon*, 160–61.

## Chapter 6

EPIGRAPHS: Ōkura, *Kōeki kokusankō*, 309; Alcock, *Capital of the Tycoon*, 1: 119.

1. See Table 2-2 in *Ibaraki kenshi, Kingendaihen*, 106–7.

2. *Ibaraki kenshi, Shichōsonhen II*, 219.

3. Docs. 2-1-12, 2-1-14, and 2-1-24, *Iwai shishi shiryō, Kinseihen I*, 193, 196, 250, 272.

4. For an example, see Doc. 2-1-11, ibid., 177–80.

5. *Iwai no rekishi*, 369–70.

6. *Ibaraki kenshi, Kinseihen*, 361.

7. Ibid., 363.

8. Calculated from figures in Doc. 2-1-12, *Iwai shishi shiryō, Kinseihen I*, 212–47. See also Docs. 3-5-1 through 3-5-5, *Iwai shishi shiryō, Kinseihen II*, 270–86.

9. Kidota, *Ishin reimeiki*, 140–43. For the family's forest lands acquired from Sekiyado, see Kidota, *Ishinki gōnōsō*, 208–10.

10. *Iwai no rekishi*, 166–67.

11. *Ibaraki kenshi, Kinseihen*, 364–65.

12. Kidota, *Ishinki gōnōsō*, 211.

13. For an account of these two incidents, see *Ibaraki kenshi, Shichōsonhen II*, 204–5.

14. Kidota, *Ishinki gōnōsō*, 212; and Kidota, *Ishin reimeiki*, 143–44.

15. Kidota, *Ishinki gōnōsō*, 210, 215–21.

16. *Iwai no rekishi*, 372, 383; Kidota, *Ishinki gōnōsō*, 214–15.

17. Quoted in Kidota, *Ishinki gōnōsō*, 214.

18. Ibid., 215.

19. *Iwai no rekishi*, 383–84.

20. *Ibaraki kenshi, Shichōsonhen II*, 208–10.

21. Kidota, *Ishinki gōnōsō*, 226, 231, 235; and Kidota, *Ishin reimeiki*, 144.

22. Kidota, *Ishinki gōnōsō*, 225.

23. Docs. 195–96, *Ibaraki kenshi, Kindai sangyōhen I*, 218–22.

24. For an example, see Doc. 4, ibid., 49–57.

25. See "Kaisetsu," ibid., 25.

26. Doc. 495, *Ibaraki kenshi, Kindai sangyōhen II*, 311–13.

27. *Ibaraki kenshi, Shichōsonhen II*, 215–17.

28. See Table 2-2 in *Ibaraki kenshi, Kingendaihen*, 106–7.

29. *Yokohama shishi*, 3 (jō): 540.
30. Doc. 492, *Ibaraki kenshi, Kindai sangyōhen II*, 308–10.
31. Kidota, *Ishinki gōnōsō*, 221–24.
32. Ibid., 229–31.
33. *Shizuoka kenshi tsūshihen*, 5: 141.
34. Doc. 8, *Ibaraki kenshi, Kindai sangyōhen I*, 60–74.
35. *Shizuoka kenshi tsūshihen*, 5: 138–39.
36. Doc. 8, *Ibaraki kenshi, Kindai sangyōhen I*, 60–74.
37. *Shizuoka kenshi tsūshihen*, 5: 139–41.
38. Doc. 488-1, *Ibaraki kenshi, Kindai sangyōhen II*, 300–301.
39. Docs. 488-8 and 491, ibid., 305–6, 307–8.
40. Table 72 in *Yokohama shishi*, 3 (jō): 538.
41. In 1879 he spent about 88 yen on cash fertilizers for his new tea groves, as well as an additional 56 yen for the labor necessary to apply the fertilizers; see Kidota, *Ishinki gōnōsō*, 226–29.
42. Ibid., 221–22.
43. According to statistics compiled for Sashima district around 1912, "industrial products" (primarily raw silk) accounted for only 25 percent of the total value of all products. See Table 4 in *Iwai shishi shiryō, Kingendaihen I*, 87–88.
44. Doc. 7, ibid., 449–50.
45. *Ibaraki kenshi, Shichōsonhen II*, 218–19. For the importance of railroads to the survival of localities, see Allinson, *Japanese Urbanism*, 35–37.
46. Kumagawa was divided into three political entities, one controlled by the bakufu and the other two by Tokugawa bannermen.
47. Doc. 13, *Tama Jiman*, 1: 24–29.
48. Doc. 47, ibid., 1: 248–56.
49. Doc. 101, ibid., 2: 579–81.
50. Doc. 243, ibid., 5: 172.
51. See the entries for 2/14/1832, 2/17/1832, 4/13/1832, and 4/26/1832 in Doc. 113, ibid., 3: 182–83, 196, 198.
52. Ibid., 3: 188–89, 194.
53. Tani, "Kamesaburō nikki," 642.
54. See, for example, the entry for 2/27/1832 in Doc. 113, *Tama Jiman*, 3: 186.
55. Doc. 71, *Fussa shishi shiryōhen, Kinsei 3*, 166.
56. Suzuki, "Edo jidai kōki," 662–81.
57. Doc. 114, *Tama Jiman*, 3: 205.
58. Suzuki, "Edo jidai kōki," 667.
59. Doc. 114, *Tama Jiman*, 3: 206–7.
60. Tada, "Ishikawa Wakichi," 435–38.
61. *Fussa shishi, jōkan*, 701.
62. Tani, "Ishikawa Wakichi," 441.
63. Doc. 171, *Tama Jiman*, 4: 62–63.
64. *Fussa shishi, jōkan*, 718–20.
65. Doc. 258, *Tama Jiman*, 5: 240.

66. Fruin, *Kikkoman*, 18–23.

67. See Table 32 in Tani, "Meiji zenki," 512–13.

68. *Fussa shishi, jōkan*, 673–87.

69. This is clear from Table III-55, ibid., 706–7.

70. For 1885 data see Doc. 380, *Tama Jiman*, 6: 25.

71. Compiled from Table III-51 in *Fussa shishi, jōkan*, 682–83.

72. Ibid., 710.

73. Doc. 411, *Tama Jiman*, 6: 103–11.

74. *Fussa shishi, gekan*, 58–59.

75. This is clear from diary entries from 1894 and 1904; see Docs. 417 and 483, *Tama Jiman*, 6: 141–42, 495–96.

76. Ugome, "Meiji Ishin to Ishikawa-ke," 535.

77. *Fussa shishi, jōkan*, 705.

78. His sake brewmaster received a salary of 70 yen in 1885; see Doc. 380, *Tama Jiman*, 6: 25.

79. For a discussion of Ishikawa's beer operations, see Ugome, "Kanagawa-ken no biirugyō," 930–37; and *Fussa shishi, jōkan*, 705–10.

80. Tani, "Meiji kōki," 905–13.

81. Ibid., 905.

82. *Fussa shishi, jōkan*, 704.

83. For a list of the largest Nadame breweries, see Doc. 419, *Tama Jiman*, 6: 172.

84. Compiled from Table III-53 in *Fussa shishi, jōkan*, 690.

85. Doc. 235, *Tama Jiman*, 5: 140.

86. The land certificates are listed in Tani, "Meiji zenki," 519–33. The Fussa city history notes that its lands totaled only 8.7 *chō*, but this figure includes only its reclaimed lands at Shimokawahara; see *Fussa shishi, jōkan*, 705.

87. *Fussa shishi, gekan*, 49–50.

88. See Ishikawa Yahachirō's introduction to *Tama Jiman*, 3: 1.

## Conclusion

EPIGRAPH: Doc. 1, *Fuchū shishi shiryōhen*, 3: 494–96.

1. For a brief discussion of the Ono family, see "Kaisetsu," ibid., (23)–(24).

2. Deyon, "Proto-Industrialization," 45–46.

3. Ibid., 42–43.

4. Hoppit, *Risk and Failure*, 42, 56–58.

5. Ibid., 53.

6. Saitō, *Purotokōgyōka*, chap. 8 passim; and Saitō, "Rural Economy," 400–420.

7. Calculated from Table 1.13 in T. Nakamura, *Economic Growth*, 21.

8. De Vries and van der Woude, *First Modern Economy*, 527–29.

9. For France, see Deyon, "Proto-Industrialization," 40–42; for Holland, see de Vries and van der Woude, *First Modern Economy*, 209.

10. For an example from Flanders, see Vandenbroeke, "Proto-Industry," 106–17.

11. Engerman and Sokoloff, "Factor Endowments," 260–304.

# Works Cited

*Local Histories, Local Document Collections,*
*Industry Histories, and Archival Material*

*Aizu shuzōshi.* By Itō Toyomatsu. Aizuwakamatsu: Aizuwakamatsu shuzō ku-miai, 1986.

*Akishima shishi.* Edited by Akishima shishi hensan iinkai. Tokyo: Akishima-shi, 1978.

*Akishima shishi, fuhen.* Compiled by Akishima shishi hensan iinkai. Tokyo: Aki-shima-shi, 1978.

*Akita-ken shuzōshi, honpen.* Edited by Akita-ken shuzō kumiai. Akita-shi: Akita-ken shuzō kumiai, 1988.

*Anjō shishi.* Edited by Anjō shishi hensan iinkai. Anjō: Aichi-ken Anjō shiya-kusho, 1971.

*Daichi ni midori no to o: Ibaraki kengikai 100-nen no ayumi.* By Emoto Tomi-kiyū. Mito: Ibaraki kengikai, 1979.

*Date chōshi,* vol. 4 suppl. I, *Ōshū sanshu honba yōsan nisshi shūsei.* Compiled and edited by Date-machi. Date: Date-machi, 1985.

*Fuchū shishi shiryōhen,* vol. 3, *Kinseihen ge.* Compiled by Hiroshima-ken, Fuchū-shi. Fuchū: Hiroshima-ken, Fuchū-shi, 1988.

*Fukui kenshi tsūshihen,* vol. 5, *Kingendai 1.* Edited by Fukui-ken. Fukui-shi: Fu-kui-ken, 1994.

*Fukushima kenshi,* vol. 2, *Kinsei 1 tsūshihen 2.* Edited by Fukushima-ken. Fuku-shima: Fukushima-ken, 1971.

*Fukushima kenshi,* vol. 9, *Kinsei shiryō 2.* Compiled by Fukushima-ken. Fukushi-ma: Fukushima-ken, 1965.

*Fukushima shishi,* vol. 2, *Kinsei I (tsūshihen 2).* Edited by Fukushima shishi hen-san iinkai. Fukushima: Fukushima-shi kyōiku iinkai, 1972.

*Fukushima-ken nōgyōshi,* vol. 1, *Tsūshi I.* Edited by Fukushima-ken nōgyō-shi hensan iinkai. Fukushima: Fukushima-ken, 1987. Idem, vol. 2, *Tsūshi II,* 1986.

*Fussa shishi, jōkan*. Edited by Fussa shishi hensan iinkai. Fussa: Fussa-shi, 1994. Idem, *gekan*, 1994.

*Fussa shishi shiryōhen, Kinsei 3*. Compiled by Fussa shishi hensan iinkai. Fussa: Fussa-shi, 1991.

*Gunma kengikaishi*, vol. 1. Edited by Gunma kengikai jimukyoku. Maebashi: Gunma kengikai, 1951.

*Gunma kenshi shiryōhen*, vol. 15, *Kinsei 7*. Compiled by Gunma kenshi hensan iinkai. Maebashi: Gunma-ken, 1988. Idem, vol. 17, *Kindai gendai 1*, 1977.

*Gunma kenshi tsūshihen*, vol. 7, *Kindai gendai 1*. Compiled by Gunma kenshi hensan iinkai. Maebashi: Gunma-ken, 1991. Idem, vol. 8, *Kindai gendai 2*, 1989.

*Hachiōji orimonoshi, jōkan*. Edited by Shōda Ken'ichirō. Tokyo: Hachiōji orimono kōgyō kumiai, 1965.

*Hachiōji shishi, gekan*. Edited by Hachiōji shishi hensan iinkai. Tokyo: Hachiōji shiyakusho, 1967.

*Hiroshima-ken no rekishi*. By Gotō Yōichi. Tokyo: Yamakawa shuppansha, 1988.

*Hiroshima kenshi, Kinsei 1 tsūshi III*. Edited by Hiroshima-ken. Hiroshima: Hiroshima-ken, 1981. Idem, *Kinsei 2 tsūshi IV*, 1984. Idem, *Kindai 1 tsūshi V*, 1980.

*Hobara chōshi*, vol. 1, *Tsūshi*. Edited by Hobara chōshi hensan iinkai. Hobara: Hobara-machi, 1987.

*Ibaraki kenshi, Kinseihen*. Edited by Ibaraki kenshi henshū iinkai. Mito: Ibaraki-ken, 1985. Idem, *Kingendaihen*, 1984.

*Ibaraki kenshi, Shichōsonhen II*. Edited by Ibaraki kenshi hensan sōgōbukai. Mito: Ibaraki-ken, 1975.

*Ibaraki-ken shiryō, Kinsei shakai keizaihen I*. Compiled by Ibaraki kenshi hensan kinseishi dainibukai. Mito: Ibaraki-ken, 1971.

*Ibaraki-ken shiryō, Kindai sangyōhen I*. Compiled by Ibaraki kenshi hensan kindaishi dainibukai. Mito: Ibaraki-ken, 1969. Idem, *Kindai sangyōhen II*, 1973.

*Itsukaichi chōshi*. Edited by Itsukaichi chōshi hensan iinkai. Tokyo: Itsukaichi-machi, 1976.

*Iwai no rekishi: Kinseihen—kingendai*. By Imai Ryūsuke. Tsuchiura: Tsukuba shorin, 1988.

*Iwai shishi shiryō, Kinseihen I*. Compiled by Iwai shishi hensan iinkai. Iwai: Iwai-shi, 1994. Idem, *Kinseihen II*, 1995. Idem, *Kingendaihen I*, 1992.

*Kawamata chōshi*, vol. 1, *Tsūshihen*. Edited by Kawamata-machi. Kawamata: Kawamata-machi, 1982.

*Kikugawa-chō chagyōshi*. Edited by Kikugawa-chō chagyōshi hensan iinkai. Kikugawa: Kikugawa chōchō, 1984.

*Kindai Ashikaga shishi*, vol. 1, *Tsūshihen*. Edited by Ashikaga shishi hensan iinkai. Ashikaga: Ashikaga-shi, 1977.

*Kindai Ashikaga shishi*, vol. 3, *Shiryōhen*. Compiled by Ashikaga shishi hensan iinkai. Ashikaga: Ashikaga-shi, 1979.

*Kiryū orimonoshi, jōkan*. Edited by Kiryū orimonoshi hensankai. Tokyo: Kokusho kankōkai, 1974; reprint of 1935 edition. Idem, *chūkan*, 1974.

*Kiryū shishi, jōkan.* Edited by Kiryū shishi hensan iinkai. Kiryū: Kiryū shishi kankō iinkai, 1958.

*Kyōto no rekishi,* vol. 5, *Kinsei no tenkai.* Edited by Kyōto-shi. Kyoto: Kyōto shishi hensanjo, 1972.

*Makabe-machi shiryō, Kinseihen I.* Edited by Makabe chōshi hensan iinkai. Makabe: Makabe-machi, 1985. Idem, *Kinseihen II,* 1987. Idem, *Kingendaihen II: seishigyō,* 1988.

*Mie kenshi shiryōhen, Kindai 3 sangyō keizai.* Compiled by Mie-shi. Tsu: Mieken, 1988.

*Mitsui jigyōshi, honpen 1.* Edited by Mitsui bunko. Tokyo: Mitsui bunko, 1980. Idem, *honpen 2,* 1980.

*Mooka shishi,* vol. 3, *Kinsei shiryōhen.* Compiled by Mooka shishi hensan iinkai. Mooka: Mooka-shi, 1985. Idem, vol. 4, *Kingendai shiryōhen,* 1985.

*Mooka shishi,* vol. 7, *Kinsei tsūshihen.* Edited by Mooka shishi hensan iinkai. Mooka: Mooka-shi, 1988. Idem, vol. 8, *Kingendai tsūshihen,* 1988.

*Nada no sakazukuri.* Edited by Nada sakazukuri yōgu chōsadan. Nishinomiya: Nishinomiya-shi kyōiku iinkai, 1992.

*Nakagami-mura Nakano-ke kinsei orimono nakagai kankei shiryōshū.* Compiled by Akishima-shi kyōiku iinkai. Tokyo: Akishima-shi kyōiku iinkai, 1985.

*Nihon sangyōshi taikei.* Edited by Chihōshi kenkyū kyōgikai. 8 vols. Tokyo: Tōkyō daigaku shuppankai, 1959–61.

*Niigata kenshi tsūshihen,* vol. 4, *Kinsei 2.* Edited by Niigata-ken. Niigata: Niigata-ken, 1988. Idem, vol. 5, *Kinsei 3,* 1988. Idem, vol. 6, *Kindai 1,* 1987.

*Nishio shishi,* vol. 2, *Kodai, Chūsei, Kinsei jō.* Edited by Nishio shishi hensan iinkai. Nishio: Nishio-shi, 1974. Idem, vol. 3, *Kinsei ge,* 1976. Idem, vol. 4, *Kindai,* 1978.

Ōhashi Kensuke Family Archives. Fukushima Culture Center.

*Okaya shishi, jōkan.* Edited by Okaya-shi. Okaya: Okaya shiyakusho, 1973. Idem, *chūkan,* 1976.

*Okayama kenshi,* vol. 7, *Kinsei II.* Edited by Okayama kenshi hensan iinkai. Okayama: Okayama-ken, 1986. Idem, vol. 10, *Kindai I,* 1986.

*Ōsaka fushi,* vol. 5, *Kinseihen I.* Edited by Ōsaka fushi henshū senmon iinkai. Osaka: Ōsaka-fu, 1985. Idem, vol. 6, *Kinseihen II,* 1987.

*Ryōzen chōshi,* vol. 1, *Tsūshi.* Edited by Ryōzen-machi. Ryōzen: Ryōzen-machi, 1992.

*Ryōzen chōshi,* vol. 2, *Genshi, Kodai, Chūsei, Kinsei shiryō 1.* Compiled by Ryōzen-machi. Ryōzen: Ryōzen-machi, 1979. Idem, vol. 3, *Kindai (jō) shiryō 2,* 1983.

*Shimodate shishi, gekan.* Edited by Shimodate shishi hensan iinkai. Tokyo: Daiwa gakugei tosho, 1968.

*Shinpen Okazaki shishi,* vol. 3, *Kinsei.* Edited by Shinpen Okazaki shishi henshū iinkai. Okazaki: Shinpen Okazaki shishi hensan iinkai, 1992. Idem, vol. 4, *Kindai,* 1991.

*Shinpen Okazaki shishi shiryō,* vol. 7, *Kinsei jō.* Compiled by Shinpen Okazaki shishi henshū iinkai. Okazaki: Shinpen Okazaki shishi hensan iinkai, 1983. Idem, vol. 8, *Kinsei ge*, 1985.

*Shinshū Ōsaka shishi*, vol. 3. Edited by Shinshū Ōsaka shishi hensan iinkai. Osaka: Ōsaka-shi, 1989. Idem, vol. 4, 1990. Idem, vol. 5, 1991.

*Shizuoka-ken chagyōshi*, vol. 1. Edited by Shizuoka-ken chagyō kumiai rengō kaigisho. Shizuoka: Shizuoka-ken chagyō kumiai rengō kaigisho, 1926. Reprinted Tokyo: Kokusho kankōkai, 1981.

*Shizuoka-ken Fuji-gun chagyōshi*. Edited by Fuji-gun chagyō kumiai. Imaizumi: Fuji-gun chagyō kumiai, 1918.

*Shizuoka-ken no sangyō kumiai*. Kakuken sangyō kumiai shiryō shūsei 20. Edited by Sangyō kumiai chūōkai Shizuoka-ken shikai. Tokyo: Fuji shuppan, 1989; reprint of 1925 edition.

*Shizuoka kenshi shiryōhen*, vol. 17, *Kingendai 2*. Compiled by Shizuoka-ken. Shizuoka-shi: Shizuoka-ken, 1990.

*Shizuoka kenshi tsūshihen*, vol. 5, *Kingendai 1*. Edited by Shizuoka-ken. Shizuoka-shi: Shizuoka-ken, 1996.

*Tama Jiman Ishikawa Shuzō monjo*. Compiled by Tani Teruhiro. 6 vols. Tokyo: Kasumi shuppan, 1985–94.

*Tango kigyōshi*. By Adachi Masao. Kyoto: Yūkonsha, 1963.

*Tatsuno shishi*, vol. 2. Edited by Tatsuno shishi hensan senmon iinkai. Tatsuno: Tatsuno-shi, 1981.

*Tottori kenshi kindai*, vol. 3, *Keizaihen*. Edited by Tottori-ken. Tottori: Tottori-ken, 1969.

*Tottori kenshi*, vol. 3, *Kinsei seiji*. Edited by Tottori-ken. Tottori: Tottori-ken, 1979. Idem, vol. 4, *Kinsei shakai keizai*, 1981. Idem, vol. 5, *Kinsei bunka sangyō*, 1982.

*Tottori-ken no rekishi*. By Yamanaka Hisao. Tokyo: Yamakawa shuppansha, 1982.

*Yamashiro chagyōshi*. Edited by Yamashiro chagyō kumiai. Yamashiro: Yamashiro chagyō kumiai, 1984.

*Yokohama shishi*, vol. 2. Edited by Yokohama-shi. Yokohama: Yokohama-shi, 1959. Idem, vol. 3 (jō), 1963.

*Yūki shishi*, vol. 5, *Kinsei tsūshihen*. Edited by Yūki shishi hensan iinkai. Yūki: Yūki-shi, 1983. Idem, vol. 6, *Kingendai tsūshihen*, 1982.

## Secondary Works

Abe Akira. *Kinsei sonraku no kōzō to nōka keiei*. Tokyo: Bunken shuppan, 1988.

Abe Takeshi. "Kinsei Nihon ni okeru wata orimono seisandaka." In *Bakumatsu-Meiji no Nihon keizai*, ed. Odaka Kōnosuke and Yamamoto Yūzō, 69–83. Tokyo: Nihon keizai shinbunsha, 1988.

———. "Menkōgyō." In *Nihon keizaishi*, vol. 4, *Sangyōka no jidai, jō*, ed. Nishikawa Junsaku and Abe Takeshi, 163–212. Tokyo: Iwanami shoten, 1990.

Alcock, Sir Rutherford. *The Capital of the Tycoon: A Narrative of a Three Years' Residence in Japan*. 2 vols. London: Longman, Green, Longman, Roberts & Green, 1863; reprinted New York: Greenwood Press, 1969.

Allinson, Gary D. *Japanese Urbanism: Industry and Politics in Kariya, 1872–1972.* Berkeley: University of California Press, 1975.

Amano Masatoshi and Abe Takeshi. "Zairai sangyō ni okeru shihon to keiei." In *Nihon keizaishi,* vol. 3, *Kaikō to Ishin,* ed. Umemura Mataji and Yamamoto Yūzō, 285–342. Tokyo: Iwanami shoten, 1989.

Arai Takayoshi. "Kinu orimonogyō no seisan kōzō to ryūtsū kikō." *Mita shōgaku kenkyū* 26, no. 1 (1983): 64–76.

Araki Moriaki. "Kinsei shoki ni okeru nōmin shihai seisaku no tenkai." In *Nihon jinushiseishi kenkyū,* ed. Furushima Toshio, 14–50. Tokyo: Iwanami shoten, 1958.

Arimoto Masao. "Chiso kaisei to chihō seiji." In *Iwanami kōza Nihon rekishi,* vol. 14, *Kindai 1,* 167–208. Tokyo: Iwanami shoten, 1975.

———. "Jinushisei keiseiki no shomondai: Bingo nanbu o chūshin to shite." In *Kinsei Seto Naikai nōson no kenkyū,* ed. Arimoto Masao, 409–73. Hiroshima: Keisuisha, 1988.

Arimoto Masao et al., eds. *Meijiki chihō keimō shisōka no kenkyū: Kubota Jirō no shisō to kōdō.* Hiroshima: Keisuisha, 1981.

Arizono Shōichirō. *Kinsei nōsho no chirigakuteki kenkyū.* Tokyo: Kokon shoin, 1986.

Banno, Junji. *The Establishment of the Japanese Constitutional System.* London: Routledge, 1992.

Berg, Maxine. "Markets, Trade and European Manufacture." In *Markets and Manufacture in Early Industrial Europe,* ed. Maxine Berg, 3–26. London: Routledge, 1991.

Berg, Maxine, Pat Hudson, and Michael Sonenscher. "Manufacture in Town and Country Before the Factory." In *Manufacture in Town and Country Before the Factory,* ed. Maxine Berg, Pat Hudson, and Michael Sonenscher, 1–32. Cambridge: Cambridge University Press, 1983.

Bix, Herbert. *Peasant Protest in Japan, 1590–1884.* New Haven: Yale University Press, 1986.

Bolitho, Harold. "The Han." In *The Cambridge History of Japan,* vol. 4, *Early Modern Japan,* ed. John Whitney Hall, 183–224. Cambridge: Cambridge University Press, 1991.

Chambliss, William Jones. *Chiaraijima Village: Land Tenure, Taxation, and Local Trade, 1818–1884.* Tucson: University of Arizona Press, 1965.

Cornell, Laurel L. "Infanticide in Early Modern Japan? Demography, Culture, and Population Growth." *The Journal of Asian Studies* 55, no. 1 (1996): 22–50.

Craig, Albert M. *Chōshū in the Meiji Restoration.* Cambridge: Harvard University Press, 1961.

Crawcour, E. S. *Kōgyō Iken: Maeda Masana and His View of Meiji Economic Development.* Nissan Occasional Paper Series, No. 23. Oxford: Nissan Institute, 1995.

———. "Changes in Japanese Commerce in the Tokugawa Period." Reprinted in *Studies in the Institutional History of Early Modern Japan,* ed. John W. Hall and Marius B. Jansen, 189–202. Princeton: Princeton University Press, 1968.

de Vries, Jan, and Ad van der Woude. *The First Modern Economy: Success, Failure, and Perserverance of the Dutch Economy, 1500–1815.* Cambridge: Cambridge University Press, 1997.

Denda Isao. *Gōnō.* Kyōikusha rekishi shinsho (Nihonshi) 119. Tokyo: Kyōikusha, 1978.

Deyon, Pierre. "Proto-industrialization in France." In *European Proto-industrialization,* ed. Sheilagh C. Ogilvie and Markus Cerman, 38–48. Cambridge: Cambridge University Press, 1996.

Dohi Noritaka. "Kinsei ni okeru bukka kisei no shokeiki." In *Kinsei kokka to Meiji Ishin,* ed. Tsuda Hideo, 51–65. Tokyo: Sanseidō, 1989.

Duran, Leo. *Raw Silk: A Practical Handbook for the Buyer.* New York: Silk Publishing Company, 1913.

Emura Eiichi. *Jiyū minken kakumei no kenkyū.* Tokyo: Hōsei daigaku shuppankyoku, 1984.

Engerman, Stanley L., and Kenneth L. Sokoloff. "Factor Endowments, Institutions, and Differential Paths of Growth Among New World Economies: A View from Economic Historians of the United States." In *How Latin America Fell Behind: Essays on the Economic Histories of Brazil and Mexico, 1800–1914,* ed. Stephen Haber, 260–304. Stanford: Stanford University Press, 1997.

Francks, Penelope. *Technology and Agricultural Development in Pre-War Japan.* New Haven: Yale University Press, 1984.

Fraser, Andrew. "Land Tax Increase: The Debates of 1898." In *Japan's Early Parliaments, 1890–1905: Structure, Issues and Trends,* ed. Andrew Fraser, R. H. P. Mason, and Philip Mitchell, 37–64. London: Routledge, 1995.

Fruin, W. Mark. *Kikkoman: Company, Clan, and Community.* Cambridge: Harvard University Press, 1983.

Fujita Gorō. *Nihon kindai sangyō no seisei.* Tokyo: Nihon hyōronsha, 1948.

Fujita Gorō and Hatori Takuya. *Kinsei hōken shakai no kōzō: Nihon zettaishugi keisei no kiso katei.* Tokyo: Ochanomizu shobō, 1951.

Fujita Teiichirō. *Kindai Nihon dōgyō kumiai shiron.* Tokyo: Seibundō shuppan, 1995.

Fukutake, Tadashi. *Japanese Rural Society.* Translated by R. P. Dore. Ithaca: Cornell University Press, 1967.

Fukuyama Akira. *Kinsei nōson kin'yū no kōzō.* Tokyo: Yūzankaku, 1975.

Giddens, Anthony. *Central Problems in Social Theory: Action, Structure and Contradiction in Social Analysis.* Berkeley: University of California Press, 1979.

Gluck, Carol. *Japan's Modern Myths: Ideology in the Late Meiji Period.* Princeton: Princeton University Press, 1985.

Gribble, Henry. "The Preparation of Japan Tea." *Transactions of the Asiatic Society of Japan* 12, pt. I (1883): 1–88.

Haga Noboru, ed. *Gōnō Furuhashi-ke no kenkyū.* Tokyo: Yūzankaku, 1979.

Hamada Toshihiko. "Bakumatsuki nōgyō seisanryoku to jinushi funō no keiei dōkō: Bingo-no-kuni Fukatsu-gun Ichi-mura Tsuchiya-ke o chūshin to shite." In *Kinsei Seto Naikai nōson no kenkyū,* ed. Arimoto Masao, 331–82. Hiroshima: Keisuisha, 1988.

Hanley, Susan B., and Kozo Yamamura. *Economic and Demographic Change in Preindustrial Japan, 1600–1868.* Princeton: Princeton University Press, 1977.

Hasebe Hiroshi. *Shijō keizai no keisei to chiiki: 18, 19 seiki no Fukushima Shindatsu chihō to sanshigyō.* Tokyo: Tōsui shobō, 1994.

———. "Kinsei kōki ni okeru kiito ryūtsū kōzō: Shindatsu chihō no kiito kaitsugi shōnin." *Keizaigaku* (Tōhoku daigaku keizai gakkai) 44, no. 3 (1982): 113–32.

Hasegawa Akira. "Bakumatsuki no Tatsuno shōyugyō." *Momoyama gakuin daigaku keizai keiei ronshū* 20 (1978): 53–74.

Hasegawa Shinzō. *Kinsei nōson kōzō no shiteki bunseki: bakuhan taisei kaitaiki no Kantō nōson to zaigōmachi.* Tokyo: Kashiwa shobō, 1981.

Hashimoto Denzaemon. *Nōgyō keizai no omoide.* Osaka: Hashimoto Sensei chōju kinen jigyōkai, 1973.

Hauser, William B. *Economic Institutional Change in Tokugawa Japan: Ōsaka and the Kinai Cotton Trade.* London: Cambridge University Press, 1974.

Havens, Thomas R. H. *Farm and Nation in Modern Japan: Agrarian Nationalism, 1870–1940.* Princeton: Princeton University Press, 1974.

Hayama Teisaku. "Shōnō nōhō no seiritsu to shōnō gijutsu no tenkai." In *Gijutsu no shakaishi,* vol. 2, *Zairai gijutsu no hatten to kinsei shakai,* ed. Sasaki Junnosuke, 41–94. Tokyo: Yūzankaku, 1983.

Hayasaka Keizō. "Meiji shoki ni okeru seishikatachi: Ibaraki-ken kindai seishigyō no reimei." *Ibaraki kenshi kenkyū* 3: 55–64.

Hayashi Hideo. *Zaikata momen ton'ya no shiteki tenkai.* Tokyo: Hanawa shobō, 1965.

Hayashi Reiko. *Edo ton'ya nakama no kenkyū: bakuhan taiseika no toshi shōgyō shihon.* Tokyo: Ochanomizu shobō, 1967.

———. *Shōnin no katsudō.* Nihon no kinsei 5. Tokyo: Chūō kōronsha, 1992.

———. "Kinsei shakai no mensaku to mengyō." In *Kōza Nihon gijutsu no shakaishi,* vol. 3, *Bōshoku,* ed. Nagahara Keiji and Yamaguchi Keiji, 171–205. Tokyo: Nihon hyōronsha, 1983.

Hibbett, Howard. *The Floating World in Japanese Fiction.* Oxford: Oxford University Press, 1959.

Hoppit, Julian. *Risk and Failure in English Business, 1700–1800.* Cambridge: Cambridge University Press, 1987.

Howell, David L. *Capitalism from Within: Economy, Society, and the State in a Japanese Fishery.* Berkeley: University of California Press, 1995.

Hozumi Katsujirō. *Himeji-han mengyō keizaishi: Himeji-han no mengyō to Kawai Sun'ō.* Himeji: privately printed, n.d.

Hudson, Pat. "Proto-industrialization in England." In *European Proto-industrialization,* ed. Sheilagh C. Ogilvie and Markus Cerman, 49–66. Cambridge: Cambridge University Press, 1996.

*Hyakushō denki, kan 8–kan 15,* vol. 17, *Nihon nōsho zenshū,* comp. Nōsangyoson bunka kyōkai. Tokyo: Nōsangyoson bunka kyōkai, 1979.

Ihara Saikaku. *The Japanese Family Storehouse, or the Millionaires Gospel Modernised.* Translated by G. W. Sargent. Cambridge: Cambridge University Press, 1959.

Ikegami Kazuo. "Meijiki no shuzei seisaku." *Shakai keizai shigaku* 55, no. 2 (1989): 69–92.

Inoue Mitsusada, Nagahara Keiji, Kodama Kōta, and Ōkubo Toshiaki, eds. *Nihon rekishi taikei*, vol. 4, *Kindai I*. Tokyo: Yamakawa shuppansha, 1987.

Inoue Zenjirō. "Kaidai 1: Yōsan gijutsu no tenkai to sansho." In *Nihon nōsho zenshū*, vol. 35, *Yōsan hiroku, Kogai kinu burui taisei, San tōkei hiketsu*, comp. Nōsangyoson bunka kyōkai, 443–74. Tokyo: Nōsangyoson bunka kyōkai, 1981.

———. "Kaidai 2: Yōsan hiroku." In *Nihon nōsho zenshū*, vol. 35, *Yōsan hiroku, Kogai kinu burui taisei, San tōkei hiketsu*, comp. Nōsangyoson bunka kyōkai, 475–85. Tokyo: Nōsangyoson bunka kyōkai, 1981.

Inui Hiromi. *Gōnō keiei no shiteki tenkai*. Tokyo: Yūzankaku, 1984.

Ishii Kanji. *Nihon keizaishi*. Tokyo: Tōkyō daigaku shuppankai, 1976.

———. *Nihon sanshigyōshi bunseki: Nihon sangyō kakumei kenkyū joron*. Tokyo: Tōkyō daigaku shuppankai, 1972.

———. "Kokunai shijō no keisei to tenkai." In *Kindai Nihon no shōhin ryūtsū*, ed. Ishii Kanji and Yamaguchi Kazuo, 1–74. Tokyo: Tōkyō daigaku shuppankai, 1986.

———. "Meijiki no Gunma no kiito." In *Gunma no kiito*, ed. Hagiwara Susumu, 79–164. Maebashi: Miyama bunko, 1986.

Iwasaki Kimiya. "Nishi Mikawa chiiki ni okeru kinsei mensaku no chiikiteki tokushoku." *Chirigaku hyōron* 58, no. 6 (1985): 349–69.

Jannetta, Ann Bowman. *Epidemics and Mortality in Early Modern Japan*. Princeton: Princeton University Press, 1987.

Kagawa Takayuki. *Kinsei Mitsui keieishi no kenkyū*. Tokyo: Yoshikawa kōbunkan, 1985.

Katō Hyakuichi. *Nihon no sake 5000-nen*. Tokyo: Gihōdō shuppan, 1987.

———. "Nihon no sake zukuri no ayumi." In *Nihon no sake no rekishi: sake zukuri no ayumi to kenkyū*, ed. Katō Benzaburō, 41–316. Tokyo: Kyōwa hakkō kōgyō kabushiki kaisha, 1976.

Kawamura Terumasa. "Kinsei Kiryū orimonogyō ni okeru shokeiei 1: Jōshū Yamada-gun Kirihara-mura Fujiu-ke." *Gunma kenshi kenkyū* 27 (1988): 55–79.

Kelly, William W. *Deference and Defiance in Nineteenth-Century Japan*. Princeton: Princeton University Press, 1985.

Kidota Shirō. *Ishin reimeiki no gōnōsō*. Tokyo: Hanawa shobō, 1970.

———. *Ishinki gōnōsō to minshū: bakumatsuki Mito-han minshū kenkyū*. Tokyo: Perikansha, 1989.

Kimura Motoi. *Kinsei no mura*. Kyōikusha rekishi shinsho (Nihonshi) 105. Tokyo: Kyōikusha, 1980.

Kitajima Masamoto, ed. *Edo shōgyō to Ise-dana: momen don'ya Hasegawa-ke no keiei to shite*. Tokyo: Yoshikawa kōbunkan, 1962.

———. *Seishigyō no tenkai to kōzō: Bakumatsu Ishinki Suwa ni tsuite no chōsa hōkoku*. Tokyo: Hanawa shobō, 1970.

Kodama Kōta. *Kinsei nōmin seikatsushi*. Revised edition. Tokyo: Yoshikawa kōbunkan, 1957.

Kodama Kōta et al., eds. *Nihon rekishi taikei*, vol. 3, *Kinsei*. Tokyo: Yamakawa shuppansha, 1988.

Konta Shin'ichi. *Mogami benibanashi no kenkyū*. Yamagata: Kōyōdō shoten, 1979.

Koschmann, J. Victor. *The Mito Ideology: Discourse, Reform, and Insurrection in Late Tokugawa Japan, 1790–1864*. Berkeley: University of California Press, 1987.

Kudō Kyōkichi and Kawamura Terumasa. "Kinsei kinu orimonogyō no tenkai." In *Kōza Nihon gijutsu no shakaishi*, vol. 3, *Bōshoku*, ed. Nagahara Keiji and Yamaguchi Keiji, 137–70. Tokyo: Nihon hyōronsha, 1983.

Kudō Kyōkichi, Negishi Hideyuki, and Kimura Haruhisa. "Kinsei no yōsan, seishigyō." In *Kōza Nihon gijutsu no shakaishi*, vol. 3, *Bōshoku*, ed. Nagahara Keiji and Yamaguchi Keiji, 103–36. Tokyo: Nihon hyōronsha, 1983.

Lloyd, Christopher. *Explanation in Social History*. Oxford: Basil Blackwell, 1986.

Matsui, Shichiro. *The History of the Silk Industry in the United States*. New York: Howes Publishing Company, 1930.

Mingay, G. E., ed. *Arthur Young and His Times*. London and Basingstoke: Macmillan, 1975.

Mishima Yasuo. *Nagahama chirimen no senbai to orimoto*. Tokyo: Chikura shobō, 1975.

Miyamoto Mataji. *Kabunakama no kenkyū*. Tokyo: Yūzankaku, 1938.

Miyamoto Tsutomu. "Sun'en cha ikken no rekishiteki tokushitsu." In *Kinsei Shizuoka no kenkyū*, ed. Honda Takashige, 379–419. Osaka: Seibundō, 1991.

Miyanaga Masakazu. *Shika nōgyōdan*. In *Nihon nōsho zenshū*, vol. 6, comp. Nōsangyoson bunka kyōkai, 3–263. Tokyo: Nōsangyoson bunka kyōkai, 1979.

Mori Yasuhiko. "Kaikō to keizai hendō: seishi urikomishō Yoshimuraya no kentō." In *Kōza Nihon kinseishi*, vol. 7, *Kaikoku*, ed. Aoki Michio and Kawachi Hachirō, 115–70. Tokyo: Yūhikaku, 1985.

Morris-Suzuki, Tessa. *The Technological Transformation of Japan: From the Seventeenth to the Twenty-First Century*. Cambridge: Cambridge University Press, 1994.

Murakami Tadashi. *Edo bakufu no daikan*. Tokyo: Kokusho kankōkai, 1983.

Myška, Milan. "Proto-industrialization in Bohemia, Moravia and Silesia." In *European Proto-industrialization*, ed. Sheilagh C. Ogilvie and Markus Cerman, 188–207. Cambridge: Cambridge University Press, 1996.

Nagahara Keiji. "Mensaku no tenkai." In *Kōza Nihon gijutsu no shakaishi*, vol. 3, *Bōshoku*, ed. Nagahara Keiji and Yamaguchi Keiji, 69–102. Tokyo: Nihon hyōronsha, 1983.

Nagatsuka Takashi. *The Soil: A Portrait of Rural Life in Meiji Japan*. Translated and with an introduction by Ann Waswo. Berkeley: University of California Press, 1993.

Nakai Nobuhiko. *Tenkanki bakuhansei no kenkyū: Hōreki-Tenmeiki no keizai seisaku to shōhin ryūtsū*. Tokyo: Hanawa shobō, 1971.

Nakamura, James I. *Agricultural Production and the Economic Development of*

*Japan, 1873–1922*. Studies of the East Asian Institute, Columbia University. Princeton: Princeton University Press, 1966.

Nakamura Masanori. *Kindai Nihon jinushiseishi kenkyū: shihonshugi to jinushisei*. Tokyo: Tōkyō daigaku shuppankai, 1979.

Nakamura Satoru. *Meiji Ishin no kiso kōzō: Nihon shihonshugi keisei no kiten*. Tokyo: Miraisha, 1968.

———. *Nihon shoki shihonshugi shiron*. Kyoto: Mineruba shobō, 1991.

Nakamura, Takafusa. *Economic Growth in Prewar Japan*. Translated by Robert A. Feldman. New Haven: Yale University Press, 1983.

Nakamura Tsunejirō, ed. *Kawamata kigyō no kōzō: yushutsu habutaegyō no jittai (jō)*. Fukushima: Iwase shoten, 1954.

Nakaoka, Tetsuro, and Kayoko Aikawa, et al. "The Textile History of Nishijin (Kyoto): East Meets West." *Textile History* 19, no. 2 (1988): 117–41.

Narita Jūhei. *Kogai kinu burui taisei*. In *Nihon nōsho zenshū*, vol. 35, *Yōsan hiroku, Kogai kinu burui taisei, San tōkei hiketsu*, comp. Nōsangyoson bunka kyōkai, 255–421. Tokyo: Nōsangyoson bunka kyōkai, 1981.

Negishi Hideyuki. "Bakumatsu kaikōki ni okeru kiito kuriito gijutsu tenkan no igi ni tsuite." *Shakai keizai shigaku* 53, no. 1 (1987): 1–28.

*Nihon teikoku tōkei nenkan*, vol. 2 (1882). Compiled by Tōkei-in. Reprinted Tokyo: Tōkyō ripurinto shuppansha, 1963.

*Nihon teikoku tōkei nenkan*, vol. 12 (1892). Compiled by Naikaku tōkeikyoku. Tokyo: Tōkyō tōkei kyōkai, 1893. Idem, vol. 22 (1902). Tokyo: Tōkyō tōkei kyōkai, 1903. Idem, vol. 32 (1912). Tokyo: Tōkyō tōkei kyōkai, 1914.

Nishikawa Junsaku and Amano Masatoshi. "Shohan no sangyō to keizai seisaku." In *Nihon keizaishi*, vol. 2, *Kindai seichō no taidō*, ed. Shinbo Hiroshi and Saitō Osamu, 173–217. Tokyo: Iwanami shoten, 1989.

Nishikawa Takeomi. "Meiji shonen no Yokohama kiito urikomishō: Yoshimuraya no keiei bunseki o chūshin to shite." *Shakai keizai shigaku* 51, no. 5 (1985): 70–89.

Ogilvie, Sheilagh C. "Social Institutions and Proto-industrialization." In *European Proto-industrialization*, ed. Sheilagh C. Ogilvie and Markus Cerman, 23–37. Cambridge: Cambridge University Press, 1996.

Ogilvie, Sheilagh C., and Markus Cerman. "Proto-industrialization, Economic Development and Social Change in Early Modern Europe." In *European Proto-industrialization*, ed. Sheilagh C. Ogilvie and Markus Cerman, 227–39. Cambridge: Cambridge University Press, 1996.

———. "The Theories of Proto-industrialization." In *European Proto-industrialization*, ed. Sheilagh C. Ogilvie and Markus Cerman, 1–11. Cambridge: Cambridge University Press, 1996.

Ogura Takekazu. *Can Japanese Agriculture Survive?: A Historical and Comparative Approach*. Tokyo: Agricultural Policy Research Center, 1980.

Ōishi Kyūkei, supplemented by Ōishi Shinkei. *Jikata hanreiroku*. 2 vols. Compiled and edited by Ōishi Shinzaburō. Tokyo: Kondō shuppansha, 1969.

Ōishi Sadao. *Nihon chagyō hattatsushi*. Tokyo: Nōsangyoson bunka kyōkai, 1983.

Ōishi Shinzaburō. *Nihon kinsei shakai no shijō kōzō*. Tokyo: Iwanami shoten, 1975.

Oka Mitsuo. "Kaidai." In *Nihon nōsho zenshū*, vol. 17, *Hyakushō denki, kan 8–kan 15*, comp. Nōsangyoson bunka kyōkai, 337–90. Tokyo: Nōsangyoson bunka kyōkai, 1979.

———. "Nōson no henbō to zaigō shōnin." In *Iwanami kōza Nihon rekishi*, vol. 12, *Kinsei 4*, 45–88. Tokyo: Iwanami shoten, 1975.

Oka Mitsuo, Yamazaki Ryūzō, and Niwa Kunio, eds. *Nihon keizaishi: Kinsei kara kindai e*. Kyoto: Mineruba shobō, 1991.

Ōkura Nagatsune. *Kōeki kokusankō*, vol. 14, *Nihon nōgyō zensho*, comp. Nōsangyoson bunka kyōkai. Tokyo: Nōsangyoson bunka kyōkai, 1978.

———. *Menpo yōmu*. In *Nihon nōgyō zensho*, vol. 15, *Jokōroku, Nōgu benriron, Menpo yōmu*, comp. Nōsangyoson bunka kyōkai, 317–411. Tokyo: Nōsangyoson bunka kyōkai, 1977.

Omura Hajime. *Hokuetsu no gōnō Watanabe-ke no rekishi*. Sekikawa: Sekikawa-mura, 1992.

Ono Masao. "Bakuhansei seiji kaikakuron." In *Kōza Nihon rekishi*, vol. 6, *Kinsei 2*, ed. Rekishigaku kenkyūkai and Nihonshi kenkyūkai, 309–39. Tokyo: Tōkyō daigaku shuppankai, 1985.

Ooms, Herman. *Tokugawa Village Practice: Class, Status, Power, Law*. Berkeley: University of California Press, 1996.

Pollard, Sidney. "Regional Markets and National Development." In *Markets and Manufacture in Early Industrial Europe*, ed. Maxine Berg, 29–56. London: Routledge, 1991.

Pratt, Edward Earl. "Village Elites in Tokugawa Japan: The Economic Foundations of the Gōnō." Ph.D. diss., University of Virginia, 1991.

Rein, J. J. *The Industries of Japan, Together with an Account of Its Agriculture, Forestry, Arts, and Commerce*. Hodder and Stoughton, 1889; reprinted Surrey: Curzon Press, 1995.

Saitō Osamu. *Purotokōgyōka no jidai: Seiō to Nihon no hikakushi*. Tokyo: Nihon hyōronsha, 1985.

———. "The Rural Economy: Commercial Agriculture, By-Employment, and Wage Work." In *Japan in Transition: From Tokugawa to Meiji*, ed. Marius B. Jansen and Gilbert Rozman, 400–420. Princeton: Princeton University Press, 1986.

Saitō Osamu and Tanimoto Masayuki. "Zairai sangyō no saihensei." In *Nihon keizaishi*, vol. 3, *Kaikō to Ishin*, ed. Umemura Mataji and Yamamoto Yūzō, 223–83. Tokyo: Iwanami shoten, 1989.

Sakurai Hirotoshi. *Seishugyō no rekishi to sangyō soshiki no kenkyū*. Tokyo: Chūō kōron jigyō shuppan, 1982.

Sasaki Junnosuke. *Bakumatsu shakai no tenkai*. Tokyo: Iwanami shoten, 1993.

———. *Bakumatsu shakairon: "Yonaoshi jōkyō" kenkyū joron*. Tokyo: Hanawa shobō, 1969.

———, ed. *Mura ni ikiru hitobito: Higashikamiisobe-mura to Hagiwara Ryōtarō*. Annaka: Hagiwara Ryōtarō kinen shuppan kankōkai, 1974.

Sashinami Akiko. "Kinsei kindai ikōki ni okeru chihō toshi shinkō shōnin." In *Shōnin to ryūtsū: Kinsei kara kindai e*, ed. Yoshida Nobuyuki and Takamura Naosuke, 125–78. Tokyo: Yamakawa shuppansha, 1992.

Shibusawa Eiichi. *The Autobiography of Shibusawa Eiichi: From Peasant to Entrepreneur*. Translated, with an Introduction and Notes, by Teruko Craig. Tokyo: University of Tokyo Press, 1994.

Shibuya Ryūichi, comp. *Meijiki Nihon zenkoku shisanka jinushi shiryō shūsei*, vol. 4. Tokyo: Kashiwa shobō, 1984.

Shinbo Hiroshi and Saitō Osamu. "Gaisetsu: 19-seiki e." In *Nihon keizaishi*, vol. 2, *Kindai seichō no taidō*, ed. Shinbo Hiroshi and Saitō Osamu, 1–66. Tokyo: Iwanami shoten, 1989.

Shinoda Toshio. "Chita shuzōgyō no seisui." *Shakai keizai shigaku* 55, no. 2 (1989): 32–53.

Shirakawa Muneaki. "Gōshō Nakano Kyūjirō no shima nakagai katsudō: 'Goyō nikki hikae' ni miru." *Tama no ayumi* 32 (1983): 22–29.

Shively, Donald. "Sumptuary Regulation and Status in Early Tokugawa Japan." *Harvard Journal of Asiatic Studies* 25 (1965): 123–64.

Shōji Kichinosuke. *Kinsei yōsangyō hattatsushi*. Tokyo: Ochanomizu shobō, 1964.

———. "Kaidai." In *Nihon nōsho zenshū*, vol. 19, *Aizu nōsho, Aizu nōsho furoku*, comp. Nōsangyoson bunka kyōkai, 219–68. Tokyo: Nōsangyoson bunka kyōkai, 1982.

Smethurst, Richard J. *Agricultural Development and Tenancy Dispute in Japan, 1870–1940*. Princeton: Princeton University Press, 1986.

Smith, Thomas. *The Agrarian Origins of Modern Japan*. Stanford: Stanford University Press, 1959.

———. "Farm Family By-Employments in Preindustrial Japan." Reprinted in *Native Sources of Japanese Industrialization, 1750–1920*, 71–102. Berkeley: University of California Press, 1988.

———. "Landlords' Sons in the Business Elite." *Economic Development and Social Change* 9, no. 1, pt. II (1960): 93–107.

———. "Ōkura Nagatsune and the Technologists." Reprinted in *Native Sources of Japanese Industrialization, 1750–1920*, 173–98. Berkeley: University of California Press, 1988.

———. *Political Change and Industrial Development in Japan: Government Enterprise, 1868–1880*. Stanford: Stanford University Press, 1955.

———. "Premodern Economic Growth: Japan and the West." Reprinted in *Native Sources of Japanese Industrialization, 1750–1920*, 15–49. Berkeley: University of California Press, 1988.

Soda Osamu. *Chihō sangyō no shisō to undō: Maeda Masana o chūshin ni shite*. Kyoto: Mineruba shobō, 1980.

Sugiyama, Shinya. *Japan's Industrialization in the World Economy, 1859–1899*. London: Athlone Press, 1988.

Suzuki Yoshiyuki. "Edo jidai kōki Tamagawa chūryūiki no orimono seisan to ryūtsū." In *Tama Jiman Ishikawa Shuzō monjo*, comp. Tani Teruhiro, 3: 661–97. Tokyo: Kasumi shuppan, 1988.

Tada Jin'ichi. "Ishikawa Wakichi to Ishikawa-ke no keiei tenkai." In *Tama Jiman Ishikawa Shuzō monjo*, comp. Tani Teruhiro, 4: 433–55. Tokyo: Kasumi shuppan, 1991.

Takamura Naosuke. "Suijō no shiruku rōdo." In *Shōnin to ryūtsū: Kinsei kara kindai e*, ed. Yoshida Nobuyuki and Takamura Naosuke, 331–59. Tokyo: Yamakawa shuppansha, 1992.

Takebe Yoshito. *Kawachi momenshi*. Tokyo: Yoshikawa kōbunkan, 1981.

Takeuchi Makoto. *Taikei Nihon no rekishi*, vol. 10, *Edo to Ōsaka*. Tokyo: Shogakukan, 1989.

———. "Kinsei zenki no shōgyō." In *Taikei Nihonshi sōsho, Ryūtsūshi* 1, ed. Toyoda Takeshi and Kodama Kōta. Tokyo: Yamakawa shuppansha, 1969.

Takeuchi Sōichi. "Kindai seishigyō e no ikō." In *Kōza Nihon gijutsu no shakaishi*, vol. 3, *Bōshoku*, ed. Nagahara Keiji and Yamaguchi Keiji, 207–38. Tokyo: Nihon hyōronsha, 1983.

Tanaka Yasuo. "Mitsui Echigoya no 'Jōshūdana.'" *Gunma kenshi kenkyū* 5 (1977): 26–43.

Tani Teruhiro. "Kamesaburō nikki ni mieru Kaseiki no shakai to minshū." In *Tama Jiman Ishikawa Shuzō monjo*, comp. Tani Teruhiro, 2: 637–56. Tokyo: Kasumi shuppan, 1986.

———. "Meiji kōki ni okeru Ishikawa Shuzō no shuzō gijutsu no kakushin ni tsuite." In *Tama Jiman Ishikawa Shuzō monjo*, comp. Tani Teruhiro, 6: 905–19. Tokyo: Kasumi shuppan, 1994.

———. "Meiji zenki no Ishikawa Shuzō to Shimokawahara kaihatsu." In *Tama Jiman Ishikawa Shuzō monjo*, comp. Tani Teruhiro, 5: 501–33. Tokyo: Kasumi shuppan, 1990.

Tanimoto Masayuki. "Bakumatsu Meijiki menpu kokunai shijō no tenkai." *Tochi seido shigaku* 115 (1987): 54–67.

Toby, Ronald P. "Both a Borrower and a Lender Be: From Village Moneylender to Rural Banker in the Tempō Era." *Monumenta Nipponica* 46, no. 4 (1991): 483–512.

Tsuda Hideo. *Nihon no rekishi*, vol. 22, *Tenpō kaikaku*. Tokyo: Shogakukan, 1975.

Tsunoyama Yukihiro. "Nihon no shokki." In *Kōza Nihon gijutsu no shakaishi*, vol. 3, *Bōshoku*, ed. Nagahara Keiji and Yamaguchi Keiji, 284–301. Tokyo: Nihon hyōronsha, 1983.

Uchida, Hoshimi. "Narrow Cotton Stripes and Their Substitutes: Fashion, Technical Progress and Manufacturing Organization in Japanese Popular Clothing, 1850–1920." *Textile History* 19, no. 2 (1988): 159–70.

Uegaki Morikuni. *Yōsan hiroku*. In *Nihon nōsho zenshū*, vol. 35, *Yōsan hiroku, Kogai kinu burui taisei, San tōkei hiketsu*, comp. Nōsangyoson bunka kyōkai, 3–254. Tokyo: Nōsangyoson bunka kyōkai, 1981.

Ugome Tsutomu. "Meiji Ishin to Ishikawa-ke." In *Tama Jiman Ishikawa Shuzō monjo*, comp. Tani Teruhiro, 5: 534–61. Tokyo: Kasumi shuppan, 1990.

———. "Kanagawa-ken no biirugyō to Nihon biiru." In *Tama Jiman Ishikawa Shuzō monjo*, comp. Tani Teruhiro, 6: 920–42. Tokyo: Kasumi shuppan, 1994.

Umegaki, Michio. *After the Restoration: The Beginning of Japan's Modern State.* New York: New York University Press, 1988.

Umemiya Shigeru. "Kaisetsu: Yōsanki yōsan nisshi no shiryō kachi ni tsuite." In *Date chōshi*, vol. 4, suppl. I, *Ōshū sanshu honba yōsan nisshi shūsei*, comp. and ed. Date-machi, 871–91. Date: Date-machi, 1985.

Unno Fukuju. "Shokusan kōgyō to gōnōshō." In *Kōza Nihon rekishi*, vol. 7, *Kindai 1*, ed. Rekishigaku kenkyūkai and Nihonshi kenkyūkai, 171–210. Tokyo: Tōkyō daigaku shuppankai, 1985.

Unno Fukuju and Katō Takashi, eds. *Shokusan kōgyō to hōtoku undō.* Tokyo: Tōkyō keizai shinpōsha, 1978.

Vandenbroeke, Christiaan. "Proto-industrialization in Flanders: A Critical Review." In *European Proto-industrialization*, ed. Sheilagh C. Ogilvie and Markus Cerman, 102–17. Cambridge: Cambridge University Press, 1996.

Vlastos, Stephen. *Peasant Protests and Uprisings in Tokugawa Japan.* Berkeley: University of California Press, 1986.

Wakita Osamu. "Kinsei Ōsaka chiiki no toshi to nōson." In *Kinsei Ōsaka chiiki no shiteki bunseki*, ed. Wakita Osamu, 295–320. Tokyo: Ochanomizu shobō, 1980.

Walthall, Anne. *Social Protest and Popular Culture in Eighteenth-Century Japan.* Tucson: University of Arizona Press, 1986.

———. "The Family Ideology of the Rural Entrepreneurs in Nineteenth Century Japan." *Journal of Social History* 23, no. 3 (1990): 463–83.

———. "The Life Cycle of Farm Women in Tokugawa Japan." In *Recreating Japanese Women, 1600–1945*, ed. Gail Lee Bernstein, 42–70. Berkeley: University of California Press, 1991.

Waswo, Ann. *Japanese Landlords: The Decline of a Rural Elite.* Berkeley: University of California Press, 1977.

Watanabe Fumio. *Yonezawa-han no tokusangyō to senbaisei: aoso shitsurō yōsangyō.* Yonezawa: Fubō shuppan, 1976.

Watanabe Kazumi. *Echigo chijimi no rekishi to gijutsu.* Tokyo: Komiyama shuppan, 1971.

Watanabe Morimichi. *Ōmi shōnin.* Kyōikusha rekishi shinsho (Nihonshi) 106. Tokyo: Kyōikusha, 1980.

Waters, Neil L. *Japan's Local Pragmatists: The Transition from Bakumatsu to Meiji in the Kawasaki Region.* Cambridge: Harvard University Press, 1983.

White, James W. *Ikki: Social Conflict and Political Protest in Early Modern Japan.* Ithaca: Cornell University Press, 1995.

Wigen, Kären. *The Making of a Japanese Periphery, 1750–1920.* Berkeley: University of California Press, 1995.

Yamaguchi Kazuo. *Meiji zenki keizai no bunseki.* Tokyo: Tōkyō daigaku shuppankai, 1956.

———, ed. *Nihon sangyō kin'yūshi kenkyū: orimono kin'yūhen.* Tokyo: Tōkyō daigaku shuppankai, 1974.

———, ed. *Nihon sangyō kin'yūshi kenkyū: seishi kin'yūhen.* Tokyo: Tōkyō daigaku shuppankai, 1966.

Yamaguchi Keiji and Sasaki Junnosuke. *Taikei Nihon rekishi*, vol. 4, *bakuhan taisei*. Tokyo: Nihon hyōronsha, 1971.

Yamamura, Kozo. "Entrepreneurship, Ownership, and Management in Japan." Reprinted in *The Economic Emergence of Modern Japan*, ed. Kozo Yamamura, 294–352. Cambridge: Cambridge University Press, 1997.

Yamazaki Ryūzō. "Edo kōki ni okeru nōson keizai no hatten to nōminsō bunkai." In *Iwanami kōza Nihon rekishi*, vol. 12, *Kinsei* 4, 331–74. Tokyo: Iwanami shoten, 1963.

Yokohama kaikō shiryōkan, ed. *Yokohama shōnin to sono jidai*. Yūrin shinsho 50. Yokohama: Yūrindō, 1994.

Yoshida Isamu. *Sanshigyō to nōmin ikki: Fukushima chihō o chūshin to shite*. Tokyo: Meicho shuppan, 1992.

Yoshinaga Akira. *Kinsei no senbai seido*. Tokyo: Yoshikawa kōbunkan, 1973.

———. "Mikawa momen to momen nakagaishō no keiei." *Nihon rekishi* 493 (1989): 46–64.

Yoshimura Jinsaku. "Bakuhansei shakai to hatasaku gijutsu." In *Gijutsu no shakaishi*, vol. 2, *Zairai gijutsu no hatten to kinsei shakai*, ed. Sasaki Junnosuke, 95–141. Tokyo: Yūzankaku, 1983.

Yunoki Manabu. *Sakazukuri no rekishi*. Tokyo: Yūzankaku, 1987.

Zaidan shōjin Ōmi shōnin kyōdōkan Chōgin-shi kenkyūkai, ed. *Henkakuki no shōnin shihon: Ōmi shōnin Chōgin no kenkyū*. Tokyo: Yoshikawa kōbunkan, 1985.

# Index

In this index an "f" after a number indicates a separate reference on the next page, and an "ff" indicates separate references on the next two pages. A continuous discussion over two or more pages is indicated by a span of page numbers, e.g., "57–59." *Passim* is used for a cluster of references in close but not consecutive sequence.

Uchida Jin'emon (Mikawa province), 122,
226n54
Ueda: area, 68f; domain, 94, 205n3,
213n29
Uegaki Morikuni (Tajima province), 55,
213n24
Ueki Shirōbei (Yonezawa domain), 20
Uji tea, 20, 52, 60–61, 72, 78, 158f,
161f
United States, 65, 69, 163, 217n81
Usuisha, 97, 100
Utsunomiya, 108

Wakao Ippei (Yamanashi prefecture), 3,
95
Wakayama prefecture, 63, 66
Walthall, Anne, 4, 206n24, 230n35
Waswo, Ann, 5, 45
Watanabe family (Echigo province), 25,
28, 60, 206n21
Watarase-gumi, 97
Waters, Neil L., 208–9n67
Wholesalers, 8f, 21f, 26, 52, 54, 78–82,
93, 96, 101, 106–9 passim, 119, 123,
128, 132, 140–49 passim, 153f, 164;
controls exercised over rural areas, 82–
86, 90–91, 127, 155–56, 182, 222n25,
220–21n15; erosion of controls, 87–90,

124–25, 136–37, 149. See also Jobbers;
Merchants; Rural agents
Wigen, Kären, 7, 63

Yamagata prefecture, 39
Yamaguchi Chūjirō family (Hachiōji area),
176ff
Yamaguchi Kazuo, 62
Yamaguchi Takakazu, 20
Yamamura, Kozo, 2
Yamazaki Ryūzō, 204n16
Yanagita Kunio, 46
Yao area, 56
Yarimizu village, 93, 157
Yasuda Riemon (Shindatsu region), 71
Yokohama, 9, 34, 56, 71, 73, 92–97 passim, 143, 154, 156, 159, 163, 175f. See
also Export merchants
Yokoi Tokiyoshi, 46
Yonezawa: domain, 20, 25, 57, 133,
213n29; prefecture, 56
Yōsan hiroku, 55
Yoshida Kōhei (Ōmama area/Yokohama),
94–95
Yūki area, 55, 67, 70
Yumigahama peninsula, 64

Zaguri, 55–56, 69f, 117, 213n29, 213n31

# HARVARD EAST ASIAN MONOGRAPHS

## (* out-of-print)

110. Benjamin A. Elman, *From Philosophy to Philology: Intellectual and Social Aspects of Change in Late Imperial China*

111. Jane Kate Leonard, *Wei Yüan and China's Rediscovery of the Maritime World*

112. Luke S. K. Kwong, *A Mosaic of the Hundred Days:. Personalities, Politics, and Ideas of 1898*

113. John E. Wills, Jr., *Embassies and Illusions: Dutch and Portuguese Envoys to K'ang-hsi, 1666–1687*

114. Joshua A. Fogel, *Politics and Sinology: The Case of Naitō Konan (1866–1934)*

*115. Jeffrey C. Kinkley, ed., *After Mao: Chinese Literature and Society, 1978–1981*

116. C. Andrew Gerstle, *Circles of Fantasy: Convention in the Plays of Chikamatsu*

117. Andrew Gordon, *The Evolution of Labor Relations in Japan: Heavy Industry, 1853–1955*

*118. Daniel K. Gardner, *Chu Hsi and the "Ta Hsueh": Neo-Confucian Reflection on the Confucian Canon*

119. Christine Guth Kanda, *Shinzō: Hachiman Imagery and Its Development*

*120. Robert Borgen, *Sugawara no Michizane and the Early Heian Court*

121. Chang-tai Hung, *Going to the People: Chinese Intellectual and Folk Literature, 1918–1937*

*122. Michael A. Cusumano, *The Japanese Automobile Industry: Technology and Management at Nissan and Toyota*

123. Richard von Glahn, *The Country of Streams and Grottoes: Expansion, Settlement, and the Civilizing of the Sichuan Frontier in Song Times*

124. Steven D. Carter, *The Road to Komatsubara: A Classical Reading of the Renga Hyakuin*

125. Katherine F. Bruner, John K. Fairbank, and Richard T. Smith, *Entering China's Service: Robert Hart's Journals, 1854–1863*

126. Bob Tadashi Wakabayashi, *Anti-Foreignism and Western Learning in Early-Modern Japan: The "New Theses" of 1825*

127. Atsuko Hirai, *Individualism and Socialism: The Life and Thought of Kawai Eijirō (1891–1944)*

128. Ellen Widmer, *The Margins of Utopia: "Shui-hu hou-chuan" and the Literature of Ming Loyalism*

129. R. Kent Guy, *The Emperor's Four Treasuries: Scholars and the State in the Late Chien-lung Era*

130. Peter C. Perdue, *Exhausting the Earth: State and Peasant in Hunan, 1500–1850*

131. Susan Chan Egan, *A Latterday Confucian: Reminiscences of William Hung (1893–1980)*

132. James T. C. Liu, *China Turning Inward: Intellectual-Political Changes in the Early Twelfth Century*

133. Paul A. Cohen, *Between Tradition and Modernity: Wang T'ao and Reform in Late Ching China*

134. Kate Wildman Nakai, *Shogunal Politics: Arai Hakuseki and the Premises of Tokugawa Rule*

135. Parks M. Coble, *Facing Japan: Chinese Politics and Japanese Imperialism, 1931–1937*

136. Jon L. Saari, *Legacies of Childhood: Growing Up Chinese in a Time of Crisis, 1890–1920*

137. Susan Downing Videen, *Tales of Heichū*

138. Heinz Morioka and Miyoko Sasaki, *Rakugo: The Popular Narrative Art of Japan*

169. Andrew Edmund Goble, *Kenmu: Go-Daigo's Revolution*

170. Denise Potrzeba Lett, *In Pursuit of Status: The Making of South Korea's "New" Urban Middle Class*

171. Mimi Hall Yiengpruksawan, *Hiraizumi: Buddhist Art and Regional Politics in Twelfth-Century Japan*

172 . Charles Shiro Inouye, *The Similitude of Blossoms: A Critical Biography of Izumi Kyōka (1873–1939), Japanese Novelist and Playwright*

173. Aviad E. Raz, *Riding the Black Ship: Japan and Tokyo Disneyland*

174. Deborah J. Milly, *Poverty of the Japanese State: Knowledge and the Pursuit of Accommodations*

175. See Heng Teow, *Japan's Cultural Policy Toward China, 1918–1931: A Comparative Perspective*

176. Michael A. Fuller, *An Introduction to Literary Chinese*

177. Frederick R. Dickinson, *War and National Redefinition: Japan in the Great War, 1914–1919*

178. John Solt, *Shredding the Tapestry of Meaning: The Poetry and Poetics of Kitasono Katue (1902–1978)*

179. Edward Pratt, *Japan's Protoindustrial Elite: The Economic Foundations of the Gōnō*

180. Atsuko Sakaki, *Recontextualizing Texts: Modern Japanese Fiction as Speech Act*

181. Soon Won Park, *Colonial Modernity and Its Legacy: Korean Workers in Japanese Factories*